THE COMPANY OF GHOSTS

THE COMPANY OF GHOSTS

STEPHANIE M. GLENNON

Contents

Photograph by James & S. R. Glennon

Quoted works are gratefully acknowledged; those not in the public domain are cited by permission and/or pursuant to 17 U.S.C. sec. 107: Kurt Vonnegut: *Galapagos & Slaughterhouse-Five, or The Children's Crusade: A Duty-Dance with Death* (Delacorte Press); John Irvng: *Last Night in Twisted River & The World According to Garp* (E.P. Dutton); Jose Saramago: *Death with Interruptions & The Elephant's Journey* (Mariner Books), *The Year of the Death of Ricardo Reis & The History of the Siege of Lisbon* (The Harvill Press); Elie Weisel: *Night* (Hill & Wang); Alejandro Zambra, *Ways of Going Home* (Farrar, Straus & Giroux); Oliver Sacks: *The Mind's Eye* (Alfred A. Knopof); Andre Dubus: *Dancing After Hours* (Vintage); Fernando Pesoa, *The Book of Disquiet* (Penguin Books), translated by Richard Zenith; *The Collected Tales of Nikolai Gogol* (Pantheon), translated by Richard Pever & Larissa Volokhonsky; Edward Gorey: *Amphigorey Also* (Congdon & Weed); Frederick Buechner, *Wishful Thinking* (Harper One); Elif Batuman: *The Possessed* (Farrar, Straus & Giroux); Barbara Kingsolver: *The Poisonwood Bible* (Faber & Faber); Primo Levi: *A Tranquil Star* (W.W. Norton & Co.); Jose Donoso: *The Obscene Bird of Night* (David R. Godine); Lawrence Block: *A Drop of the Hard Stuff* (Mulholland Books); C.D. Wright: *Steal Away: New and Selected Poems* (Copper Canyon Press); Marilynne Robinson: *Home* (Farrar, Straus & Giroux); Carol Ann Duffy: *Collected Poems* (Picador); Thomas Wolfe: *You Can't Go Home Again* (Harper & Bros.); Thornton Wilder: *Our Town* (Gardners Books); Ranier Maria Rilke: *Sonnets to Orpheus*, translated by Edward Snow (Farrar, Straus; & Giroux); Kiran Desai, *The Inheritance of Loss* (Atlantic Monthly Press).

Harborside Books

ISBN/SKU 979-8-218-57659-2, ISBN/SKU 979-8-218-03787-1

Part I: Before You Were a Ghost

Photograph by James R. Glennon

1

Before You Were a Ghost

The last unscathed evening fell on June's final Thursday. It must not have been humid enough to make us uncomfortable as we sprawled on the crimson couch that occupied the length of a carpet my husband Jim bought when our firstborn fit comfortably between his palm and forearm.

A toothed triangle had gone missing from the carpet's corner, where a Ficus taller and sturdier than I had towered in the home our first three children had known. There, it had succumbed to over-watering, its selvedge unsalvageable after water stewed in wool before seeping into perfectly intersecting modern floorboards.

Here, the phantom Ficus hovered over deep brandy pine boards hewed and hammered into place no later than 1805, before the home Jim had always searched for harbored any ghosts at all.

A single sea change had been in sight: at summer's end, for the first time, our closely spaced sons and daughters would all be at different schools. One would be hours away. Family nights were growing rare as our older children began venturing out on their own.

Jim started up a movie, *Raising Arizona*.

The night before, I'd slept as well as I ever had, and ever may again.

That night I did not look out the west-facing windows and beyond my handsome husband's shoulder, to see whether dusk had turned to fire before settling in deep rose and violet.

I rarely used to look beyond the people in my presence.

I did not glance at a sun that would have been perfectly balanced atop the church spire across the street before disappearing behind it.

Our yellow house's previous owner, a physician like my husband, had been keeper of the church's bell. He'd wound its clock until human hands no longer were needed to mark time.

I did not take Rufus and Brady out that evening. Jim had run with our rescue beagles after work and they'd settled down to sleep, curled into each other. Yin and yang.

I neither took a single photograph that day, nor wrote a word unrelated to work. I may have shopped for groceries. I mailed two birthday packages. The probability I cooked is not far above zero.

I didn't know my healthy husband had for six weeks felt a ping of lingering, localized abdominal pain. Or that his instincts suggested it wasn't due to muscle strain from outdoor tasks and adventures which filled his nonworking hours. In summer they tended to include carrying Rufus uphill. Our first rescue's initial enthusiasm to take off running often surpassed his mastery of the hills.

I did not know my husband had an ultrasound that morning at the hospital where he worked.

He didn't know, when the movie's kinetic, twangy score and spirit began unwinding into the late-darkening night, what the scan revealed.

The movie zoomed in on plump babies bathed in orange light. Jim answered his phone, then paused the movie and disappeared. When he returned, he sat next to me and laughed along with us as it resumed. It was as if he, like our children, was seeing it for the first time.

Not the last.

~~~~~~

Later that night Jim looked especially thoughtful. He sat on our four-poster tiger maple bed with an expression that told me he was working through a problem. Focused, without a hint of alarm. Propped up against a king-sized pillow, he wasn't reading the open book on his lap or wearing reading glasses he'd recently acquired on what was known in-house as a 'Birthday of Significance.'

This serious a look ordinarily meant he was puzzling through a work issue. An internist as well as his hospital's first Chief Medical Officer, he foresaw and addressed complicated system-wide issues, from Electronic Medical Records to pandemic response.

We met in New Jersey, where we'd migrated from different parts of Massachusetts for college. I was almost seventeen. We married four years later, after first he returned to Boston to work, then we both began graduate school.

After more than two decades, I could look at him from across a room and identify such nuances as 'the beagles are overdue for their shots face' and 'tuition face.' The latter was among the less luminous aspects of parenthood which he'd always spared me. But this wasn't a look I'd seen before. Not even when one of our children had been critically ill in a Boston hospital where he'd once trained.

"That was Patty on the phone."

I didn't immediately link his internist to the earlier call. She'd joined his and his partner Bob's internal medicine practice a
~~~~~~

decade earlier, when my husband began his transition from full-time (and then some) practitioner by adding part-time (and then some) administrator. He'd created his own niche by combining them, and was dedicated both to each patient and to improving the systems they're compelled to navigate.

He described an oddity on an ultrasound I was unaware he'd had that morning, after six weeks of a twinge of abdominal pain that had neither evaporated nor intensified. Patty had called to tell him something in the image seemed to "disappear" near his pancreas. His spleen was enlarged, likely accounting for his pain.

I pictured a glowing blur lurking in his scan. I think I knew that if I'd looked too closely at him, I might have seen the space between what he'd deduced and what he was telling me. Having known me all my adult life, and better than anyone else ever could, he was telling me what I was then able to hear. The way he drew out his words, although only slightly more than he usually did, lodged in my heart and drowned out everything but his always steady voice.

"Should I panic?" I asked him.

~~~~~~

Jim was well aware of my tendency to catastrophize. I'd always been the family worrywart, having been reared in a family with unusual levels of perpetual consternation. My theoretical physicist father's mind continuously churned as he mathematically contoured the chaotic state of the unseeable--and therefore impossible adequately to supervise--matter that makes up our Universe. My mother worried more passively about everything else, from chemicals leaching into food to nuclear meltdown. Until returning to visit them with a child of my own, I'd somehow failed to notice that despite this perseveration, my brothers and I managed to emerge physically intact from a home that was a death trap. The
~~~~~~

door through which we'd been dispatched to play outside was surrounded by insecurely capped containers of lawn chemicals emblazoned with skulls and crossbones. A plugged-in chainsaw casually leaned in a corner by the low bookshelf which still housed children's books.

I remembered how, despite my mother's never-explained visceral aversion to silver tinsel (which I eventually assumed she considered either a choking hazard or an invitation to holiday pica), she crafted her signature World's Deadliest Christmas Ornaments. They were both weightier and less balanced than Ninja stars. She made them by slicing off Maxwell House coffee tin tops with a rusty can-opener. She used gardening shears--although we'd never maintained a garden in our small backyard green space--to engineer scalpel-sharp fringes whose edges she curved with surprisingly little bloodshed. She let my brothers and me loose to gather these metal starbursts with our tender, fleshy toddler fingers. We pried apart their razored tentacles to bend and inadequately anchor them in clumps of fresh evergreen. It's a wonder none of our abundant unsupervised time ended in exsanguination. I suspect it is a rare physicist-artist/musician team that's born to shepherd children into adulthood.

Unsurprisingly, one Christmas my older daughter gifted me with the same book I'd just given my mother: *The Complete Worst-Case Scenario Survivor Guide.* Why give oneself over to the tepid calm of not sweating the small stuff, and forego lying awake while contemplating wildly improbable disasters for which one is unprepared? My first car, for Stephen King aficionados, was Christine. She'd had a habit of switching on a single headlight and draining her battery overnight before my morning commute. She once abruptly shed her front bumper on the Southeast Expressway for no apparent reason. Sometimes unlikely mischief does occur.

In *Julius Caesar*, Brutus mused that "between the acting of a dreadful thing/ And the first motion, all the interim is/ Like a phantasm or a hideous dream." In his role as family administrator of practical things, my husband developed a simple and elegant system to keep me from envenoming my days by worrying about low probability future misfortunes. To avoid my frittering away time (and, all too often, vitriol) at perceived injustices and problems ultimately unlikely to be panic-worthy, he agreed to simply alert me when the time to panic arrived. The overflowing glass to my two-thirds empty one, the even-keeled antidote to my rambling worries, he'd say, "I'll tell you when it's time to panic." I could put my worries on hold. We both understood he'd never tell me the time to panic had come.

Whenever I was unsure if panic *might* be situationally appropriate, I needed only ask.

"Is it time for me to panic yet?" I might ask about an IRS return address, a process server at the door (long story), or the results on a glucose tolerance test during a pregnancy. He'd smile and shake his head, no matter how badly I'd screwed up or what the not-so-worst-case scenario might then have been. If it could be fixed, he'd take care of it. If it couldn't, there wasn't any upside to my losing more sleep over it. Meanwhile, a "Steph blackout" would remove the discrete matter from my radar. Everyone in the house could be spared my pointless agita.

During our marriage's early years, long before difficult pregnancies and a near-catastrophic delivery, I'd exhausted myself with anxious questions he always patiently answered. Jim had codified the formula by the time he sat at my side as I was unsuccessfully anesthetized for a crash C-section after 45 ½ hours of hard labor. Not that I was counting.

"I'll tell you when it's time to panic."

And then I was okay. Peace was restored. To the operating room, the household, and any space we were lucky enough to share.

But on that late June night, for the first and last time, he didn't say "No" when I asked if the time to panic had come.

~~~~~

Despite my rich lineage of worrying about almost everything else, I'd never worried about cancer. That night, Jim mused while our children slept. In his tone I heard what must have been circling in his mind when he returned from speaking to Patty and resumed the movie as if nothing had changed or was about to. I wasn't even close to understanding what had already changed. That he--that we six, and so many more--had already crossed the divide from the Before.

"So, what could that be?" I asked when he described whatever had been too murky to read on his ultrasound.

It is easy to picture something that can be measured against what one expects to be there, like a mildly enlarged spleen, and the husband who should have grown old along with me. It's difficult to describe, much less grasp, what's gone missing.

"There aren't a lot of things it could be." Very carefully phrased. He must have known exactly what narrow possibilities could account for the data he already had.

He paused. "Pancreatitis is a thing that generally only happens with heavy drinkers."

"Maybe you should drink more?"

He looked at me in a way he never had before. I would see that look only once more, not many months later, as we stood frozen together in a storied Boston hospital's lobby while strangers swirled around us. Staff and visitors. Patients and people who were
~~~~~

indifferent to them and people who loved them. The lucky, the un-lucky, the more-or-less lucky in that moment.

"I think we have to prepare for the possibility this is a tumor."

This did not fully compute with me. I knew not all tumors are cancerous and not all cancer is malignant. I wouldn't even have been able to identify a pancreas by shape or location had our son Noah not remarked upon the clay sculpture his brother brought home from school after his class made non-piggy banks. Given the commodious belly required for his uncoiled snake to collect pocket change, Noah had blurted out, not disapprovingly, "That looks like a pancreas."

The only sign of my husband's recent birthday milestone had been his reading glasses' acquisition. He'd never smoked. He spent all the time he could outdoors, and worked out every day. Apropos of a dedicated BSA Troop 158 leader, he lived like a Boy Scout. He wasn't far under the perfect weight for his height, about 6' 3" or 6' 4." He never told me his exact height because he wanted me to think the difference between us might not be vaster than a foot, and knew I do not like to think of myself as insubstantial.

"Could it be some kind of complication of what you had?" My brain unspooled an episode years earlier, when he had a one-in-a-million adverse reaction to a medication. His white blood cells had been wiped out. For three days his condition had been perilous.

"You gave us a scare," a colleague had told him once it seemed clear he'd recover, and masked visitors safely could enter the room where he'd been isolated.

"I gave myself a scare," Jim said lightly from the hospital bed where he sat reading a medical journal.

In fact, he feared nothing.

~~~~~~

"Well, I've never heard of *pancreatic* complications."
~~~~~~

Jim, like all born teachers, lacked any impulse to make others feel foolish. But his subtle head shake told me this wasn't a medically sensible possibility.

"I'd like to go with that," I said, nodding to convince myself of my mythical diagnosis.

He was quiet.

"Do you want to talk to someone? Do you want to call Bob?" Bob--Dr. Bob--was his primary care partner, married to our children's pediatrician. We'd followed them in rapidly producing a boy-boy-girl-girl household. Some later hires might have been scared off by concluding such bounty was either expected or a settled habit within the practice.

Jim said he'd talk to a general surgeon at his hospital in the morning. In retrospect, I understand he already had begun to ease me out of the nascent news blackout. He understood what the shock of the probable next piece of data would do to me. That my mind's eye would go straight to the tunnel's end. My husband knew what the limited medical possibilities were, but was able to contend with whatever he faced at any given moment. In death's anteroom, he knew I'd see only black. I would battle the present and fight fruitlessly back into the past, trying to undo what couldn't be undone. I would abandon hope, as I understood hope then.

"*Show me the data*," I only late learned, but should have known was his professional mantra before deciding on a course of action.

"And you'll call me?"

"Of course."

He turned out the bedside light, a teak lamp given to us when we married. After so many moves, its base was just enough off-center that it rocked with an audible *clank-clink* reminiscent of Law & Order's opening notes when he tugged its weary metal chain. He put his book aside, closed his eyes, and quickly was asleep. I'd been an insomniac since I was nine, and always envied his ability to drop off, for a nap or for the night.

"How do you *do* that?" I'd asked over the years.

Each time he would smile and say to me--the career prosecutor, the crusader for justice--"I sleep the sleep of the just."

2

Lightning Strikes

My husband had attended a medical conference in Washington, D. C., soon before the June night when all we could do was wait for what, in differing ways, we both knew Monday would bring.

Although he never described the glass atrium he occupied on the conference's final night, I picture him in a cathedral-like space several stories high, built from glass panes leaded at their seams and conjoined at angles. He'd have had at least one book on his lap, atop a stack of conference materials annotated with a pencil in his left-leaning half-script. Crossword puzzles and Ken-Ken problems swiftly were rendered in ink. As to everything with less certain and ready answers, he always was open to thoughtful revision.

I still see him surveying an intense storm in a sky darkened by purple shelf clouds. He sits in a pristine white chair, like those in the church across the street from our home, watching rapid-fire lightning all around. The earth rumbles as bolts undo at least the surface of the ground beneath him.

His hospital's CEO later told me he'd approached my husband about heading with him to the day's final meeting after noticing

12

he'd missed dinner. He told me my husband said, "There will be more meetings. Let's watch the storm."

Jim was always attuned to the benefits of watching a storm, just as deliberately as he paid attention to the sometimes less turbulent spaces around him.

They were no worse for missing the conference's final meeting. And there would be more such meetings for the rest of them.

~~~~~~

"Last night it did not seem as if today it would be raining."

I often think of Edward Gorey's couplet and wonder if we do register signals of an incoming storm, in the same way I now detect harbingers on the horizon--infinitesimal signs of a sunrise simmering in the undifferentiated darkness preceding it. Perhaps we shiver them off, at least when not paying very close attention. A goose walking over our graves.

On June's final Friday Jim worked his usual very full day, stopping in to see a colleague who agreed he should speedily see a specialist and have an abdominal scan. She connected him with a surgeon just outside Boston who was willing to squeeze him into her Monday schedule. Meanwhile, over the weekend, Jim would make a fifteen-hour round-trip drive to drop off one of our daughters in Pennsylvania. He always did the family driving. He was unfazed by high speeds and the unpredictability of those who share roads with us. Almost nothing unnerved him.

But I already *knew*. I know that because after the two of them left, I wandered upstairs to the suffocating attic and began gingerly going through piled boxes. Paring down was not something I did. My subconscious was ahead of me in discerning we'd cleaved off from Huckleberry Finn life as a family of six in the yellow house. I understood even then that I'd need to begin the never-ending task of knowing what to keep and carry.
~~~~~~

The attic was a yawning unfinished space, clogged--always by me--with artifacts of our children's younger years. Jim occasionally would scrawl *Fine Emotables* on boxes he retired to the attic, knowing he could never talk me into tossing away anything that captured even a fleeting facet of our children.

Downstairs, he'd sometimes cast his eyes upward in the direction of this sanctified and increasingly unwieldy hoard. He'd say, "You know, we can never move."

~~~~~~

On our first wedding anniversary, we lived in a tiny apartment a cobblestone's throw from Mass General Hospital and the Charles Street Red Line stop. Jim had to duck under our door frames. He barely fit in the closet-sized bathroom or quarter-bowling alley of largely neglected kitchen space. Long before I could envision the old fireplaces and beehive oven he would tend to years later, once he found the home his soul had long sought out, I gave him an old copper pot for Christmas. I found it in a dusty storefront near the Charles, on the flat portion just below Beacon Hill--ground that will never be as stable as what lies inland and uphill.

Lower Beacon Hill's geology led early builders to fill the anchoring river's shallows with sand and soil. But such earthly limiting boundaries are not so easily expanded. The process ensured that the area's oldest structures would someday be first in line to sink back into their liquid origins. It is not so much a fallacy of sunk costs, as it were, but plot-commanded: once mortals took it upon themselves to convert water to land, elaborate wood foundations had to be built to steady their creations. But the substitutions left the wood insufficiently suffused, too brittle and weak to protect what was built from being buffeted and felled by natural forces. Entropy endured, as it always will. The result, as a 1970s ge-
~~~~~~

ological study of Boston's groundwater and wood foundations put it, was "An Unending Need for Vigilant Surveillance."

At the ground floor of any momentous choice, when it may not appear quite so pivotal as its branching consequences sometimes reveal, one needs to understand the terrain and pay attention. That attention should solidify, not cease, once the commitment's been made. Placing a foundation, developing a talent, taking or declining a job. Marrying, becoming a parent, acquiring and maintaining a friendship or coming to grips with its loss. Letting go. Never letting go. A course worth undertaking will rarely become less complicated or less worthy of our considered devotion.

In paying attention, Jim was the measured voice to my impulsive takes, the steady counterpoint to my sometimes ill-considered reaction in a moment he understood would pass. His four younger sisters, I had learned early on, were way ahead of me on this. When faced with challenges, they considered then, as now, *What would Jim do?*

~~~~~~

Eternal vigilance is, of course, ineffective against stealth disease. But my husband understood the importance of attentiveness even to what hovers beyond what our traditional senses detect. It is not so much--if at all--being "in the moment," but its opposite: an instinct to see eternity in whatever is within our grasp. William Blake's grain of sand: "Infinity in the palm of your hand."

But back to the copper pot.

It was wide enough to hold kindling, or a pair of companionable babies. It would have been a tight fit for our first apartment's bathroom floor. Its interior had dulled to a quiet, deep brandied ash. On its surface, mottled patches floated on burnt sienna storm clouds and swirled with constellations of oxidized green dots--the reverse image of the bright eyes I still cannot believe no longer
~~~~~~

look back into mine. Jim's eyes could be deep emerald and in strong sun turn to amber flecked with green. Sometimes it was the reverse.

I always, always see his eyes first.

I noticed few of those aspects of the pot when I gave it to him, or for decades afterwards. Not until I had packed and unpacked it at least once by myself after relieving it from duty standing sentinel in the dining room fireplace of our New Hampshire home. The room where my husband would die, yielding back to my care all his earthly belongings and all that only the two of us shared.

The pot now sits empty, but for dust and ever-replenishing spiders, in the crook of an 1802 fireplace in a house he never saw, in a seaport city he never called home. Now I've truly examined it, perhaps the way he did, considering the way outside forces changed its shape over time. How it was created by hand from the earth's offerings and passed down with care, accruing family memories along the way. How it held its stories. How it meant something to someone else before it meant something to my husband, and therefore to me.

How we are but stewards of others' stories as well as unlikely treasures.

~~~~~~

Did my husband know, before he *knew*? Did I? Do people who perpetually focus their attention outside themselves read cues no one else can, or is willing to? Did his body--that of a supremely skilled clinician--tell him? Or his heart?

Jim always viewed omens differently than I do. As with the lightning storm he urged his colleagues to stop and savor, he saw the first lightning strike at our yellow house--our about-to-be family home--as a positive thing. He wasn't tied to many inanimate things, but he was deeply attached to the only place we ever called
~~~~~~

home as a family of six, and then eight with our beagles. The house was solidly built, anchored in a granite foundation far uphill from Great Bay's then heavily wooded shores. It was just inland from the narrow slice of seacoast upon which New Hampshire staked a claim, marking the arguably wise separation between Massachusetts and Maine following the Commonwealth's ultimate insults to the Crown-gifted Maine colony during the War of 1812.

Samuel F. B. Morse was said to have painted portraits in what became our living and music room. Daniel Webster reportedly acquired the main house for $1200 and sold it four years later for $900. In a part of New England where nearly as many houses boast an affiliation with Daniel Webster as sport signs that an apparently perpetually weary George Washington there rested, the story had the ring of circumstantial truth: that interval coincided with Webster's house in neighboring Portsmouth perishing and rising again from the ashes after the Great Fire of 1813.

Fire can be at least as perilous as over-watered earth.

Before we moved there, Jim and I had lived in apartments of fewer than 500 square feet; a claustrophobic 1950s house; a single room his height exceeded; and a contemporary house fronted by highway but backed by an oasis of conservation land. Throughout those years he always seemed to have had something else in mind. A home imbued with history and made by devoted hands. A place that reminded him, I think, of the colonial New Hampshire house he as a teenager had spent a summer restoring with a beloved uncle and cousin.

He found it.

I knew he'd already made up his mind, and suppressed my reluctance to move, when our first family visit to the house turned into a scene out of a John Irving novel. On a mid-August weekend, he brought us to a 2:00 appointment to see The One. The house faced a tiny triangular town green. Its hexagonal gazebo was surrounded by cross-hatched lattices colonized by Morning Glory vines on which blue buds bobbed and their white star centers glowed even when there was no sunlight. It was an improbably perfect movie set version of a tiny New England town.

Small-town life was and remains a mystery to me, as does much of the Live Free or Die state itself, but Jim was smitten. He pulled into a narrow strip by the gazebo, facing the property of his dreams. It was fronted by a sunny yellow house of Federalist style. The front path was of unsettled bricks untethered by mortar and long left to the companionship of soil. A dark emerald door was topped by a fan of slatted wood. The house was the most recent addition to the property. A section of its wood skeleton was visible upstairs and inside, where a thin wood frame set into the surrounding horsehair plaster revealed its 1805 provenance. The numbers had been carved by someone who had stood where we did when we first saw the handiwork.

Attached to the back of the house was a foundation-free, brick-floored, wood-beamed room that listed well short of round and led to a late 1600s barn through which high winds didn't merely whistle, but carried like baying hounds. The barn's second story bore a plaque identifying it as having originally been owned by William Pickering. Beyond it was a series of small wooden outbuildings painted a lightly creamed bright teal, and a hill that sloped down to almost 33 acres of woods surrounding an eight-and-a-half-acre pond. Jim seemed most interested not in any of these lovingly preserved structures, but in the pond that instantly exerted a pull over our children as well.

Despite gathering storm clouds, which never deterred my husband, we wandered down the hill and past a carved wooden owl keeping watch over well-tended gardens of fruit trees, concord grape vines, and clusters of asparagus stalks as large and solid as silver dollars. Beyond the gardens were wild grasses which grew higher as we trekked downhill and neared the sustaining water, until they towered over all of us but Jim.

Our son Noah stared at clear wavering water at the hill's base. The pond's outer reaches were beyond our sight and around a bend, and to our children it must have seemed as boundless as the Atlantic. When we all reached the pond's reed-cluttered shallows, Noah dipped one hand in and drew out a wriggling perch, startling himself as much as any of us. By instinct, and as he always would, he immediately let it return home.

By then it was almost 2:00, so we scurried up the hill and piled back into the car. Rain began not with a spatter but with a deluge. The realtor was just pulling to the side of the road across from us.

Directly across from the yellow house, the church bell rang twice.

Craaaaaaack.

Jim and I watched a lightning bolt strike the white-painted wood fence in front of the house. Instantly, a section of stalwart fence that had stood for almost two centuries splintered and collapsed. I looked at him. Neither of us was particularly superstitious, but surely he couldn't have considered this a good sign.

But he was no less smitten. He'd probably told our forever friend Randy, "I've found a house," with the same lightly-scarred left eyebrow arch and to-the-core smile that accompanied his coming home from college and telling Randy, "I've met a girl."

Jim would have seen it more like T. S. Garp did, when he watched a small plane crash into his prospective home and decided it was the perfect time to buy it. After all, what's the chance of lightning striking twice? As he had announced to his beloved, they were bound to be safe in such a "pre-disastered" home.

~~~~~~

By the carved wooden owl that oversaw the garden, Jim would plant quince and pear trees and berries and vegetables. During some seasons the bounty would disappear just as each fruit and vegetable reached its prime. Deer might consume them. If the deer were insufficiently attentive, gophers might stake a claim. My husband was mildly less tolerant of the gophers, who were far more disruptive, tunneling with abandon among his carefully arranged plantings, tearing away roots and thoroughly disrupting what was left behind but still standing.

Uphill, Jim planted flowers in every color but black and blue, which he supplied in blue-black berry bushes closer to the nourishing pond. Over the years he maintained all these growing things, sacrificing their renewable fruits with equanimity to wildlife visitors rather than safeguarding them in a way that might alarm or endanger skittish critters emerging from surrounding woods. It was a minor cost of his side-gig as a gentleman farmer.

He cooperatively enlisted and supervised less visibly complex organisms. He tapped maple syrup, tried his hand at brewing beer; and tended to sourdough bread starter until he unwisely left it in my care during an out-of-state conference. He built bird-feeder cities, meticulously matching their contents to their guests' tastes and dietary sensibilities--far better than I ordinarily did when attempting to feed the humans inside the house as we looked out the kitchen windows. Outside, supremely contented winged families feasted, started their own families, and always returned.

~~~~~~

In autumn my husband would hay the steep hill, so that even in his last winter he could coax his nieces and nephews--and even his mother--to sail on sleds just above its slick snowy surface and catch air as it gave way to sprays of ice which skittered away with the wind along the frozen pond. He taught our children to paddle kayaks and identify each season's birds and flora. He'd show them and their friends and our multitudinous nieces and nephews how to skate and pay attention to all that surrounded them.

In the brick-floored barn he would build netted goals. He hammered together low benches to drag out onto the ice so children could sit with their mittens pressed to them for the illusion that it would make gravity hold them more tightly.

He'd glide over to them on the same hockey skates he'd been wearing the only time I ever saw him intentionally make contact with an opponent. When we were students--and only after Jim's clear warnings had been ignored--he'd return-checked the administrator who'd boorishly checked a petite friend in a faculty-student game. (I have since heard, and can confirm, that the aggressor went on to become a defense lawyer.)

~~~~~~

Jim's winter jackets were always open, his cheeks as rosy as the children's as he pulled tightly on their laces and double and triple-knotted them before smoothly skating backward, holding small hands ensconced in the bright hand-knit frog-shaped and dinosaur-patterned mittens their Grandma Jackie knitted for them. One sunny winter day, Jim's skates smoothly kicked up ice crystals arcs while mine settled awkwardly in pigeon tracks on the pond's thick frozen plates, which groaned at their tectonic seams. Under inches of ice Jim had carefully measured and tested to withstand human weight, I saw a cluster of bright orange fish, exuberant and plump. Their almost translucent feathery fins fluttered and wove beneath us in brilliant blue water stippled by overlaid ribbons of liquid silver.

The pond and surrounding woods attracted animals of all kinds. Jim, who had an amazing photographic eye and often used
~~~~~~

real film even in a digital world, would take his camera gear down the hill and patiently wait. He never disturbed any creature as he zoomed in from a vast distance and snapped portraits of dedicated pairs of swans, red fox parents and newborn kits, heron families, and beavers assembling the formidable dams they built to reshape the water and surrounding soil as they found it.

For awhile, at least.

~~~~~~

The sun rose beyond Jim's bountiful bird-feeders. When he could no longer eat, and likely knew it would be the last trip he would make on his own, he'd made a purchase I found much later inside a paper bag tucked behind his driver's seat. He'd bought blocks of seed-encrusted suet so artfully presented that at first I thought they were gourmet human treats.

His truck contained his stethoscope, those fresh cakes of bird-seed, and a music system he had so fiendishly well-wired that both I and the car dealer were powerless to disconnect it.

~~~~~~

I had never watched sunrises and sunsets so easily within my reach as I did during my husband's illness, when the fear of missing a waking moment with him, even as he still slept, seemed over-whelming. When my frantically cycling mind wouldn't let me sleep, my heart had me stand at the upstairs bedroom window overlooking the pond. After several hours, I sometimes could sense whatever light underlay the blackness. Until then I would watch his shoulders rise and fall, holding my breath the same way I had as time stilled between our sleeping infants' shimmering movements, no more than whispers in their tiny bodies as their perfect hearts beat the ceaseless measure of the blessings their lives brought.

3

Monday Morning

Heat assaulted us as we walked into a hospital just outside Boston early on June's final Monday morning. We occupied a claustrophobic bubble because so few people knew what had come to pass and what might lie ahead.

Jim registered for his more detailed abdominal scan. We were pointed to a charmless corridor off a partitioned area with stiff benches. Two women were playing a farm game on tablets, perhaps harvesting ever-resilient crops or tending to animals who wouldn't perish no matter how long they went without attention. If crops withered, they might instantly be restored to full bloom. Jim pointed out to me what they seemed to be playing, having previously and with equal good cheer told me that one quality he was certain he hadn't been looking for in a spouse was the ability to maintain a virtual farm.

We made our way to a small white waiting room with a bowed window. A low table held a fan of magazine covers featuring young people with inventive names and mysteriously sourced celebrity. Jim spirited himself away to prepare for his scan. He would not emerge for almost two hours. My only job was to wait, preferably without coming undone. There would be more than enough occasions for both.

Irony already had absented itself from my waking persona. I carried an Elizabeth George novel, *This Body of Death*, its black and blue cover adorned with a deeply bowed stone angel. A cemetery marker. In the empty waiting room I stared at the printed pages, but my glazed mind stalled and the words blurred. I'd read George before. I knew someone would perish at villainous hands, in some atmospheric British way. Detectives would gently speak of "sussing out" information--which distinctly was not the way the detectives with whom I work speak.

This perishable body, I whispered to myself.

~~~~~~

Finally, the double doors *whooshed* as Jim emerged. In a T-shirt and khaki shorts, he didn't look quite like either a doctor or a patient. He looked no different than he had when he'd disappeared from my view. I don't know why I thought he would have.

We waited together. He read medical journals. I paced, reading plaques of homage to unspeakably generous hospital donors. Eventually we decided we might as well migrate to the downstairs office suite where a surgeon had been kind enough to squeeze us in for an appointment during her lunch break. Jim sat and read as I wandered in another strangely empty white waiting room.

Just after noon, a woman in a bright orange linen sundress summoned us into a windowless conference room and left us to wait there for the surgeon. We sat in conjoined molded chairs. I was slightly closer to the hallway door, having always favored proximity to exits. I felt nauseated.

Minutes later, a woman who looked much younger than I'd expected of a surgeon of such renown opened the door and introduced herself. She told Jim she'd heard he was the medical director
~~~~~~

of a group she knew of and was glad to meet him, and sorry it had to be under these circumstances.

That should have been a tell for me. It must have been for him.

She was no more than a table's width away when she moved a cursor. A scan appeared on a computer screen we faced from across the narrow room.

"This is your tumor." Gently, with kindness.

Jim looked intently at the screen. My interior self must have been a few steps ahead of my jittery, leg-shaking, hand-clutching physical self, because I heard myself crying before I was aware that I was. He put his arm protectively around me as I burrowed into his shoulder.

Without a hint of panic, he signaled the time had come when I needed to know he could no longer protect me from the truth we had to contend with and would soon have to explain to our children.

He kissed the top of my head and said, "I think it's time to panic now."

~~~~~~

I've never actually seen the tumor. I never looked at that screen. But nor have I been able to discard the cardboard sleeves which house his copies of its images, any more than I can let go of any of our children's pictures from the before and after.

My own occupation isn't without trauma. I've been with brutally injured people and seen the dead dismantled. But to look at even a black-and-white image of what I knew would kill my husband would have swallowed me up. I carry only an abstract vision of it at any stage--a malevolent tentacled mass stretching out in all directions, knotting itself wherever it chooses. I couldn't even assign it a color. If it were a color Jim or I or our children favored,
~~~~~~

it would have poisoned everything else in that hue if there came a time I'd be able to feel color again.

~~~~~~

The surgeon had pivoted her wheeled chair toward both of us. She pointed at portions of her screen. Jim looked intently at his abdomen's contents. I turned away and buried my head under his chin, next to his heart. My tears were already pooling in dark blotches on his soft burnt orange cotton shirt. He held his arm around my shoulder as he leaned closer to the screen as she showed him how his tumor had wrapped so tightly around his portal vein that it couldn't be surgically removed.

The surgeon suggested a PET scan and offered to set it up later that week. After looking at us for a few seconds, she said she might be able to schedule it earlier. Jim nodded and thanked her; he said he'd rather have the information as soon as possible. She left the room and somehow coaxed someone upstairs to extend their day into night.

~~~~~~

When I could speak, I asked my husband what the PET scan meant. It's the only question I ever asked him that he was hesitant to answer. Given the physicians' back-and-forth, of course he knew, but I did not, that if the shadows on his liver the surgeon had pointed out were to light up on a PET scan, that would mean his pancreatic tumor had already metastasized. Surgery would never be possible. He would die within months, perhaps weeks or days.

Jim had been a Biology major. I'd found myself in the Plant Biology class in which I met him only because our undergraduate institution sensibly required even liberal artsy types like me to expand our understanding of science and the world by taking at least two laboratory classes. I foolishly had thought that plants, ubiquitous to the point of exhibitionism, would be easier to see and evaluate--and therefore understand--than the natural world's better kept and more theoretical secrets. I ended up writing a term paper about plant tumors after being caught up in the visible artistry and poetry of our science library's collection of antique watercolor renderings of their sculptural external configurations. Tumors were depicted clustered outside their arboreal hosts. Cartoonish, bulbous appendages layered themselves over healthy bark. The intruders stacked themselves to solidify their hosts from outside, instead of insidiously attacking them from within.

I had little understanding of what the known biological data meant about what would happen next. When Jim hesitated after my question about the PET scan, I read his eyes. I then knew enough to say, "You don't have to tell me now."

~~~~~~

Jim sat in an upholstered beige chair in a modern two-story glass-paneled front lobby. Broad spaces between the world outside the hospital and its inner floors were rendered in excruciatingly neutral tones. Not a scrap of oxygenated blood-red, a flesh tone, or even bones' yellowed ivory.

Dry-eyed, he intently read journal articles about pancreatic cancer on his laptop. I gestured to him that I was going outside, where the unbearably hot afternoon air remained unleavened by clouds. I watched him from the other side of the glass while he calmly pored over his screen.

~~~~~~

I leaned against a prickly pillar studded with pebbled cement. The sun was high and heavy and far too bright. I haltingly left phone messages for two close friends.

Eventually, a woman in a vivid orange shift dress emerged from the building and walked my way. I was still trying to hide my face between glances at my husband as he read inside. Her dark hair was tied back in a long pony tail, and she was slim in a healthy way, not in the way I already felt I was beginning to disappear at the edges, while Jim even then had begun to bulk up for what might lie ahead.

It was the not-quite-stranger from the surgeon's office, who must finally have reached the end of a very long day. Everyone else who'd glanced my way had given me a wide berth. She must have recognized me, shaking and stricken, as the sun was close to its highest point in an empty sky. Wordlessly, she walked over to me, wrapped her arms around me, and let me weep into the bright linen on her shoulder.

~~~~~~

I tried to breathe deeply and returned to the atrium. Jim looked up at me and calmly said that whatever the PET scan showed, it looked like he would need a significant course of chemotherapy. I grabbed a handful of tissues from a nearby box.

~~~~~~

On the way home, as always, Jim did the highway driving. We'd been at the hospital for almost twelve hours. He wouldn't know the PET scan results until the next day, at the earliest. Our sons would be home that night. Our daughters were hours away.

In our darkened kitchen, as Brady--our less intellectual beagle-- snored loudly at his feet, Jim had our boys sit with him.

"I have a kind of cancer, and it's not the kind I would have chosen, but there is treatment I can get. It's not genetic, and you're not more likely to get it because of this. It's just bad luck."

Only in looking back did I see how carefully he'd chosen his words for our children's sake, to let them know, should they ever wonder, that this was not more likely to be visited upon them.

"This is still all very new, and I don't know exactly what the treatment will be, but it will probably involve some chemotherapy and some surgery after that, and probably some more chemotherapy after that."

We had to tell our daughters next. One arrived home the following night. We could reach her sister only by phone, several states away. Her dad had dropped her off at a summer program only a day earlier and driven another seven hours back to us. He called and told the staff why he needed to talk to her and asked that they please look out for her after the call.

Our not-technically-related nearby family, Randy and Judy--friends to whom we were so close we'd moved an hour-and-a-half north of my office to be able to spend more time with them as our families grew--would have to know, as would our siblings and parents. But not immediately. Jim was hoping to have more data by the following day.

~~~~~~

Later that night, we lay down on the tiger maple bed Randy had helped Jim put together after we moved into the yellow house. The room hadn't perceptibly cooled after the sun went down. We were atop the quilt I made just before we married, in blue fabrics already out of vogue. Its surface swam with hand-sewn pieces in the light blue of our first apartment's walls, which we'd duplicated in our first home. The fabric had thinned in spots by the time we spread it out over the grass at Prescott Park a little more than four weeks later.

On an August night, Jim sat in a camping chair atop the quilt, beaming and relaxed. We listened to Richard Thompson playing an acoustic guitar on a stage just a few feet in front of us, singing of taking his chances on the *Wall of Death*.
~~~~~~

No one who saw Jim there would have realized anything was amiss. A potent chemo cocktail was being infused into his body through a nest of plastic tubing connected to an innocuous-looking fanny pack. He ate cheese and crackers and sipped flat, warm beer, because a sip of any cold liquid would have made him feel as if he were swallowing shards of broken glass. He drummed his fingers on the chair's dark orange canvas arm, closed his eyes in the high sun, and smiled.

~~~~~~

But on that last Monday night in June, it was only the four of us, cocooned with this bottomless news. Our sons were asleep in the room they shared and we were atop the well-loved wedding quilt.

"I'm slightly radioactive, you know." He spoke very seriously, as I pressed myself as tightly as I could to his shoulder. I could feel, and may already have been trying to memorize, the vibrations of his voice and the cadence of his beating heart. He sounded as if he were worried about my getting too close to him after he'd been injected with radioactive dye for the PET scan.

I smiled, as much as I could for quite some time, because this time the parry fell to me.

"That's the second worst pickup line I've ever heard."

~~~~~~

Exactly eight years later, I would find myself at Boston's John Adams Courthouse, at a conference whose keynote speaker described trauma in surviving victims of violent crime. Such trauma can reorder the brain and alter consolidation of memory. Time may be rearranged. Some images and sensory memories will be indelible. Other fragments may eternally be missing, never having formed, leaving blurred and disordered spaces like the indeterminate *bokeh* beyond a sharply focused photographic image.

The speaker paused. "So, what's the essence of trauma? What is trauma?"

For a room filled with lawyers, it was uncharacteristically quiet.

"I'm willing to wait."

Not much of a wallflower, nor comfortable with a void, my hand flickered.

"It's the violation of expectations, something you don't see coming and can't prevent."

She nodded, as if reading my mind.

~~~~~~

Another June 28th. So early in the morning as to have been deepest night for most people, even on solstice days with little external darkness.

I awakened from a nightmare that baffled me until the date registered on my waking self. I'd dreamed of imagined calamities of my own doing. My dream self had steered obliviously backwards, veering off a sandbar into the ocean, and endangering the three of my children who sat silently in my rear seat. In the next nightmare reel, I drove furiously in the wrong direction on a highway, aggrieved--as Boston drivers are wont to be--at other drivers, who in this rare instance were only innocently in my way. Another cut and I was back in my driver's seat, but this time at a beach. I occupied the same faithful blue Honda I hadn't acquired until years after my husband was gone, and in which I had by then already safely navigated another 120,000 miles alone at the wheel. I saw Jim walking on a jagged cliff's edge, weighed down by a bright green backpack. I eagerly called out to him. He looked at me in a way he never had, abjectly disappointed, and used words he never would have spoken, in a tone he was incapable of using: "Why would I want to go with someone who can't even drive children safely?"
~~~~~~

Once awake, I tried to shake off the dream. I tended to a very sympathetic Rufus, who was by then my lone beagle. I left for work from the second home I'd moved to without Jim. I turned on my corporeal car's radio--92.5, The River. On came *Last Kiss*.

That's when I thought about the date and reconsidered the dream. In the yawning space between that indelible day of diagnosis and its most recent anniversary, my focus had been askew. I saw only the blur of disruption and mistakes and thought not that my husband *would*--because I know he would not--but that he should have been disappointed in me, although I know he was never disappointed in me when he was here. I miss that, too. How lucky I was to have spent my entire adult life with someone who always saw in me the best person I was capable of being.

He would have wanted me to bring the other pieces into focus. His hand's steady strength as he held mine and we walked into the hospital. The high glass doors sliding open to give us far more space than we needed, when he must already have known what we'd learn. The buoyant tiger lilies, which had arrived ahead of schedule that year, back-lit by sun and tickling our bare legs as we brushed past a stone bench. The two carved statues of cherubic children atop it, which someone had gifted with Red Sox caps and fresh summer flowers. And the kindness of the woman in the orange dress who found me weeping outside the hospital that last Monday in June and chose not to look away.

4

The Space Between

My husband's default position, even when he knew he was dying--indeed, especially then--was to consider his good fortune. It was more than inherent optimism; it was a state of grace. Three days after his PET scan surgically confirmed his diagnosis, he continued eating heartily. He was trying to bulk up his lean, healthy frame for a chemo regimen no one had yet suggested would be reasonable to attempt. At the same time, I--the physically healthy spouse--began to disappear. I didn't see any point in trying to sustain my own body, not because it could have betrayed me just as suddenly as his had, but perhaps because it was as much as my subconscious could do to feel some sliver of what might lie not far ahead for him. I readily would have traded places. Not only in treatment, but later, when he would lose the capacity to eat and drink. It was a nonsensical, fruitless solidarity, as with those said to feel some of the physical travails of a partner's pregnancy.

We're one but not one when the chips are down.

~~~~~~

The first radiology consultation took place in the same hospital complex where the diagnosis had been delivered.
~~~~~~

This time the office was in a subterranean suite off an atrium open to light through a cut-out to the ground floor above us, which thudded with the weight of the lucky and unlucky making their way through the hospital wing's entrance that day.

I wondered if the large open waiting area was designed to accommodate already hospitalized patients being ferried down on gurneys and in wheelchairs. Perhaps tall fountains along the path from the elevators had been designed to mimic coastal waters' cycling, soothing sounds. The world outside as it continued on an early summer day.

The waiting room chairs were stiff and tightly spaced.

I rigidly sat, holding Jim's hand. We were surrounded by patients. Pale, balding, thin. Patterned with older and newer bruising. Most were hooked up to IV towers which further locked us into the waiting space.

My non-judgmental husband read my thoughts as I silently surveyed the otherwise antique crowd, lingering on the couples. He leaned down, forehead to forehead, and gently whispered to me.

"Other people are allowed to get older."

He knew my imperfect soul so well, and loved me nonetheless.

~~~~~~

More than once, I looked at my husband, thinking we youngsters had vowed always to be together.

"I know. Promises were made," he would say, when I hadn't said a word.

And I could read in his face the practical caveat his lawyer spouse refused to confront.

But that was only until death do us part.

In jest, we'd occasionally augmented our vows. Jim had promised not to lose his thick, wavy hair, which hadn't receded at all. And because we'd both been genetically gifted with metabo-
~~~~~~

lisms that made it no effort to comply, I'd promised not to become morbidly obese.

The distance between a dream come true and a nightmare come to life can be a thin space indeed.

Stories like *The Gift of the Magi* and *The Monkey's Paw* suggest the difference may lie in a failure of imagination. Wishes may become horrifically twisted when one neglects to consider unintentional ways in which they could be made to come true. Suddenly it was as if Kafka had collaborated with O. Henry. Jim needed to gain weight for the treatment he'd deduced would be recommended, and after the shock of his diagnosis I struggled to eat at all. Chemo wouldn't make him lose his hair, but it would turn white nearly overnight, and curl in smaller waves, like the surface of low grasses on sand dunes in high winds.

Of course, it had never mattered to me or to him if he'd lost all his hair.

As I internally railed against what was happening to my husband--a process that escaped me in tortured thoughts and crying jags while he slept--he recalled patients even younger than he and considered himself lucky to have married, to have lived to see our children's very different personalities and thoughts and interests emerge, and to have found his calling in service to others.

To have lived "this life," with us, as he would tell me when its end was near.

~~~~~~

We waited over an hour beyond the appointed time for our consultation before being pointed to what turned out to be just another underground waiting room closer to the radiologist's office. A quilted wall hanging with a checkerboard border was of sailboats pieced from squares and triangles. White and shades of blue. It wasn't unlike a quilt I'd made for our first baby.
~~~~~~

Eventually the radiologist beckoned Jim into a corner office. I followed. For the first and not nearly the last time, I realized I would have been equally invisible had I been absent. The doctor addressed Jim, outlining a course of radiation in likely combination with chemo. The only words dispatched in my direction were dismissive: "You don't have to write this down."

I said nothing.

I was aware I didn't "have to" write down what he was saying. My husband was a physician and could answer any medical questions I had later, but as a patient, he should never have been put in that position. I wasn't writing because I "had to." I wasn't clutching a pen in my white-knuckled, shaking hand, and writing down snippets of unfamiliar words and sketching quilt blocks of clipper ships because I needed to write down anything this doctor said. On that point he was both technically correct and crushingly wrong.

I was writing because I wasn't in a position to heed my body's command to run from that suffocating underground room. I was writing because the continued effort of pressing down a pen point was all I could think of to do. To focus my attention and keep myself from derailing the business at hand by telling the doctor how singularly unhelpful it was to be instructed in what I did or did not "have to do" in such moments.

I was pressing the blue point nearly through-and-through my orange notebook's then nearly empty pages because I had no other way to try to steady myself enough to resist the impulse to flee the room as the physician discussed intensive radiation as if it were something abstract. As if it were unconnected to the body and soul of the person I loved, who sat so close to me that I could sense his core temperature was higher than mine that day.

It would not be even close to our worst experiences as patient and partner.

5

Three Words

I have twice laid eyes on a renowned surgeon who on each occasion sent a total of three one-syllable words in my general direction. I can't say we weren't forewarned. When a local oncologist heard we planned to go to Boston to meet with him, he warned not that my husband should be wary, but specifically that *I* should be aware this wouldn't be the most personable consultation.

How bad could he be? I wondered.

The evening before the traffic madness of the extended July 4th weekend, Jim assembled his own medical records, including printouts of his labs and cardboard-sheathed copies of the scans he'd already collected in two hospitals and states. He drove us to a Boston hospital close to an especially alarming Storrow Drive offshoot. There, most out-of-towners' frantic attempted exits are met with strenuous honking and bouquets of emphatically extended middle fingers. Jim was an old hand at handling this.

We took an elevator from the main hospital tower's nearly empty lobby. It was wide enough for six-lane gurney races and adorned with larger-than-life portraits of copiously bearded silver-haired men from centuries past. Vaguely encouragingly, all of them seemed to have enjoyed medical care of a quality that carried them well into their golden years.

The bell dinged on a floor high enough to guarantee a stellar view of the day's remains. When the elevator doors slid open we heard heels to our right. A scheduling assistant who appeared to be the only human on the entire floor told us the surgeon was on his way into the city. She led us to stiff gray chairs in an alcove adjoining a room we didn't then know was an examining room. I twiddled with an old paperback of Kafka's *The Trial*, still failing to appreciate how far my subconscious had bounded ahead of me and jettisoned nuance--at least when grabbing reading material on our way to venues where indeterminate waits would lead to verdicts in which we had no input. Jim was grateful the surgeon was willing to meet with him. I felt sick and vaguely dizzy and dehydrated.

The surgeon eventually arrived and nodded a greeting to Jim, who I could not possibly have been shadowing any more closely. He gestured for my husband to follow him to a closed door at the hallway's far end. I asked the surgeon--or, rather, the back of his silvered head--whether I should come, too.

"If you like."

He didn't look my way. Two of the worst parts of the worst days of our lives would be spent in this space, and a total of six words sent in my general direction from this master of the surgical universe. I trailed into a conference room with a magnificent view of a rapidly darkening city. The table was an enormous oval of distinguished dark wood, topped with thick glass beveled in layers at its outer edge, like a Roman Colosseum's cavea. The walls bore tastefully spaced awards. Dust-free shelves held artifacts from travel to five-star destinations around the world, possibly commemorating the surgeon's own adventures, or perhaps those he made possible for patients gifted with his handiwork.

Black leather chairs were so wide I couldn't comfortably reach Jim in his seat immediately next to mine. He leaned forward, in animated discussion with the surgeon across the table from him. I fiercely dug my right hand's fingernails into my ringed hand's nail beds, to have some physical sensation to divert my attention. But I couldn't escape their conversation about my husband's tumor's complicated construction: it had engineered its way around his veins so intractably that surgery would be impossible even at this surgeon's hands. He seemed to perceive no downside in advising a hyper-aggressive course of chemo to try to shrink the tumor. After that, he announced, he could operate; he could even "zap" the tumor directly with radiation while Jim was "open on the table."

These images of my husband flayed, delivered as if promising an early bird bonus prize at a July Fourth fire sale at the Honda Barn, made me feel physically ill. I was certain I was about to vomit on that gorgeous conference table. I began to rise, slightly off-kilter, so I could reach across the chasm of our side-to-side cushioned chairs' arms. I clutched Jim's left arm, startling him as I felt my heartbeat go into staccato. A wash of pinpricks worked its way down from my dizzy head to my toes as I judged the distance to the hallway door behind him.

The surgeon glanced at papers on his side of the table, deeply frowned, and looked directly at the man whose lab results were recorded on them. He casually said, "Of course, these numbers are concerning."

Had I heard only the tone of that single word--*concerning*--I knew enough to understand it was a euphemism I didn't want to hear from a pancreatic surgeon. He was referring to initial CA 19-9 levels, which I didn't yet have the burden of understanding were blood protein markers for the tumor's presence. The same markers which *The Last Lecture*'s author had known signified his swiftly impending death from pancreatic cancer when they'd "skyrocketed" to a "horrifying 208."

Jim knew what those numbers meant. And that his were had been between 1700 and 1900.

A scan of his tumor floated on the surgeon's small laptop screen, across the gulf of the glass-topped table. I looked away and tugged at my husband's arm, leaning toward him as far as the chair permitted while lurching to my feet and whispering, "I have to leave." Equal stress on each word.

And I fled.

I opened the door and sped back down the hallway, back to the unyielding gray chair. I sat and bent forward and wept, trying to take in air around the immovable weight of what I already knew.

I knew how this would end, even as my physician husband genuinely believed this surgeon would be cutting into his abdomen, possibly before winter came.

After an interlude I couldn't begin to measure, the surgeon's assistant emerged from another direction. She wordlessly handed me one of the legendary hospital's insufficient thin cardboard tissue boxes as she echoed her way to the elevator to leave for the long weekend.

I've never felt as ashamed as I did in the hallway of that surgeon's suite. Strictly speaking, there was no "fight" option, other than the figurative, quixotic one-sided "battle" against his tumor. I despise such war terminology, and what it unfairly implies about the options and agency of those who don't survive their biological killers. But I need not have left my husband's side.

When he finally came out of the conference room, he knelt on one knee in front of me as I cried.

"You never would have left *me* alone in there." I lifted my aching head.

He took my left hand and looked up at me. As always, he understood. He reassured me with the simple truth: "We're made of different stuff."

6

Whirlwind

Unlike my work, in which almost every word I utter or file is a matter of perpetual public record, Jim's work didn't lend itself to outside observation. I'd always thought of him as being economical with language, and was surprised to learn that at work he habitually spoke and wrote at great length. His colleagues told me that if they got an email from him--ordinarily late at night--they knew to sit down, settle in, and scroll all the way to the bottom so they wouldn't miss anything.

Fewer than twenty-four hours after his diagnosis, he sent an email to the eleven physicians who would be dividing up his administrative tasks during what he told them would be an indefinite medical leave. He said he'd been diagnosed with cancer, and likely "will need a combination of chemo, radiation and surgery, although in what order, where, and when are all details that have yet to be decided upon. Today I feel pretty good, but I anticipate worse days ahead. In a way, I'm kind of looking forward to an enforced vacation, knowing I need to boost my physical and emotional resources. I'm battening down the hatches for the storm that will hit next week."

Soon afterward, he made a call to arrange for us to meet with an oncologist at his hospital and get a jump on preparing for pulverizing chemo no one technically had yet recommended.

"Denny, how are you? I have good news and bad news. I'd like to make a referral to you. The bad news? I'm the patient."

~~~~~~

Rufus, born in Indiana and equipped with a New Englander's stereotype of Midwestern calm, abruptly stopped eating.

It is an understatement to say beagles are highly motivated by food--or anything possessing the vaguest aura of being edible. I couldn't help wondering whether he knew something was wrong. I considered who would tell the beagles once a beloved human was no longer within their senses' reach? Who could look into those mournful brown eyes and explain why they no longer had someone who ran with them uphill, and had the strength to carry them home if they ran out of steam?

I called the vet, who thought a two-day hunger strike sufficiently concerning to bring any beagle in to be seen--which was stricter than my own guidelines for consulting my internist. I walked Rufus down to the vet, to Brady's howling consternation. He seemed to be under the impression his big brother was being taken on a grand outing. It wasn't until we walked into the examination room that Rufus's recollection was refreshed enough for him to realize it was a Place Where Bad Things Happen. He mightily quivered, possibly recalling unceremonious probing of deeply personal areas, and having his nails clipped to such protestation one would think their rotini-like appearance had been a deeply thought-out statement of personal identity. The vet looked him over and recommended an x-ray to make sure he hadn't swallowed a foreign object (as beagles *do)* that may have lodged in his gastrointestinal system. I waited, listening to his heartbreaking yelps.
~~~~~~

The vet emerged and beckoned me to a wall-mounted light box where his films were displayed only inches away from me. Looking away wasn't an option. She pointed out that his spleen was enlarged, and something seemed to be pushing forward on his stomach; his pancreas looked a bit enlarged as well.

I could tell from her reaction as I stared at the x-ray that she was puzzled by my level of dismay.

~~~~~~

Brady also sensed something. He'd whimper, and seemed to grow unusually anxious if Jim left the room and closed the door behind him. On the night before chemo began, Brady began emitting a high-pitched whine whenever Jim left his sight. My husband knelt down and sat on the floor with him, gently rubbing his impossibly soft ears.

"What's the matter, Brady? Is it all this cancer business? Is that what's bothering you?"

Brady lowered his caramel-swirled head and rested it on Jim's lap, putting his front paws protectively around him. He burrowed in for a nap as Jim arranged himself on the floor for the longer haul and patted his velvet brow.

~~~~~~

Even before he'd discussed possible chemo with any other physician, Jim had arranged to have a port surgically implanted under his collarbone. It left a rigid, perfectly circular button-like protrusion above his heart, like a penny pressed upwards, or the taut covering of a miniature drum. I always feared I'd hurt him as I rested my head there, although he assured me I never did.

He knew from his own survey of the medical literature that the recommended course would be a very high dose of chemical cocktails. He also must have known how terrible the side effects might be. Jim soon introduced me to his local oncologist, a gentle and kind man nearing retirement, who had treated a young friend of ours whose children were our daughters' classmates and friends. We sat around a circular table in a small white waiting room adorned with nothing but a far larger and plusher box of tissues than I'd been handed at Mass General. He talked to us both, and asked about our children. He recommended a regimen of three-day infusions, beginning with twelve hours at the hospital and followed by continuous portable infusion. He prepared us for side effects I wish remained outside my imagination. Copious prescriptions would need to be filled to address those alone.

My husband could not wait to get those poisons running through him. He would update the hundreds of health care providers in his group during his first hospital infusion, when colleagues stopped in to offer encouragement. Before he felt any effects at all, Jim pulled out his laptop and began to compose a message to his colleagues. He began by expressing gratitude and concentrating on his good fortune: "While it is true, as they say, that cancer sucks, it's also true that there are a few things relating to this for which I can be thankful. My cancer is curable with aggressive treatment, which I'm receiving even as I write this. I'm fortunate to have accrued something of a dream team of cancer care, and I'm ready for whatever's next."

In the efforts of close to two dozen physicians to fill his size 13-plus shoes, he assured them it would take some time and error, and to be forgiving of themselves: "There may be some missteps and some balls that hit the floor, but in the big picture, I'm not worried."

~~~~~~

My cancer is curable with aggressive treatment.
I knew even then, with as much certainty as I could know any objective truth, that it was not curable, but am convinced my
~~~~~~

husband genuinely believed it could be--that despite his lab results and the objective odds, he expected to return to work and have significantly more time with us. He was convinced he'd have surgery after that torturous course of chemo, which he endured with his usual equanimity. Each long day in the brightly colored pods would end with the same alarming closer: after the final drug cocktail, his tongue thickened and his skin turned bright red. A heavily pregnant nurse in triple layers of protective gloves and blue scrubs would rush to administer something to counteract the symptoms as he tried to wrap his swollen tongue around an explanation that he thought he was having a neuropathic rather than an allergic reaction. And I'd bring him home in a state beyond any previous incarnation of exhaustion--even beyond the perpetual weariness of his rotations in emergency medicine and obstetrics. There, a portable pump would release its toxins into him with a low hydraulic *whoosh* exactly every two minutes, all day and all night. As he slept and I did not.

~~~~~~

For months after the shock of the diagnosis, it was I who had sieve brain. I was unable to keep track of objects measuring fewer than three-by-five inches. Cell phones and bank cards were in constant peril. Yet in those immediate days and weeks, we had to make profoundly important, informed decisions--soliciting second opinions; updating provisions to entrust to others the future care of our minor children and management of Jim's medical care if neither of us could; and managing a complex series of medications. I would need to muster the discernment to know which symptoms signaled possibly life-threatening complications from treatment and required emergency care. I was astounded at how much both a patient and grieving *sous*-patient were required to keep track of
~~~~~~

and logistically coordinate. And those were the burdens most patients and their families experience.

I didn't anticipate that I'd also need to call upon my adversarial core and skills just to contend with some of the very people who were managing my husband's care, yet resisting his specific wishes, which I would have seen through to my own dying breath. I shouldn't have had to. No one should.

~~~~~~

After six weeks, the remaining scheduled chemo abruptly was canceled. The process had been relentless and debilitating, and no lab results even hinted it had helped. Worst for my husband were the days lost to sleep. It wasn't the pain or nausea or less common side effects which disturbed him, but I could see he felt that sleeping for so long--sometimes eighteen hours a day--marked another day with us in this world that had slipped through his fingers.

I waited for hours in a hospital hallway during a post-chemo ultrasound at his hospital, clutching his wedding band and under the mistaken impression he couldn't wear it while being scanned. He must have known that when he handed his ring to me, and that I'd want to hold it anyway. Only someone who knew him well would have seen even a trace of the lingering physical exhaustion from his treatment regimen. He finally reappeared in the hallway, having spent almost an hour staring at his own scan, which at least two radiologists had weighed in on. One of them agreed with him that there may have been a slight reduction in his tumor's size, but it sounded to me like his agreement had been tentative--more an unwillingness to entirely exclude the possibility it had infinitesimally receded.

~~~~~~

Jim once again gathered his own medical records. He scheduled an appointment to follow up in Boston with a surgeon who was an associate of the surgeon who'd held court in the hospital suite from which he looked down upon the city. The following week we returned to Boston, where we waited for more than an hour past our appointment time before being led into a smaller waiting area. We waited even longer there before being ushered into a tiny examining room where, eventually, five oncology residents filed in like Robert McCloskey's ducklings. Behind them was not the surgeon with whom the appointment had been made, but a gastroenterological oncologist who introduced himself. We recognized his name, which my physician uncle had given to us; the oncologist had been kind enough to speak to Jim by phone early on, as we'd scrambled to try to figure out where it was best to go for more information. He appeared puzzled that the surgeon hadn't been in to see Jim.

A resident whose name tag identified her as a radiological oncologist spoke, explaining that the new scan hadn't shown any reduction in the tumor's size, and they recommended a seven-week course of radiation to see if it could be shrunk.

I watched Jim absorb the information and nod.

"And if it doesn't work, I would be sad, but..." My husband left it there, with a light shrug. Instantly adapting.

It was all that remained reasonable to try.

The residents soon filed out. The oncologist lingered and walked us back to the empty inner waiting room. He said he'd ask the surgeon at least to come out and meet Jim. He soon returned, looking slightly abashed, and said the surgeon wasn't able to come out for Jim's appointment with him. By that time, we'd been there more than three hours past the scheduled appointment with the unseen surgeon, who evidently couldn't be bothered even to introduce himself to an unlikely candidate for his or his associates' scalpels. I did not excavate the hundreds of papers already piled on Jim's desk to see what we and his health insurance provider, in some combination, had been billed for that afternoon's non-consultation.

In the end, three supremely skilled Massachusetts physicians spoke a total of ten words to the spouse who would carry the story of how they treated one human being.

"You don't need to write this down."

"If you like."

And I would not have recognized this surgeon had he looked down on me on Boston's streets.

~~~~~~

My husband was, but was not nearly only, a technically skilled physician. Bridget, a nurse practitioner, told me about one of his earliest patients: "I remember him getting down on one knee to comfort an elderly woman who was lonely but otherwise had no medical concerns. He gave her uplifting advice and told her she could come see him anytime and that he would always help her. She left relieved and admitted to me she had always had a crush on that 'beautiful man.' He had mastered the art of medicine."

Another early patient balled up her young internist's prescription for high blood pressure medication. She instructed him that she had done just fine without it for her many years, and topped off the appointment by throwing it at him. Jim was unfazed and pleasant to his cantankerous assailant. I learned of this event decades later, from that patient's daughter, who had been with her mother in the room at the time and had given birth to a son years after the crumpled curve ball incident. He'd grown into the teenager who met our daughter in high school and became like another son to me and a brother to her siblings.

Compassionate care endures, as does its haunting absence.

~~~~~~

Forever after that, or in truth just months into widowhood one year later, I was on a playground with a physician friend and her three-year-old. A little boy neither of us knew showed me the green wooden sailboat he'd made, which was the same sailboat one of our sons had made as a Cub Scout. I watched him hold it aloft on an imagined sea as he ran and kept cycling back to where we stood to tell me more stories about his boat.

"He's imprinting on you," my friend said. She grew quiet and told me about the night her husband, one of the physicians who'd taken over a portion of Jim's tasks, had been the first of the two of them to see his "Extended Leave" email. Visibly shaken, he'd told her of Jim's cancer diagnosis.

"Maybe it's prostate cancer?" She told me she'd hopefully offered up. It was more plausible than the imaginary disease I'd conjured up that first night.

Anything but this.

But they knew him, and what it would take for him abruptly to stop doing the work he loved, and begin to delegate his many tasks so patients' care would seamlessly continue.

~~~~~~

After his first missives to his colleagues, Jim was an entirely open book about his diagnosis. It wasn't until much later, when only Bob could answer the question, that I understood this, too, was protective of us. He told me Jim had wanted to hold off telling even the wider world of his colleagues the precise nature of his cancer only at the very beginning, and only until he had enough information to help others get their bearings about it. People immediately had begun flocking to Bob with questions about his partner, and Bob had asked Jim what he wanted him to say.

"Why didn't he want you to say it was pancreatic cancer?" I asked Bob, who looked at me and hesitated. "Did he say?"
~~~~~~

Bob paused. "He said he didn't want people measuring him for a box."

And then I understood. Jim hadn't wanted me immediately immersed in his own hospital's world and surrounded by his medical colleagues, many of them longtime friends. Their fear for him would make it impossible for us not-in-the-medical-know to share his unassailable hope in those moments. Before more data came and he recalibrated what could be hoped for and began preparing us for the next irrevocable medical truth.

Although he soon began referring to his cancer as "the worst-kept secret" at his hospital, I suspect the original sin of full disclosure lay elsewhere. The colleagues involved in his diagnosis and treatment carefully guarded his condition. I think the shock of his diagnosis had promptly filtered down from a much broader community of family and friends who had no reason to think that Jim, being Jim, would closely hold that information. But most civilians, unlike his colleagues as they read his first message to them, wouldn't immediately have understood what his diagnosis meant, and how little time he likely had. Because I'm made of different stuff, I did.

~~~~~~

It cannot be easier to be the gravely ill or dying spouse than it is to be the surviving one, but Jim truly believed my role was harder. He must have known how he would suffer, but also knew his suffering and his time were limited, while my capacity for worry is infinite. He believed it would be harder for me because I'd have to go on without him for whatever came our way next, and he knew how hard that would be for the person he chose to spend his life with. He knew how lucky he was to have his family and so many friends. He had time to plan, and the clarity to make sure I understood exactly what he did and did not want at the end of his life.
~~~~~~

That he would want to come home when that time came if he were anywhere else. But he never believed he was the unluckiest person in the room. Not even, and indeed especially, in the room to which he would come home to die.

7

Two Words

The future dissolved in two words.

That November day began in the Happiest Place on Earth. On the preceding evening, Jim had given me the key to the Kingdom. The Magic Kingdom. A key attached to a brilliant blue card on a carnation-pink lanyard. It had been a few weeks since his course of radiation had ended. He'd had a follow-up scan in Boston the day we flew out to Orlando for two days. We would fly back and go straight to the pancreatic surgeon's office, where Jim expected to be told he'd be scheduled for surgery in December.

My tension level as we prepared to leave Florida was so high that I became frantic when the airport bus hadn't arrived by the scheduled time.

"It's okay," Jim told me. "We've got plenty of time."

He read on a bench while I dashed back across the street.

"We can't miss our flight," I told a man at an outdoor desk. He asked when our flight was, checked some schedules, and deduced the shuttle bus had come and gone earlier than scheduled, while I'd long been awake and Jim still peacefully slept.

He picked up a phone. "We'll get you a cab to the airport," he said. "We'll pay. Don't worry. We'll get you there in time." He looked at me intently, reading a distress deeper than a possible missed flight. "Will that make you feel better?"

I think somehow he knew it wouldn't. That nothing would. But his kindness helped.

~~~~~~

How do you tell someone he's dying without saying a word?

I wish I didn't know an answer to this riddle.

Almost exactly four months had passed since I fled the same surgeon's office. Jim's chemo and radiation had been in service of two hopes: that his tumor would shrink enough to make surgical removal possible, and that meanwhile no metastatic disease would "declare itself," as some doctors euphemized. Jim was so certain he'd have the surgery that he'd told family and colleagues he planned to return to work in January, after recovering from it. His four sisters had arranged to take consecutive weeks off from work to help us.

From Orlando's heat we flew into Logan and drove to the hospital, where we emerged for the second time from the elevator into the surgeon's office suite. It was at first as echoingly empty as it had been almost four months earlier, in July.

We were instructed to wait in the same gray chairs, in the same hallway alcove where I'd become undone. We promptly realized there was no soundproofing between the examining room and the hall, and no other place for us to wait. We couldn't escape hearing the surgeon cheerfully speaking to a patient who'd recovered full health after his masterful surgery, and telling her to come back for a check in another five years. Laughter. Lightness. Assurances. He told her there was no increased future risk to her despite a close
~~~~~~

relative's death from pancreatic cancer, just as Jim had been careful to tell our children on the night of his diagnosis.

Even had the conversation beyond the door not been crystalline to anyone waiting outside it, the patient, who looked about Jim's age, was so visibly buoyant when she emerged that there couldn't have been any doubt about what had been communicated to her. The cured do not tend to carry themselves like the afflicted. Indeed, in all the waiting rooms in all the hospitals we occupied, it was the only time I ever heard a lilt in a patient's voice. Or a doctor's.

Then it was our turn. The surgeon nodded at Jim, who stood and walked into the examining room with me. He sat on its table as I deposited myself on another uncomfortable chair, inches from his knees. The surgeon nodded again at Jim, never looking my way--which required some effort in a room about the size of a modest walk-in closet or undersized prison cell. One small, high window looked out toward the Charles River. A bright painting of flowers in a vase was rendered in large strokes of primary colors above a scarlet book shouting the upper-case title: "PANCREAS." How festive. And I'd thought my mother's Renaissance-inspired collages occupied a niche art market.

Down to business with my husband. "So, has anyone talked to you about your CAT scan?"

"No."

The surgeon, his back to me, handed him a few sheets of densely printed paper.

Jim began to read what I gathered was the radiologist's report on the scan he'd had in the same building just before we flew south. He looked up at the surgeon--who was still standing and had migrated slightly toward the door--and evenly said two words: "That's disappointing."

He later told me he'd stopped reading when his eyes reached a different two words: "metastatic disease," describing lesions on his liver.

For the second time in my life and those never-ending months, I heard myself crying before I realized I was doing it.

~~~~~~

Before quickly completing his exit from the room, a short jumble of words flew from the surgeon in Jim's direction: "I didn't see those myself at first, but I can show you on the scan, there's one that's about one-and-a-half centimeters and one closer to the biliary duct, about two centimeters."

After the surgeon vanished into the hallway, I stood to take the single step to my husband, who still sat on the examining table as we held onto each other. He looked at me and I knew he wanted to see the scan for himself.

I choked out, "You can go. I don't want to see it."

"I know." He put his hand to my cheek and bent down his forehead to mine, then went to the conference room.

He materialized a few minutes later, which was longer than the surgeon had spent with us in the examining room where I'd stayed behind, leaning against the wall and staring at the loud framed 'PANCREAS' print. I could only see the red in it.

As Jim took my hand, the surgeon stepped infinitesimally back into the room, with one shoe barely over the threshold. The consultation, such as it was, was over. He shook Jim's hand, said "Good luck," and disappeared.

~~~~~~

When I was nine, I lived in Meudon, Hauts-de-Seine, with my older and younger brothers while our father was on sabbatical and teaching outside Paris. My mother did not tell me that my close childhood friends' father, who was married to her close friend Eva back home in Massachusetts, had died after a long illness that even now I can only suspect was cancer. The nature of adults' travails was never discussed in front of the children. On the only day snow fell that year around Paris, promptly melting away so no one who hadn't seen it transform the city would have noticed, my mother handed me an already opened letter to her from Eva. It had been refolded into a nearly translucent powder-blue airmail envelope. My mother left me alone in the room to read it. A third of the way down the second page, in a tall, thin script that reminded me of my mother's friend herself, I read, "Alan died," and knew those were the words I was meant to see. My mother never spoke to me about it; I merely absorbed it, and was terribly sad, tearful at the unfairness of my friends being without a father during his extended illness, and then forever. I can still see the handwriting on the light blue page.

I imagine my husband carried the computer-printed words "metastatic disease" with him until he no longer held such images.

My parents were not physicians. They weren't in the business of communicating such news, and my mother was pained for her own friend. This surgeon's disengagement put my husband in the position of not only having instantly to absorb such devastating information himself, but also having to explain it to me. I shall never forgive the imposition of that additional burden on him.

Neurologist Oliver Sacks grew up in a physician-filled household which he wrote about in *The Mind's Eye*, noting that his parents did not talk about their patients as just "cases," but as beings, with medical conditions and in circumstances which uniquely "became biographies, stories of people's lives as they responded to illness or injury, stress or misfortune." I know my husband was that kind of physician. But some physicians treated him as a "case." And sometimes much less than that.

By the time we emerged outside the hospital's main building after the second non-examination in an examining room there, it was deep dark. Jim wanted to walk to a neighboring building where the oncologist who'd met us with the flock of residents had an office. Having been left with an unironically delivered "Good luck" and no hint of a next step, Jim wanted to try to make an appointment with the oncologist to discuss the radiologist's report folded into his jacket pocket, and what, if anything, we were to do. Would someone at least be referring him to hospice care?

But first I stilled myself against the cold cement wall at the garage's entrance. The thought of going home was overwhelming. Our children were various distances away and we needed time together to figure out how to answer their questions and get them all back home.

I leaned my head under Jim's chin, which required I stand on tiptoes, and held onto him tightly and looked up into those green eyes.

"I'd really rather you run off with an Argentinian mistress instead of this," I wailed. (At the time, it was somewhat more topical.)

He looked steadily at me. "Nah, I think you'd still kill me first."

He had a point.

~~~~~~

It was after even hospital business hours when Jim took my hand and we walked, my two-to-three steps to each of his strides, toward the oncologist's office--a place where patients receive news and advice about some of the deadliest kinds of cancer. Inside the building, the lights were far too bright. A few people were still waiting in a large room behind clear floor-to-ceiling glass along a hallway with an unobstructed view of lower Beacon Hill. We walked to the front desk, where Jim protectively held my quiver-
~~~~~~

ing shoulder and explained he wasn't a patient, but had talked to the doctor before and was hoping he could make an appointment to come back to see him.

The receptionist looked at both of us, signaled for us to wait there, and disappeared for a moment.

She came back and said the doctor was with his last patient of the day and would stay and talk to us for as long as we needed.

"Can I get you anything?" she asked me, not my husband.

I couldn't speak.

"She'll be okay, thank you," Jim told her, leading me back to the hallway outside the glass door, where we sat and waited on a white bench overlooking Mt. Vernon Street, where I'd presented my groom with the copper pot during that joyful first winter of our marriage.

~~~~~~

As we talked with him in his inner office, we immediately ruled out clinical trials even before the gastroenterological oncologist (two-thirds of a haiku for his specialty alone, I marveled) had called up Jim's recent scan on his computer screen. I did not look at it. As he scrolled on a second screen, he quickly ticked through the disqualifiers which ruled out each ongoing clinical trial, but still did not beat us to our synchronized side-to-side shakes of our heads.

We had not in fact asked about trials, and had no intention of traveling to any more hospital spaces.

This kind oncologist's only misread was his apparent assumption that we were interested in such probability tails. We wanted to understand how much time there likely was, and how and when to get palliative care, and not waste a minute more loosing time with those we love while chasing an unavailable cure.

Jim had a different winning hand in mind.
~~~~~~

~~~~~~

After meeting with the oncologist, we returned to the hallway bench, in a building that hadn't been even a glimmer in some architect's eye when we began our married life in a tiny apartment on the same block the window overlooked. I leaned into Jim. I'd been crying so hard that sharp pain had cemented itself behind my eyes and I felt sick to my stomach.

Two women, perhaps a mother and daughter, emerged from a neighboring office and walked past us in the otherwise empty hallway. The younger woman, who had straight strawberry-blonde hair, looked at me, collapsed against Jim, and said understandingly, "We got bad news today, too, dear."

I wanted to say, "I'm sorry."

I wish I had.

No words came out.

~~~~~~

That night we each answered just one phone call, briefly and numbly. I spoke to Randy and Jim spoke to Bob.

The next day, the first of our children arrived home ahead of schedule, while Jim was asleep upstairs. He began asking me about the CAT scan and what would happen next.

"How long will it be before they can look again?"

He sat on a high stool in the kitchen, facing the glass-paned door that looked out to towering trees beyond his father's plantings, which remained improbably lush and green. Snow hadn't yet smothered them.

Seated there, my son was at just the height where I could wrap my arms around him from behind and rest my head on his shoulder, feeling the vibration of his deepening voice as he spoke.

I paused. "Do you mean…. Are you asking if they could operate sometime later?"

Of course he was. I thought I felt him nod. My own aching eyes were closed as I leaned on him. Before I answered, I could feel his shoulders begin to tremble.

"Honey, he's not going to be able to have surgery. There may be some treatments he can have to give him more time and help if he has pain, but this means he can't be cured."

It was the hardest question I've ever had to answer.

I would never again fear such anodyne annoyances as testy judges yelling from high benches.

~~~~~~

It was a three-day marathon of breaking the news to our children. Finally, Jim and I were beyond emotional exhaustion. We were upstairs in our all too quiet house, which by then harbored more than two centuries' accrued ghosts along with our newly somber beagles.

I turned to him. "It's a good thing we didn't have eight children."

But we couldn't have been luckier than to have these four.
~~~~~~

8

Into the Words

I often direct grammatical corrections toward defenseless inanimate objects. Scoff if you will--and should--but I believe I owe my avocation to a single word I included in a post-interview letter enclosing a writing sample just shy of the final version. Decades later I saw the word (penultimate) had been circled in blue, with a scrawled note that Charlie, the head of my division, would like to hire me.

Words, and their delivery, can be pivotal.

Serious illness has its own language, spoken and written. It has its own tones, and even melodies.

~~~~~~

"It's *Jupiter: The Bringer of Jollity,* and you're playing it like a *dirge.*"

Mr. Cirillo, our sons' Percussion Ensemble director, delivered the verdict by loudspeaker after the Portsmouth High School Clipper Marching Band had spent another eight hours going through several movements of *The Planets Suite.* His tone supplied the wink, the good humor accompanying a canny critique of the exhausted musicians' phrasing. So much lies within tone.
~~~~~~

In our household, as it justifiably would have been in the home in which I was reared, the very word "tone" came briefly to be shorthand for "the way in which a child between the ages of roughly thirteen and fifteen addresses her mother but no one else." In the odious alphabet soup of medical terminology in which I'd unwillingly been steeped, doctors applied loaded inflections to terms like "cyber-knife" and "stereotactic radiation." Trotted out to another audience at a different hospital, the same words would be rolled around on another physician's tongue and spit back out in a manner that seemed to embed rivalries among professionals I naively had thought were all on the same team.

At teaching hospitals, my husband tended to be addressed as "Mr." rather than "Dr." An institutional ethos was expressed by hyperactive verbs, attached to aggressive options. New things to try; new places to go.

"Oh." one physician raised his eyebrow when Jim mentioned a previously suggested course of treatment. "They're very big on *stereotactic radiation*," the two words intoned as if the other hospital were promoting rain dances or insisting upon yodeling therapy. (My inner haiku generator would flash: *Stereotactic/ You would think they'd suggested/ bleeding by leeches*).

Well, there's tone and there's *tone*.

I confess to having occasionally found my husband's unflappability disquieting. I've always been far more overtly reactive. As a new lawyer at "trial camp" in Boston, I aced the content, while every single attorney and judge on hand for the week observed that I was going to have to devote myself to mastering the courtroom poker face, save the attitude for closing argument, and even then take it down several notches.

~~~~~~
~~~~~~

What's the opposite of a loaded question? Surely it isn't "unloaded." Maybe it's closer to "neutral" or "antiseptic." It had taken me years to decipher my husband's habit of delivering a dry, "Hi. How are you?" to me in the same business-like tone in which he delivered those four words to anyone and everyone else at the beginning of a telephone conversation. This applied no matter how attached he was to the person on the other end of the line. It could be me, our children, or a stranger being summoned to encourage the departure from our home of red squirrels who'd barricaded themselves in an old fireplace like doomed revolutionaries in *Les Miz*.

Someone listening to my end of a conversation, on the other hand, would immediately know if I were talking to a colleague, a cyber menu, someone I love, or someone from whom I want promptly to disengage. Eventually I realized that with the people closest to him, this was just Jim's "pause" button--his rhetorical conversational breather as he gathered his thoughts to transition from work mode to family mode.

Initially he hadn't even wanted me to call Bob and "burden" him with the emotional weight of his diagnosis. I called anyway. We all needed him, although we did not immediately understand how much, and he was with us from that moment on. It was the tone, not the content, of the message I left for him that caused him to call back late that night, on the last day of June, as Jim soundly slept after his confirmatory surgical biopsy that morning.

"We just got in and I didn't want to call you back this late, but it sounded like it was important. Are you okay?" were the words Bob got out before I fell apart.

He'd been able to read what I was unaware my tone had given away about the neutral words in my message.

Thinking back on that conversation, I can hear what he did not say and picture what I could not have seen. His gestures to Myra as he spoke to me, Charlie the German Shepard looking intently at him as Bob mouthed or wrote the words 'pancreatic cancer' so Myra would know how to interpret the look she would have seen on her husband's face and the edge she would have been able to detect in a voice that on my end was completely steady as Bob asked me questions and began to absorb the answers.

I had a very long way to go.

I had only just learned the correct pronunciation of "adenocarcinoma."

~~~~~

Not so many years earlier, Jim had broached the subject of life insurance with me. Our youngest child was on board in the form of a priceless cluster of cells already causing profound physical upheaval of the kind my obstetrician warned me should, once again, be taken very seriously. Although a certain Duchess hadn't quite caused hyperemesis to be in vogue, he advised me it had caused the death of one of the Brontë sisters. As parents of three-and-one-ninth children likely headed for educations beyond dreams of indebtedness, Jim thought it wise that we buy life insurance for both of us. He approached the subject with what I hoped was comical understatement, without a smidgen of unseemly sentimentality.

"You know, if you were to die, not only would I miss you, but I'd take a tremendous financial hit."

Of course, it was not that our family would have been impoverished by the absence of the fraction of public servant's salary remaining after childcare costs, but that he would need to hire someone to do all I did during his very long working hours. Cooking, along with the household's physical maintenance, such as it ever was, presumably could continue to go by the wayside.
~~~~~

Bob told me he'd once asked Jim how he did it all. He'd responded by gesturing at the chaotic mess in my portion of the home office space and said, "I learned a long time ago, some things just have to be let go."

The time we had at home together as our children grew would be short, at least in retrospect. One day we would miss the maelstrom.

I had no objection to signing up for life insurance, but reminded him neither of us was going anywhere, ever. Sacred vows were involved. I may have mentioned being a bit taken aback by the fleeting and dispassionate subordinate clause ("not only would I miss you...") leading up to the "financial hit" chaser. I know now that the calmness of his language reflected his unparalleled capacity to accept life's changes in plan. My physicist father specialized in chaos theory; my husband lived with the understanding that life intrinsically is unpredictable, chaotic even in a purely physical, biological sense.

My husband's words about the grown-up need for life insurance did not mean he wasn't passionate about his life and the family that was its core. He saw no need to bring emotion into that discussion. It was as straightforward as T.S. Garp's mother explained to her son: "Everybody dies.... The thing is, to have a life before we die. It can be a real adventure having a life." Some adventurers will perish unexpectedly, and far too soon, with people still depending on them; that was among the things Jim could plan for.

I saw and better understood his preternatural acceptance when I heard him speak in the same even tone as he reacted to devastating events when they came to pass. My husband himself never hid behind or among words. Sometimes he came so directly to the point that I recoiled, as I did when he tried to teach me his meticulous bill-paying system. When I balked, he said I'd need to know how to do it "after I'm dead."

I beseeched him not to use *that word*, until a more impartial listener who also loved him urged me to understand that he needed to use the vocabulary that was right for him to describe his own disease. It wasn't a fault of the language, or of any word or turn of phrase, that it would be hard for me to hear. And in using the same vocabulary with everyone, including our children, he was giving them the dignity of being able to talk about anything--including his death--with him, to give voice to their own fears and feelings.

~~~~~~

Jim was always a planner, for all of us. I'm certain he left behind exquisitely detailed notes and records and ideas at work, so multitudes there could carry on. He tracked accounts for our children's educations, to culminate in graduations he wouldn't live to attend, and for a retirement he would never enjoy. When I had to fire up his computer after he was gone, his screen flashed reminders of weekly meetings and conferences which went on without him. It asked me for passwords I didn't know. I was startled when I successfully tried one that echoed what was written inside the wedding band that gives me gentle ballast on a chain around my neck. My heart hurt when I saw financial files with handwritten notes like, "What to do if I can't." He had cushioned them for my eyes by using an "if," and not a "when," in case I had seen them too soon.

~~~~~~

Everything, with Jim, was so straightforward and unlayered.
"We have to prepare for the possibility this is a tumor."
"If it's metastasized, I would be sad, but..."
"That's disappointing."
"When I'm dead."

Early in his medical leave, he wrote out a long list of all the out-door chores which needed to be done in each season. Not unlike the need for eleven physicians to divide up his job's administrative component alone, we had to scale up to fill his shoes. Nineteen friends and nieces and nephews and sisters and brothers-in-law spent an entire day on a trial run of his autumn list. Jim supervised, although we allowed Rufus to think that he, as the senior beagle, was in charge.

~~~~~~

"I should show you how to do this. And this is a list of things I do by season outside."

From his out-sized computer monitor, Jim had called me over to his desk from my unkempt neighboring workspace. I stood at his shoulder, not accepting the thought of any season without him.

"I can't. It won't make it any easier." I protested, not wanting to see the list, my head down.

He spoke so very intently, looking up at me from his wheeled desk chair, which squeaked every time he sank into it, even as he grew thinner, but does not now make a sound for me.

"But it would be easier for me."

Anything that makes it easier for you, I thought, but didn't say, as I tried to stop my tears from plunking onto the old pine floorboards.

~~~~~~

I hope my husband understood the way he would be missed. "Miss" is not a big enough word; no tone could make it so. An entirely new word or phrase would need to be coined even to dance around the vast expanse of emptiness. As it was in José Saramago's *The Stone Raft,* in which a previously unimaginable blackout required that a new descriptor be coined: it was "later referred to as *apagón* in Spain, *negrum* in a Portuguese village that still invents words." Or the words and cadence attached to the otherwise inexpressible experience of yearning to hold on in John Irving's *Last Night in Twisted River*: "*she bu de* meant something like 'I can't bear to let go.' You say it when you don't want to give up something you have."

I could not bear to let him go, to grasp how big the lacuna would be, even when I whispered in his ear at the end of his life that we would be all right. Even when I lied and said I would be. Even now.

I don't have the words for it.

~~~~~~

Tone is forever entwined with the words a family holds and the experiences they encode.

Our extended families can revisit our son Noah's two-year-old incarnation whenever they hear the unadorned word "back." An assurance that one is soon to return. A declaration that those left behind should not worry, because the declarant will not be gone for long. Packed within its single lingering syllable I see our toddler son's earnest, enormous cornflower blue eyes as he made his smiling rounds of a room at Papa Dick's house that brimmed with boring adult conversation and bitter beverages. Then he would rejoin his siblings in more amusing endeavors, which usually involved running around on the front lawn no matter what the weather held.

But before crossing the threshold back and away to such adventures, he would pause to reassure us and avert any stress we might experience during his absence. He'd perch at the door sill and wave to us all with a big smile, then lift his right index finger. On the heel of his lingering "back" he made not a sharp swoop, but a slowly floating concave dip to his right and a longer one diagonally downward, like a number "7" or a tracing of a swan's grace-
~~~~~~

ful throat line. A conductor warming up Lilliputian woodwinds. It was a flourish we'd see repeated and refined over the years, his hands poised aloft with mallets, solidifying the stretch of time just before he struck the first notes to *Festive Overture* or *Firebird Suite*. He directed it at everyone in the room at his Papa and Grandma's house as he improbably elongated the word "back."

So the tone of the word "back," to those of us who shared those years, will always mean much more than a promise to return. It means, "I know you'll miss me, but you'll be okay. I have places to go, and you have my blessing to carry on without me."

9

Penguins on the Equator

Days after my husband's diagnosis I had spoken to our friend Elizabeth, who'd spent almost five years living with hers, and told me of her occasional wish to "just take a vacation from cancer." As soon as Jim learned he wouldn't have surgery, he began planning a vacation. Between his birthday and New Year's Day, our children's school breaks would overlap. He looked and felt astonishingly healthy. More than once in this in-between world, he was introduced to someone who reflexively asked, "How are you?" He answered, "For a guy with metastatic pancreatic cancer, I'm great." And he was.

Although he must have known horrific symptoms would soon set in, we were going to take his dream vacation. Off to the Galápagos.

As a Biology major, he'd studied creatures great and small. He'd applied their lessons even to his administrative work, and was so dedicated a student of Darwin's that I sometimes wondered if he'd subliminally laid the groundwork for the rest of us to find beagles irresistible. He understood natural selection is more nuanced than "survival of the fittest." It's not the strongest or hardiest individual organism that endures, but the most *adaptable* organisms which are most likely to flourish together. He himself was endlessly adaptable. When thrown a difficult, nasty personality or work crisis, he thrived on fixing what could be fixed, and working creatively with what remained. He saw problems in context, as parts of systems, and would gather data to fuel adaptations in those systems and serve patients within them.

So we would spend a Saturday night navigating a blizzard in order to watch Mr. Gagnon, our children's beloved band director, guest-conduct the Boston Pops, then immediately travel south to days unbound by time, where majestic frigates glided through jeweled lavender clouds above an emerald sea.

~~~~~~

Jim had quickly planned the trip, necessarily on very short notice. He hesitated only once, when he'd tallied up the costs. He turned to me with the numbers.

"We *are* taking this trip. If we need more money I can always find other work... later." I stumbled on the last word. We both knew what "later" meant.

Then he asked if I thought he should get insurance for the trip.

"But we have insurance." I didn't immediately understand he meant not health insurance, but insurance in case he died there and we had to bring his body back with us. I shook my head from side to side, splashing more tears on the old pine floorboards.

A week after his birthday, off we went.

~~~~~~

Jim was a true artist as a photographer. Growing up on Massachusetts' South Shore, and only in part to occasionally escape his battalion of younger sisters, he'd commandeered a basement where he could disappear into a darkroom to develop his own film. Soon after we met, I noticed he had a particular gift for rendering his surroundings in black and white, although I decidedly am the one who conducts myself as if the world were thus divided. He often focused on the macro, highlighting constituent parts and elevating core components which tend to go unnoticed--like the stuff of which a leaf or butterfly or shell is made and connected to what surrounds it.

Because we'd shared the same undergraduate campus, and then conjoined life, from different vantage points, I have a good idea of what lay outside many of those captured frames. Each photo had been of the ever-candid outdoors. In all the years we shared, the only photos he took in artificial light were of our children. He only once inveigled them to pose for him indoors, against our front room's white folding doors. Against them he took black and white portraits he gave me for Mother's Day not long before his diagnosis.

~~~~~~

Jim never lost sight of the illuminative power of whatever traces of light remain in even the objectively darkest skies. Many of his photographs captured storm clouds. Our youngest child inherited his eye for and love of outdoor photography. During his illness they scoured the internet to trade off lenses at the most fortuitous prices, so she would be best equipped to carry on.

In addition to his photography gear, Jim had collected and consumed tomes about the species and environments we were about to encounter. He listened to Spanish lessons, the better to catch up with our children. I packed fiction, unknowingly including a meditation on relationships begat by chance, which in its way encompasses all encounters among sentient beings. During our first day aboard a small boat, John Irving's *Last Night in Twisted River* would introduce me to a character who literally fell from the sky into another's life. Not a bolt of lightning but a source of enduring light--
~~~~~~

"the same sudden way we lose people, who once seemed they would always be part of our lives."

Greg Brown's lyrics in *The Poet Game* use flying birds as symbols of lingering regret and past mistakes, but in his imagery even the densest congregation of birds still leaves the sky at least half-light. At sunset in Ecuador, gliding frigates filled the skies, but the sense of light remained undiminished.

The choices we're empowered to make are in some ways unbounded. They include the friendships we forge and maintain and how we seek shelter in a storm. Both the people we hold dear and those who deeply wound us might never have fallen into our lives. During that last winter, the six of us nested together, treasured reconnecting with people we'd known in our earlier lives, and made new enduring friendships.

And we happened to encounter the Most Interesting Man in the World.

~~~~~~

His name is Hantzel, and the Dos Equis gentleman has nothing on him. He was our guide, and knew every crevice of the Galápagos, including a tiny remote island upon which his superhuman sight had detected signs rare Pacific birds soon would be nesting in a small crevice high on a cliff. Hantzel's scuba diving skills, impeccable multilingualism, total recall of facts and global events, and entire mien all strongly suggested to me that his prior life had involved *very* interesting work both above and well below the waterline. Even the way other guides would respectfully bow and back away with even a look from him, lest he adjudicate they had stepped a millimeter beyond where they were authorized to tread, made it clear he was a Legend even as he walked among us.

We rowed to the island where he'd gauged from prior binocular observation that offspring were likely recently to have hatched.
~~~~~~

As Hantzel directed him with military precision, Jim carefully clambered to the cliff's edge while the rest of us stood at the short distance the island's circumference allowed. He beamed at the rest of us, his backpack providing the counterweight as he leaned seaward over a sheer drop-off to blue-green water and ragged volcanic rock. I held my breath as my husband slipped almost entirely out of view while leaning away from the cliff's edge at a respectful distance from the nest, which was built into the cliff's face and none of us could see. Jim may well have been the only human ever to have had that vantage point and beheld those new lives.

I watched the sun glint off something out of sight--almost certainly his wedding band--as he clicked his camera's shutter with his free hand. I shouted into the wind for my terminally ill husband to *be careful.*

I'm sure he grinned if my voice carried his way.

~~~~~~

Had I not seen them the way Jim saw them and his camera captured them, I'm not sure I would have warmed to the majestic albatross. Until we climbed another cliff and saw them nesting, molting concentrically from the tops of their heads like balding monks, I had credited the rap on their species that likely originated in the *Rime of the Ancient Mariner,* in which one poor fellow was compelled to carry an enormous dead bird around his neck. Nor had I been nearly as enamored of large reptiles who shed strips of mustard-hued dragon scales as they lumber forward, moving as if bearing the weight of chain mail armor. To capture one of them for us on film, Jim had folded himself sideways, kneeling in stone-strewn sand so he could discretely zoom in on a festively mohawked iguana impervious to our admiring attention. The iguana rested his armored chin on the rock, clasping it between splayed claws aligned with the royal ruby ridges in his neatly appointed
~~~~~~

crest and caudal spines. *"My rock. My world, here in my grasp in this moment. I am satisfied. What more could I need?"*

Jim gave us the world through his eyes. The family rock, knowing he wasn't far from death, felt not just peace, but pure joy. *What more is there than to be with my family in this place in the sun, in this moment?*

When we later uploaded thousands of pictures from no fewer than five cameras, they arranged themselves by date and not source. But I could pick out every one of my husband's photos, no matter the subject, even when several of us took pictures from the very same spot.

~~~~~~

After we'd spent three days at sea, a flotilla of raucous dolphins arrived to see off our first companions, a lovely family of six from Vancouver with their own eldest child Sam, at 3:30 a.m. It was one of those rare occasions when my insomnia was fortuitous.

That night, two new families arrived by rowboat to take their places in the narrow below-deck bunks: a family of four from New Jersey and, from the opposite coast, world traveler Audrey and her grandson, promptly dubbed Noah 2.0. Our new friends were equally as tolerant with our more offbeat evening festivities following our treks under the equatorial sun. Our children toned down some of the wordplay for Noah the Younger, who was exceedingly bright, but still only ten. Our son Sam's drawing game brought us to tears of laughter. Soon three generations were laughing uproariously into the silent starlit night as enormous wings *thwapped* overhead and our Sam spun out an intricate premise of a crime syndicate made up of Orcas and blind Emperor Penguins.

~~~~~~

Jim snorkeled among white-tipped sharks, giant tortoises, and schools of neon puffer fish. When we paddled through mangroves, I noticed he'd position himself to make sure he spent an equal amount of time sitting next to each of our children. Every time I looked at him, he seemed not just relaxed, but blissful.

On Christmas Day he climbed 375 steps, to the top of an unpopulated island. He saw a Mars-like volcanic landscape on one side and a dazzling view of young volcanic islands and land formations on the other. He and our daughter jumped off the boat's upper tier into clear teal water. He learned to do an uncanny impression of a barking baby sea lion; taught Noah 2.0 to snorkel; and played riotous word games with our new friends. We weighed theories about why manta rays leap and spin over deep ocean. Hantzel explained how *halucinojenos* can be extracted from bright hanging flowers. When we returned to Quito, Jim gave a sip of his adult beverage to a son who pronounced the sweet, fruity concoction reasonably tasty--except for the alcohol's battery acid flavor.

We were so lucky.

~~~~~~

*.... Go together,/ You precious winners all; your exultation
Partake to every one. I, an old turtle,/ Will wing me to some
wither'd bough, and there
My mate, that's never to be found again,/ Lament till I am
lost.*

In our own *Winter's Tale*, on the cusp of Ecuador's rain season, we were introduced to Centenarian Lonesome George, the Darwin Research Center's best-known resident. His heart-shaped pool was set in among cactus gardens. Occupying a different angle on the scene, I hadn't appreciated the decorating touch of its shape until I saw a picture Jim took of the entire bachelor enclave. Thought
~~~~~~

to be the last of his species of giant land tortoise, George lacked a mate. It was not for lack of trying. Indeed, unseemly public attention had been brought to his mating misses. Hantzel explained each tortoise species has a uniquely configured carapace. Lack of fit between mates is, as it were, an insurmountable issue. Poor *Solitario Jorge* would have required an engineering feat to partake of "joys with like relation."

George gave no sign his days were numbered. But this prince among tortoises, who despite his enduring solitude had betrayed no indication of illness or distress, and might have lived another century or so, would perish of natural causes the following year. There was not, after all, "time enough for that."

He left behind no like companion to lament until she, too, was lost.

~~~~~~

I would eventually read the stacks of books I'd brought Jim that fall and winter and remained on his bedside table. It was one of the few ways I could be certain what had occupied his mind, at least for a time, when he was too exhausted to do anything but read. In Carl Hiaasin's *Star Island*, I discovered a lead character was nicknamed "Chemo." In another effort to bring my husband light reading while he was in treatment, I'd also brought him David Sedaris's *Squirrel Seeks Chipmunk*, which had him chuckling so heartily that I asked what he was reading. He told me about a short story: "The Sick Rat and the Healthy Rat," the former a credulous white rat with pancreatic cancer, and had heard limericks cure heart disease, and some forms of cancer.

What were the odds?

Given its title, another book I'd given him, as he planned our last family trip had seemed an inescapable choice: Kurt Vonnegut's *Galápagos*. I didn't read it myself until much later, when I
~~~~~~

once again felt lost without my husband and wondered what he'd thought when he read it. I discovered how Vonnegut had designated characters whose time was short. A small black star before a name signified when each was about to be dispatched through a blue-tunnel-to-the-Afterlife. In one passage, a heartbroken widow fled from a hopeful suitor because she didn't want to contemplate being married to anyone other than her husband: "even if Roy was dead, she still didn't want to be married to anybody but Roy."

Her husband, suddenly diagnosed with an inoperable tumor, had yearned to stay alive long enough to make one last trip, to the Galápagos.

"Let me see penguins on the equator,' he said. 'That'll be good enough for me.'"

~~~~~~

Blue-footed boobies, I'd thought as we winged our way to San Cristobal for our last adventure as a family of six visible to the rest of the world. *That'll be good enough for me.*

The trip brought him such joy. Every second with us. Every photo he took and sense he engaged. He didn't permit present time to be supplanted by what he, better than any of us, knew lay ahead. It was as if by force of will he banished his cancer until we had to complete the circle back into winter in New England.

In *Wishful Thinking*, Frederick Buechner wrote about joy, taking the Gospel of John as his starting point. He stressed that the words were spoken not in a setting in which the concept of joy would readily spring to mind, but at the Last Supper. Joy may be found in unlikely surroundings. Jim had not, to my knowledge, read Buechner, but he discerningly, faithfully lived a life of joy.

I know this much of joy: it travels hand in hand with wonder, occupying the same boundless space as love. And, like grace, it can-
~~~~~~

not be gifted or sought out, but only felt, by the attentive and wherever it presents itself.

~~~~~~

Both within and outside the frames Jim created each time he sparingly clicked his camera's shutter, there was love. This was not anthropomorphism (although the scene as female frigates gathered around a scarlet-throated male echoed what I understand to be the premise of a reality show involving distribution of a limited number of roses). Inside each frame is something Jim loved and preserved about his window on this world: brilliant colors and creatures, plants and geological formations, and the spectacular beauty of sights he'd never seen before and never would again. At least from this earthly vantage point on all that grows and erodes and decays and grows again around us.

On the other side of the lens was a man relishing everything about a trip he knew would be his last with the family he loved and will forever love him. Each of his photos can transport us back to the warmth of that sun, the sounds of sea lions, and the feeling of being able to reach out and touch his arm or the back of his shirt as he found himself among winged and earthbound creatures near the end of the visible world and his time in it.

~~~~~~

The artist's frame allows a viewer to recapture the world it holds. It also lets us see the artist outside each preserved moment, whether capturing something real or imagined, aspirational, or merely magical. If I study an Ansel Adams photograph or a Georgia O'Keefe painting, I see the artist, too. If I look at my great-grandfather's oil painting of my mother as a blonde-curled toddler, I also see him painting portraits, the same way I picture Samuel F. B. Morse painting portraits inside our yellow house, at a wood easel like our daughter's, facing windows to the church across the street when its clock was wound by human hands.

Art travels in time, sometimes even more readily than we do. Only in looking back from a considerable distance in traditional time do I realize this trip was when I began feeling called to take and create my own pictures of what lies out there beyond the beloved people in my view.

~~~~~~

We left Ecuador and returned to the recent remnants of another epic Nor'easter. We pulled our down coats on over the morning's thin cotton clothing, flip-flops still on our feet as we stepped out of Logan Airport's sliding doors into dense, quarter-sized snowflakes still drifting down over more than a foot of fresh snow. We headed home to repurpose a lightly tinseled discarded tree for a delayed Christmas celebration, and to two delighted beagles. They didn't seem to know exactly what was amiss, but only that we'd all returned to them and would never leave them for so long that they wouldn't be joyful to see us again.
~~~~~~

10

Interregnum

In January, on our firstborn daughter's birthday, Jim handed in his beeper. He hadn't yet experienced any new symptoms other than weariness, or at least didn't tell me if he had. Once summer's chemo drugs had dissipated from his system, and throughout radiation and our family trip, there hadn't been any external sign of illness. Yet something told him he would not, after all, be going back to work, a hope he'd maintained right up until we returned home.

He handed his beeper to the beeper lady. I hadn't known such a position existed. Apparently, his hospital was big enough for more than one keeper of beepers.

"Are you sure?" she asked.

He nodded.

~~~~~~

My husband had always favored my giving new adventures a try, and resisting the urge to focus on possible bad outcomes. Until his diagnosis, he'd ask, "What's the worst thing that could happen?"
~~~~~~

I began to understand this had always been a gentle way of helping me prepare. Of letting me rehearse possibilities, and conditioning me to walk myself back from a worst-case scenario that might never come to pass. It's a surreal feeling to occupy the space in which the worst-case scenario assuredly would arrive.

Not long after turning in his beeper, we drove to an appointment with his oncologist. For the first time in our lives together, Jim leapt straight to a sinking revelation. I later understood the urgency: he knew his body was telling him I'd need to begin taking over tasks he'd no longer be able to do himself.

At the wheel of a truck I'd never driven, or even known how to drive, he told me he'd been having abdominal pain. It was a far more searing version of the 'ping' that preceded his diagnosis.

I retraced what he'd told me that Thursday night in June. "Wait, when did you know it might be a tumor? Did you know *before* the first ultrasound?"

"I was still trying to protect you then," he told me.

There had been no protecting me for quite some time when he told me the pain had returned, with enough force to wake him and require pain medication. And he had a very high pain threshold, and had always slept the deep sleep of the just.

"What kind of pain?"

I looked at him. He was driving no differently than he always did, face set forward and attentive to everything around him.

I used the in-house pain scale terminology, which originated when our son's siblings had visited him in a pediatric hospital. His brother had made him laugh for the first time in weeks by pointing to the Wong-Baker scale taped to the wall and supplying his own adjectives to account for the ever-less smiling faces younger patients could point to.

"Was the pain heart-stopping... or catastrophic?" I asked my husband.

"Just a two or a three."

He'd never confessed to more than a 'two' before. Ever. Nor would he have been awakened by or taken medication for anything below the top tier. Facing into hail as we traveled the muscle-memory route to his hospital, he continued.

"The pain makes me a bit more pessimistic."

He'd been hesitant even to mention it to his oncologist. He explained that voicing the symptom would "pull the trigger" on a recommendation of palliative chemo, which wasn't likely to be nearly as terrible as the regimen he'd been through, but could only be undertaken for so long, and was of uncertain value. I was puzzled this would concern him: he knew he could say no. He knew exactly what he did and didn't want. We'd discussed it in excruciating detail for whenever I might need to speak for him.

Only much later did I put together the pieces and realize he hadn't told me, because he knew I wasn't yet ready to hear, that the degree and acceleration of his pain likely signified a very rapid decline. He'd instantly recalibrated his hopes to what he knew the sudden onset of such pain meant. His youth, his strong body and abiding heart, and all the other positives at the time of his diagnosis clearly would not garner him anything close to the time his wildly over-optimistic colleagues had told him he likely had, and he in turn had told me and our children he might still have.

He'd adjusted to the present reality of his condition, although still not sunk even close to the bottomless baseline where I'd dwelled since he told me about that first call from Patty. It was crushing to have him join me even partway there. To see his initially reasonable optimism leave him as he followed the evidence his body supplied. I realized how terrible it must have been for him to have watched hope evaporate from me at the outset.

There was nothing I wouldn't have done to make sure every remaining wish he had would be honored. It was just as well I didn't know how difficult some outsiders would choose to make that for us.

~~~~~~

Jim's experience would bear out with uncanny mathematical precision the research Dr. Atul Gawande had described in "Letting Go," a *New Yorker* article that was the precursor to his book, *Being Mortal*: physicians routinely overestimate how long their own patients will live with terminal diseases. The better they know their patients, the more they tend to overstate their projected survival. Indeed, he noted, they regularly do so by more than 500%. Overestimation, even to a far lesser degree, seems to me far more problematic for patients and their families than underestimation. I believe it is better to be pleasantly surprised than to have unrealistic hopes dashed, especially when one is an outsider who puts faith in the physicians to whom we entrust ourselves and those we love.

The numbers were dizzying for me, the household's only mathematically challenged human. As Jim's symptoms began to develop and multiply, we used the same non-whimsical numerical shorthand. "What's your pain?" or "What's your nausea?" would yield not an adjective, but an unadorned number from one to ten. Much later, discussing palliative options, Jim and his doctors spoke in numbers which by that point passed for conversation: "What are you looking for?" "Well, I have no problem with a baseline 2 or 3 for pain, and a 5 or 6 for nausea if it's only, say, two out of seven days, Five or six out of seven I'd have to think about, and above a 6 on pain."
~~~~~~

I'll forever be able to tick off a blizzard of numbers thrown out in my presence by physicians--including that at least 80% of pancreatic cancers have metastasized by the time they're diagnosed.

~~~~~~

Dr. Gawande's article described patients' end-of-life care, including that of a pancreatic cancer patient who had in the end hoped only for a taste of strawberry ice cream. He cited a study of such patients' doctors' advice: 63% overestimated their patient's survival, by an average of 530%. On November 10th we learned Jim's condition was terminal. Over the next days, our children and other family members understandably pressed us for numbers: how long would he live? Left to our own devices to divine such information, Jim told them he believed it would be less than a year. In part from having read *The Last Lecture*--which also involved a prognosis of pancreatic cancer that metastasized to the liver--the two of us were convinced it would be at best between three and six more months, no matter what Jim's doctors said. His oncologist, who was also his colleague, had ticked off the comparatively good news: Jim hadn't yet experienced symptoms from the liver lesions, and on physical examination there was no palpable mass. His blood work remained "fine" (if only in comparison to the dizzying heights at which his blood markers initially had been measured). So, the oncologist told us, he might well have another eighteen months-to-two years left.

He had fewer than ten weeks.

Two years, 730 days, is 553% of 132 days. Put another way, the doctor we adored could be said to have overestimated Jim's survival by slightly more than 550%. Of course, there is always a right tail in discussing median survivals. Stephen Jay Gould memorably focused on that tail in his essay, "The Median Isn't the Message." Someone will survive longer than expected. Gould himself was that
~~~~~~

low-probability long-term survivor of an initial rare and deadly form of cancer before succumbing to a different one decades later.

In this paradoxically, pathologically optimistic health care edifice that my husband also occupied, I always knew how this would end, and had a very good idea of when. But had I truly immediately understood the medical import of the numbers doctors bandied about at the beginning--like those "concerning" CA 19-9 levels--I couldn't have seen around them when I needed to, and when I needed to be functional for our children. Jim, knowing full well what such numbers meant, still could. He could see the positives in his health, fitness, youth, and prompt response to that 'ping' of pain, and realistically consider the possibility he'd have significantly more time with us by subjecting himself to the treatment he endured and the surgery he'd hoped then to have. But he also never failed to prepare for what evolved despite those positives.

It was the things for which my husband--and in turn the rest of us--hoped that adapted and changed. He had plans and hope throughout, but hope could never be and was not the plan itself, any more than my depressive resignation could have been. As our enduring college friend and poker companion David, a University of Colorado math professor (and a darned good player), told me after Jim's diagnosis, "As for how to handle the tail of the distribution, when I teach probability, I recall the old adage, 'The race is not always to the swift, nor the battle to the strong. But that's the way to bet.'"

~~~~~~

It's not only the numbers. We saw evidence that physicians are often treated differently than other patients. For us, the orphaned upside of this was that Jim likely was seen much more quickly (on those occasions when he was seen at all). He understood where to start, what tests to prioritize, how to amass his own records and
~~~~~~

ferry them to different medical institutions, and what treatment--standard or wildly experimental--*not* to chase. Thanks to my uncle Robert, a cancer researcher, we were able to get through to hard-to-reach physicians and swift second opinions. Along with those medical resources came the peace of mind of knowing that no matter what the outcome, Jim couldn't have received better technical medical resources and advice. But those turned out not to be the resources that counted most.

Not nearly.

11

Winter's Weighted White

Jim's pain broke the dam. Within a week I'd taken over all the driving. The last time he took the wheel was on the day we drove to visit friends in Peterborough, New Hampshire, which in its guise as Groves Corners was the setting for Thornton Wilder's *Our Town*. Gary and Elizabeth had invited us and other longtime friends for a rollicking recording session in the home studio Gary built, within the old house and barn he and Elizabeth had restored. Jim spent the day playing guitar with a reunited Biff Jackson Group made up of friends we've known and made music with since all of us were teenagers on staff at a church summer camp in Deering. "Quality Through Volume" remains the group's motto.

It was an overflowing day of music, belly laughs, home-made pasta and sauces, and an exegesis on the difference between People Who Like Parmesan and People Who Like Romano. (As a guest and the niece of an etiquette columnist, I did not poke the bear by inquiring about the acceptability or atrocity of either cheese in powdered or mixed form.) Precious quantities of each nectar had been carefully segregated and transported from Boston's North End like bank robbery bounty or Michael's fresh cannoli.

We all ate supper at a long oak table in a house easily a century older than our own, returning again to our Deering church camp staff days, when we'd laughed just as hard. And my husband laid down some amazing guitar tracks on *Psycho Killer*--which he'd once been mildly surprised to hear our pre-verbal infant daughter singing, in her way, as she repeated tones which spoke to her musical soul.

Neither Jim nor I ever laughed as consistently loud and long as we always did with this group of beautiful souls. I didn't know it would be the last night he'd spend out with friends, and will always be grateful to have spent it in their company. When we finished our lingering goodbye bear hugs and trudged up the icy driveway to where Jim had parked his truck, he went to the passenger side.

Despite the moonless dark, I could see something etched in his face as he handed me his keys. He braced himself and paused, one hand flattened against the door, wincing. He was in too much pain to drive.

~~~~~~

After a second and final fruitless neural block to try to alleviate his pain, Jim asked me to drive to his nearby office, where he cleared out the few things he wanted to keep: our older daughter's large painting of a folk art golden wooden bird; family photographs, almost all of them of our children; and a gift from one of his very first patients. It was an old-fashioned doctor's bag made from weighted clay. *DR. GLENNON* was painted on it in gold.

He took two of the books in his six-shelf collection: Atul Gawande's *The Checklist Manifesto* and Dennis Perkins' *Leading at the Edge*, about the Antarctic expedition aboard the *Endurance*. A book about precise goals to manage day by day, and a tale of leadership and bravery into the perilous unknown.

~~~~~~

Even my husband needed guidance as we considered how to talk to our children. In retrospect, I think he also needed to know I'd have a calm, objective sounding board after he was gone. Someone who'd seen and spoken to us together and would be able to understand the depth of the darkness I'd soon occupy and the breadth of a loss I might never be able to describe. We went together to speak with a therapist whose office was close to our daughters' school.

Two of my longtime friends lack filters. Synapses fire; words are ejected. Coincidentally, they both have high-powered jobs in New York City, where I imagine a rapid response time comes in handy. Professionally, and notwithstanding my hair trigger for righteous anger, I try to maintain an overactive filter so I can frame my words precisely before I utter or file them on an enduring public record. But at times during Jim's illness, I completely lost my filter, occasionally for the better and sometimes very much for the worse. Within the therapist's tastefully decorated brick walls, where fresh flowers improbably found themselves in vases during deep winter in New England, I sat pressed into Jim's side at the far end of a leather couch somewhere between green and brown, giving him barely enough space to breathe deeply. I spoke perhaps the most ridiculous words I'd ever said aloud, to my dying husband: "You'll never be alone. You'll never have to be without us, but we'll have to be without you forever. I'll be alone forever."

Jim considered this very seriously. "I don't think it helps to think in terms of 'forever.' You'll get through this. Lots of people do."

What I meant, but never found the words to say, was that I would never leave his side, and could never accept being without *him*--of not having him at my side, for the rest of my life. I never have, and never will.

~~~~~~

Our fifty-some minutes ended. In lovely quiet winter light we held hands and walked across the snow-hushed street to a bakery where I couldn't eat even my favorite food (at least among chocolate-bereft offerings). I used a coffee stirrer to dissolutely disassemble a pumpkin muffin as Jim finished a second bagel and described the two most likely ways he would die. I envisioned both and thought I would never eat again.

"Will you be home?"

"Yes," he said instantly. "I'll be home with you." Not just a promise, but a vow.

It wasn't only that he gave me the gift of assurance he'd be home, but that we had the gift of knowing there was never any doubt about what he did and didn't want. So whatever obstacles arose, we'd make that happen. It was, at least and at last, something we *could* do for him.

~~~~~~

Weather-wise, too, it was an especially harsh winter.

Jim initially had decided it would be reasonable to try two rounds of palliative chemo. They hadn't relieved his increasing pain, and left him incapacitated by exhaustion. I already felt he'd been betrayed by physicians' assurances his pain could and would be managed. The first time I saw him in the kind of pain his medications couldn't touch, I went in search of new ones, walking miles along the empty middle of Route 33 head-on into a vortex of needled ice. A blizzard had rendered the highway impassable by vehicles.

My mission failed.

Days later I needed to get him to the Emergency Room for the first time. It was only the second time I'd driven his truck. I had to navigate a near white-out, inching along the highway with my husband doubled over next to me in the horrifying silence of intractable pain. Along the way, emergency responders were gathered around cars which foolishly had ventured above a few miles an hour and were angled off the highway at the losing ends of swerving tire tracks. I couldn't imagine what had been important enough for those drivers to be out in such a storm.

During his second emergency admission, and after both of us had repeatedly asked for a referral to hospice that had never come, Jim picked up the phone in his hospital room and referred himself to hospice care.

~~~~~~

Soon before he was discharged, I returned to his room on the PCU floor (another ill-fitting acronym--for 'Progressive Care Unit'--that I could have lived decades more without having to learn). He lay very still in his bed with his eyes almost closed and his arms disquietingly folded crosswise on his chest. A man in a professorial jacket stood next to him and did not look at or identify himself to me. Jim quietly told me he was a hospice physician.

The man held out a piece of paper to my high-fevered, prone husband. I heard the entirety of the end-of-life advisory; to call it a conversation would suggest it had two active participants and involved an exchange between them.

"I know you have a DNR but you're going to need a portable DNR, too. If they have to resuscitate you, it won't be pretty."

The man slid the paper across the empty plastic faux-wood surface of the wheeled table where other patient's meal trays went. Jim could no longer eat. He mustered a shadow of a nod and managed a scrawl.

The man picked it up. Without a word, he swept past me as if no one occupied the compressed space where I stood between my husband's bed and the door.
~~~~~~

~~~~~~

A different disconnection was evidenced by some well-meaning physicians who knew Jim. As his medical complications accelerated and compounded, even those who specialized in the highest-mortality diseases seemed incapable of referring to his death. By then all his colleagues knew his cancer was terminal. They knew when they saw me at the hospital that he was there, too. In one hallway I ran into a surgeon who mentioned how difficult it was to have learned of my husband's "disease being one which would eventually bring about his demise." The last word called me back to a beekeeper's death in R. T. Smith's *Sourwood*, a poem that reminded me so much of my husband, tending to others to the very end and contemplating not his own fate, but the possible consequences for the hive if they were unable to comprehend or come to grips with his absence.

I like ten-dollar words as much as the next lawyer, and I never stopped wanting to run from the room when my husband talked about when he was "dead." But one of the lessons I'd worked hard to take from him, even before he became a patient, is that a problem can't be analyzed and addressed until it's been identified and voiced and discussed. Magical thinking and euphemism have no place in matters of mortality. Physicians can, like my husband, be compassionate without giving false hope. They can review realistic, if limited, options without being heartless. Patients and their families ought to be extended the dignity of understanding that entering hospice care is not giving up hope but acknowledging the reality that what is hoped for no longer encompasses a cure. And one does no harm by acknowledging that all of this is hard to talk about, even for physicians.

~~~~~~

Days after my husband's self-referral to hospice care, a visiting nurse and a social worker sat at our kitchen table with their admission paperwork. More than once, they looked at each other in a way that suggested the intake procedure was not quite what they were used to. Jim's hopes did not encompass any possibility he would "beat" metastatic pancreatic cancer. In the time it took him to read the words "metastatic disease" in November, he'd been ready to sign up for hospice care. Inexplicably, despite our repeated explicit requests, none of his physicians had even brought it up. His hope was to use his remaining time as he wished and was able to; to have as few incapacitating symptoms as possible; and not to linger by artificial means. And, most of all, to be home with us in the yellow house.

The hospice visitors had arrived separately, bearing identical rose-colored binders with a print of watercolor flowers slid underneath their clear plastic covers. In addition to the usual array of tedious forms, they included a few sheets describing the physical process of dying. The single sentence that made me close the binder forever noted that family members "might even feel tearful" when the person we love dies. I thought it was a belittling way to characterize the bottomlessness of what any witness to such a death is likely to feel. Beyond that, I thought the reckless understatement would make those beyond merely "tearful" at such a moment feel they were pathologically overreacting.

I would keep the insurance paperwork, and toss the binders away with the recycling.

The hospice nurse told Jim they could "pronounce" him. He nodded. The same words floored me. They asked us about medical directives and what we planned to do with "the body," as if it were an entity independent of the person to whom they were speaking. As they spoke to my husband about his upcoming death, he matter-of-factly took in what he no doubt had known since he stepped into gross anatomy lab as a first year medical student. I stood at the kitchen table, next to him, the beagles adorning his feet while I sewed tiny stitches in a quilt for newborn baby Elin next door.

~~~~~~

A day earlier, I'd approached Jim about what everyone else referred to at a linguistic distance as "arrangements." I'd come up behind him as he sat at the kitchen table and put my hands on his shoulders. We both watched the cardinals at his bird feeders. I began, "If it were me...." (In family life I occasionally drop my grammatical fanaticism.) I paused to breathe before lurching into the next clause: "I'd be fine with being scattered in the ocean, or going to a medical school."

He alerted to the idea of donating himself to his alma mater, where his group of first-year medical and dental students spent a year with a donor named Max. We'd been married then, and I knew how much he and his fellow students had honored those donors and the sacred process of learning human anatomy from their bodies. Although Jim likely had known far better than I how to go about the donation process, he told me I should "look into how that's done," and whether Tufts needed bodies. He knew I needed to be given some task that made the concept of "arrangements" concrete, and would think I had the bandwidth to handle. Understanding paperwork and law relating to anatomical gifts remained within my dissipated wheelhouse.

Jim, a man of tremendous faith who no longer took part in many of the official sacraments of the church in which he was raised, knew we were going to have to come up with something creative to produce a memorial service that would mean something to both of our families and all our friends. With a nod to a
~~~~~~

favorite family sport he'd long coached, he produced his own concept: I could begin planning his "Closing Ceremonies."

After I'd gathered all the anatomical donation paperwork, for both of us, I told him we 'd probably get the ashes back within two years. He said it would be nice if it were earlier, perhaps in a year, so I and the kids could do something in remembrance then.

"You could do it earlier. You could do something in a year," I immediately said.

"No, *you* can do it." He smiled with his immeasurably loving twinkle. "I won't be there. You can do whatever you want."

~~~~~~

Between emergency room visits, I'd brought Jim to medical practices where specialists performed three different kinds of outpatient neural blocks to try to control his pain. Each gave him some immediate relief, but only over dwindling increments of hours and, finally, mere minutes before he was revisited with pain no medication could touch. I drove home from the last of those appointments, armed with more prescriptions that offered no relief. Freezing rain streaked the windshield. Thick chunks of gray slush wormed from side to side with the overwhelmed, weary wipers.

We were at a red light just before one of New Hampshire's notorious unadvertised lane merges--the better to challenge out-of-towners' skills. Jim knew what else had recently taken root in my mind. At a concert in Portsmouth which our daughter Emma had gifted us--the last concert he would attend in any traditional way-- we happened to have been seated next to a man he knew, who'd introduced us to the woman he married after his wife died of cancer when their children were of similar ages to ours. This had not fazed Jim but deeply unnerved me. On our way home, he read my mind: *How could he? How could he replace his children's mother in their home? How must their children feel?*
~~~~~~

Seeing me sobbing in his driver's seat during another ice storm clearly was not striking my husband as a safer alternative to his taking the wheel, even in his condition. He gently suggested I pull over. I made it to a deeply slushy spot in a nearby lot and cried mightily. The wipers continued protesting. I left the heat on to try to warm Jim, who seemed suddenly to give the illusion of being dwarfed by his winter jacket. I grabbed his hand tightly with my cold, gloveless one. I could never find both gloves on my way out into winter.

"You know, seriously, you might meet someone, and that would be fine with me."

I shook my head in an emphatic *no*. The breath shuddered out of me: "You've ruined me for other men."

He patted my knee and didn't say anything until I finally locked eyes with him. and he smiled. "You've ruined me, too, dear."

I came close to laughing. "That sounds so very wrong."

But I was soon back to full-on sobbing. "But we're supposed to get old and crusty together."

"Well, *you* get to get old and crusty... and you'll still be hot."

Those eyes. The way he smiled, even then.

~~~~~~

There were continuous misfires among physicians and pharmacies. Once Jim had been signed out from his oncologist's service, all his medication had to be ordered through hospice. Some essential prescriptions took several days to fill. One critical medication was so rare in the elusive liquid form required to inject it that, only after I'd driven from pharmacy to pharmacy for hours, a pharmacist eventually explained he couldn't find a pharmacy within three states that could fill it.

"Is this for your dad?" more than one pharmacist asked when I sought certain medications.
~~~~~~

"No, my husband. He's young," I'd robotically and unnecessarily add, then thank them for trying.

~~~~~~

During the next emergency hospitalization, the air warmed enough to reduce the day's storm to violent wind and rain. Accumulated snow turned to deep, filthy slush that spilled over and into my inadequate boots. For over an hour I trudged across busy roads and dodged Live Free or Die drivers who seemed to think serviceable windshield wipers would be a sign of weakness. I waited in lines at every pharmacy and medical supply store I could locate, trying to find a DNR bracelet for my husband to display at all times so long as pain management might require another emergency room visit.

At the last store I tried, which was dedicated to and housed by far the most extensive medical supplies I'd seen, the man at the register told me they had no DNR bracelets on hand.

"But I could order you one."

"How long would it take to get it?" I asked.

"We could have it in two weeks."

"I'm afraid that'll be too late."

I thanked him and left the store, back into a hard rain. I didn't cry until I was outside and tears could disappear in the deluge.

~~~~~~

On Monday night, Jim was back home. His pain was off-the-charts. He could neither eat nor drink. When Bob stopped by after work, he said I should bring him to the hospital.

"We'll get you buffed again," Bob told Jim, who sat, folded forward on the crimson couch. He barely nodded.

Bob followed us there, and we were quickly brought into a room inside the ER, which was strangely empty except for children literally bouncing off the walls in the next room. Bob and I once again went through the litany of failed medications and regimens of patches and injections and infusions. We turned off the lights and sat in the dark together.

Both of them had only sisters, biologically speaking. A nurse came into the room and clicked on an overhead light. She looked at the two of them as she turned to tend to Jim's IV pole and smilingly said, "*You're* not related."

Anyone would have taken them for brothers.

~~~~~~

At home, winter nights seemed to strip away our last lingering defenses. Sometimes we were able to share naked pain we couldn't voice in daylight.

"Are we still going to go to Papa Dick's house?"

Almost every Sunday afternoon we'd continued to gather at Jim's parents' house with bumper crops of cousins who were all steadfast friends.

"Why wouldn't we still go there?"

"Because it's going to be so strange without him."

I nodded. "Everything's going to be strange without him."

"That's *his* family."

"It's *your* family, too. Always."
~~~~~~

12

A Green Carnation

Just before Jim's final emergency hospitalization, he sank at the top of our staircase, experiencing a level of pain anyone would call a '10.' But neither the language of numbers nor any other sufficed.

Since those moments, on more than one continent and in a smattering of states, I've presented my freshly, klutzily broken bones and been asked to numerically describe my discomfort. "Maybe a 5 or 6," I'd say, even if the pain pierced and shattered me like a band saw and I could almost see it vibrate through my body the way two days of piggy-back labor once did. "It hurts, but I've seen a '10.'"

I see and hear it still.

Whoever is doing my ER intake ordinarily pauses with a head tilt, looks again at me and my visibly swollen and askew body part, enters the '5/6,' and moves along.

Whenever I'm asked to lodge a pain complaint, I'm haunted by sounds that attend the kind of pain that forecloses words. It exceeds their descriptive power.

On the Ides of March, I took the phone from my husbands hand as he sat on the top step and heard Bob's voice telling me to go straight to the Emergency Room. Once we arrived, I repeatedly had to tear myself from his side to beg the desk nurse to check on whether pain medication had even been ordered. It would be almost an hour before any was injected, although he was one of only two ER patients on that quiet night.

Bob, who'd raced over from his house, sat with Jim as I corralled the nursing supervisor: "How could you make anyone wait that long when they're presenting with a '10' for pain?"

She looked at his chart and told me, "But it was just a '3'."

I pointed to the entry, which I had made on arrival and triple-checked was correctly recorded. I hissed, "No, and this is *your* form. The '3' is his *baseline* pain level. We're only *here* because it's a '10,' for God's sake." I pointed at the '10,' weeping with frustration and rage for his added suffering.

~~~~~~

Jim was admitted late that night and assigned a 4th floor room. He was scheduled for an upper GI series, which required him to ingest a large amount of barium in the hope it would reveal what was causing his inability to eat. Almost all of it came right back up. Bob and I waited in the dark, otherwise empty waiting room while he was scanned. Bob explained we were *hoping* for an obstruction because it would be treatable. A stent could enable him to eat again. But he also explained the medical reality: it simply didn't make sense to him, given that there had been no obstruction on a scan just two weeks earlier. I realized Bob was echoing what Jim had done with me earlier, when he still could: explaining the probable result while giving me time to absorb the reality I'd need to begin conveying to our children and parents and siblings very
~~~~~~

soon, so there might be a chance to get them to us before he died.

Jim was left alone with us in the room. It was a terrible night. Bob, attentive to everything he saw and read and elicited from Jim with careful questions, warning me that the imaging might be misleading because very little of the barium had made it into his system. Just as he'd predicted, the scan was read as showing an obstruction, and in the morning Jim was alert enough to seize what turned out to be a false hope that a stent could give him some quality time. He quickly underwent the procedure.

But, as Bob had warned me might happen, the gasteroenterologist explained that the only obstruction he'd seen was much smaller than expected from the imaging, and there was not much hope he'd eat again. The pancreatic tumor had invaded even further.

Physician or not, in his immense discomfort as a patient, Jim was at that point vulnerable in a way he'd never been. The failed stent had been his last hope for better days. For even one tolerable night. Not only did it not give him relief, but he awoke from surgery febrile, agitated, and in respiratory distress. I had to take over as medical proxy.

Bob and I sat with him. No one came in to check his vital signs. I could tell from touching him that his fever was still spiking. His temperature was close to 104, and a single sip of water set off more vomiting. I had to extinguish the belief he'd live to see our son graduate in May, which I'd expressed to the Reverend who I'd asked to conduct his "Closing Ceremonies" at Phillips Church.

This time, our roles reversed. I had to become the medical realist.

Bob took me aside and explained what was likely happening.

"You don't mean he could die tonight?" I asked.

"His blood pressure could drop out. It could happen." Bob urged me to get our children back home. Calls were made to family up and down the East Coast and West to Chicago.

Vigil began.

~~~~~~

When all our children finally arrived that night, picked up from rehearsal and in two neighboring states and deposited at the hospital by their aunts and uncles, they shed their down coats in the stifling room and sat around their father's bed. He was only lightly conscious. When it was time for them to be driven home, they all kissed their father goodbye. Our daughter, who was last in line, knowing full well what it would mean when her dad came home-- the same prospect that filled me with unremitting terror about what would happen there--bent down to kiss her father's burning forehead and spoke eleven words to him. It was the purest expression of love I've ever heard.

I'm certain he heard and understood her.

~~~~~~

When Bob and I were alone with him again, Jim was dysregulated and completely serious. Feeling the absence of the spirit and humor that had always animated him undid me before I recognized what else had gone missing. As they had during earlier hospitalizations, Randy and Bob would appear quietly overnight to make sure Jim was never alone when I followed our children home. Both of them must have been making calls to family and friends who, by the time I returned to the hospital, had begun appearing in a waiting area on the hospital floor. Bob spent hours answering their questions and preparing them for what lay ahead.

Days sealed inside hospitals are difficult to distinguish from one another. At almost midnight, Bob walked me out to the parking lot during another snowstorm. My heart hadn't been able to process the answer I heard him give when Jim whispered to him, "How long do I have, two weeks?" Bob had told him, to the day, the lesser time he likely had.

I told Bob I wasn't ready. He said he wasn't ready, either. I leaned lightly into his shoulder, knowing he'd keep vigil with us despite his own excruciating back pain. I could think of nothing to say but that he was like a brother to Jim, which by some transitive property made him my brother, too.

～～～～～

I spoke to the on-call hospitalist and found myself briefly hoping a different scan might reveal something that could provide a reprieve: maybe he had brain metastases which could easily be "zapped"? Perhaps then he wouldn't grow dizzy and disoriented when he tried to lift his head from the pillow.

When one is hoping for 'brain mets,' as the hospitalist supplied the shorthand, the bar has been lowered considerably on what counts as good news.

"You know," the hospitalist, who was not so much younger than his patient and colleague, told me, "I've always wanted to grow up to be like Jim."

"Me, too. We all want to grow up to be like him," I said.

So I stood at my husband's side again, holding my hand infinitesimally above his while he was wheeled to the radiology department, afraid the weight of my touch on the light blanket over his still feverish body would somehow hurt him. As we arrived downstairs, a flash of his humor resurfaced.

"What's a little more radiation?" he quipped on his way to the brain scan.

～～～～～

I deduced it was Saint Patrick's Day when a carnation of variegated bright green appeared on a white cloth napkin laid over an empty cafeteria tray in Jim's room. Although he couldn't have even a drop of liquid by mouth, the lag in transferring and recording rapid-fire medication changes meant nursing assistants continued showing up with medication in forms he couldn't take. He was still intractably nauseated and in pain. His small corner room remained wildly overheated.

4:00 was the appointed hour. I'd asked the doctors treating him to help set up a meeting with the hospice physician and a social worker about bringing Jim home.

It was his wish, and by God we were going to make it happen.

The meeting would not go exactly as planned. At one point Bob would have to physically restrain me from leaping across the bed to underscore my response to a point. I settled for words, which it's possible I delivered in the manner that more than once had prompted my husband to observe he never wanted to see me armed with less figurative weapons.

One family member might have alluded to willingness to commit a low-level misdemeanor, at least in the state we were in, should anyone's sixth and final variety of pain receptors--the cannabinoid--need assessing.

Jim's sisters would watch for the most part in stunned silence, as if tracking a nightmare tennis match.

~~~~~~

Bob had used much of the day to organize everything we'd need to care for Jim at home. Many of our closest friends still hovered in and around a waiting room, and most of Jim's immediate family had arrived. My parents and brothers had appeared at the hospital, where I ushered them in and out for brief visits before the afternoon meeting.

My father, who was so fearful of hospitals that he hadn't crossed their threshold even to see his wife and recently delivered children,
~~~~~~

came into Jim's room and gently touched his socked foot, from which a thin waffled cotton blanket had fallen away. Given my father's deep lifelong fear--which my grandmother had told me dated back to surgery gone wrong when he was five, requiring him to be isolated without her for weeks in a New York City hospital-- I know how brave an act of love that was.

Emerging from the room, my younger brother stood with his back to the hallway wall, slid down it with planted feet as if sinking into a chair, and bowed his head toward his bent knees. He was not much more of a fan of hospitals than our father.

My older brother asked if there was anything else he could do before he had to return to Chicago. I asked him if he could come back for the service. I told him it would be soon.

~~~~~~

The meeting began on time. The hospitalist reviewed Jim's medical status. Squeezed into the room were floor nurses; the hospice physician who'd told my husband, "If they have to resuscitate you, it won't be pretty"; a hip, purple-haired, nose-ringed hospice nurse; a hospice grief counselor with the misfortune to be standing in for another staff member; Jim's sisters; Bob; and me.

I began reviewing the evidence.

Jim's medical needs couldn't be accommodated within the level of care any non-hospital medical facility offered. It was equally clear no hospital could meet his needs, because none had. When his pain was under reasonable control, his nausea and vomiting became intractable. When the latter were successfully treated, his pain became intolerable.

Immediately, the hospice physician took a *tone*, announcing, "Well, we've covered everything but the cannabinoid receptor."

I am not sure why he used a "we."
~~~~~~

"Oh, we've covered that, too," piped up an attendee whose van bore a Catholic school sticker (and who resided in a nearby jurisdiction in which a small quantity of the relevant plant product lawfully may be held and had).

A brief silence. The physician looked at Jim, lying in bed, stiffened by pain, stewing in fever, lightheaded and confused, and spoke around me and directly to the patient who could no longer speak for himself.

He addressed my disoriented and desperately ill husband, for whose needs and wishes only I could speak, and suggested that he have still another upper GI series--the same fruitless procedure that had resulted in his precipitous decline and brought us to this catastrophic juncture. And our only chance to get Jim home, where he wanted to be.

It was not truly a question he posed, but more of a verdict he delivered: "What's the downside?"

In that instant it felt like Jim's professional persona, augmented by a whopping dose of attitude from my adversarial core, had taken over. I started to rise from my chair in a diagonal movement toward this man.

Bob put a hand on my lower arm, while mine lightly rested on Jim's foot, and I realized the room's ungodly heat was emanating at least in part from his continuing high fever.

I stood, no longer willing to be the broken, fragile self I'd grown to despise, but instead the more complicated person I'd been eight months and forever ago. The person I'd need to reconstitute myself to be, who brooked no intentional infliction of harm to the innocent, and who our neighbor Hobb once described as his "100-pound 800-pound gorilla" when I'd stood up for him. I heard the words escape me, at last with the steel that disappeared on that late June day when I already knew *this* day would come.

"What's the *downside?*"

I glared at the man, who still didn't look my way. My blood bubbled. When I was a tween (before the word existed), a physicist friend I adored brought us an hourglass blown into hollow Clementine-sized orbs at both ends of a tightly corkscrewed clear tube. It was filled with isopropyl alcohol, tinted cardinal-red. If you placed the bottom in the palm of your hand, the bright liquid's low boiling point made it bubble until it quickly shot up through the coiled tube, roiling at the top. That's what I felt like.

"Let me be really clear on this."

The man briefly glanced in my general direction, as I spoke directly to him.

"This isn't Bob's decision, and if you believe you need to hold anyone responsible for what's going to happen, that would be *me.*" I was working up to courtroom volume, although the room was about a twentieth the size. "No *downside?* I've got some to start. One is discomfort, pain, the quality of his time. Look at what the first GI series did to him. Bob and I have been here to see it." (The unspoken coda: *You haven't.*)

"Two, you're opening him up to the possibility of more complications. He could get an aspiration pneumonia...."

The man straightened his back in his chair and began speaking in a way he might have thought was professorial. I grew up around professsors. He was merely patronizing.

"Well, it's a legitimate point that there could be some complications...."

I cut him off like the Massachusetts driver at my core. "And third, and most important, *where does it possibly get us?* He is *not* going to have a feeding tube put in." I let the words settle. "So, here's where your role ends. There will be *no more procedures, no more tubes, no more surgery.*"

I zeroed in for the summation. "And we're going to get him stabilized here tonight and get his medications in the right goddamn form and know he can tolerate them. If you start subjecting him to anything else, we will never get him home. *And we are taking him home tomorrow.*"

Silence.

"Well...." The man agreed there was no point in more imaging "if" we had decided against more procedures.

"There's no 'if.' It's not happening."

You are done putting your hands on him. I thought.

"He's going to need 24-hour-a-day coverage." He continued digging in. Dubious, frowning, pursing his lips and cocking his head slightly toward the familial array, as if thinking they were about to jump in on his side against the patient's lunatic wife.

"We can do that." An instantaneous chorus from Jim's sisters.

We'd have Bob, our concierge physician, with us. I'd been trained to administer injections. If Bob needed relief, we were blessed with physician friends who'd come and take shifts. Jim's sisters would alternate all day and night. Our children would all be there. Their father would never be alone, and never out of reach of those who love him.

I had not imagined we'd need to go rogue on hospice.

But here we were.

And we were ready.

And we did.

13

The Last Lap

"You might as well, for your last lap."

It was a grotesque thing to say. At the end of the St. Patrick's Day meeting, after I'd spoken, I did not hear the hospice physician direct one last question straight to Jim: did he want to drive home with *me*, or instead want him to arrange for an ambulance? When Jim, incapable of answering, did not, the man chose the ambulance. Out of my earshot, but within Bob's and my sisters-in-laws,' he told my husband, "You might as well, for your last lap."

His casual cruelty--his trivialization of my husband's wish to come home and contempt for my insistence he would, and perversion of the fundamental unit of an unending journey for what we all knew was a one-way trip to an imminent and early end--makes my heart race even now.

~~~~~~

Among many privileges of parenthood has been getting to know my children's friends, including Johanna, whose graduate school presentation years later would introduce me to a Holocaust survivor's account of a uniquely healing moment. Gérard Miller's
~~~~~~

film, *Rendez-vous chez Lacan,* shares her story of having been haunted for two decades by nightmares of the Gestapo seizing her family. As she described her recurring nightmare to Lacan, he rose from his chair and gently ran his hand along her cheek, converting the terrifying power of the word "Gestapo" into, in her native French, a tender touch--a *g'este à peau* she thereafter could recall as a superseding physical memory.

On the way home in the ambulance late that afternoon, I'd clutched the electric-pink portable DNR in my left hand, rolled like a diploma and splotched with my tears.

I had touched my right hand to my husband's left temple and cheek. A *g'este à peau.*

~~~~~

The ambulance arrived at the hospital late that afternoon, an hour-and-a-half after we'd been assured it would. Meanwhile, this time, we had peace. No one appeared awkwardly at the door or tried to administer medication in a form I had to explain again my husband hadn't been able to take for quite some time. No machines buzzed or beeped. I had not realized how unaccustomed we'd grown to being undisturbed.

We lay on the narrow hospital bed. Outside the room's single window, snow had been wind-whipped into rolling waves complete with rounded crests of granulated ice.

Exhausted, but less agitated and febrile once the room had cleared and we were alone and he knew he'd come home, Jim somehow mustered the energy to stand and, leaning on me, very slowly walk a single circle around the small unit floor. Every physician and nurse and staff member who saw us looked up from what they were doing, some putting their hands to their hearts.
~~~~~

Our children and friends had been at our house for several hours, arranging everything for his return. My brother had driven Jim's truck back to our house from the hospital.

The ambulance's two-person crew finally appeared at the open entrance to Jim's room. They seemed surprised to see me there. I picked up a plastic bag with the few belongings he'd arrived with.

"Is it okay if I ride with you?" I asked the men.

"Yes, but you understand you have to ride in front. You can't be in back."

"That's fine." A drained monotone that no longer sounded like me .

I walked alongside the gurney and into the elevator, one hand on Jim's shoulder and the other gripping the a portable DNR. At the ground floor we passed through gently *whooshing* sliding doors into clear skies and sudden, intense sunlight. I squinted and turned away just as Jim's boss, who was also our friend, was speed-walking into the hospital for a rare Friday evening meeting that Jim surely would be attending or running if only none of this had happened.

She immediately reached out and hugged me, and I became undone, crying hard into her shoulder, "He wants to go home, and I just can't stand the thought...." I didn't mean the thought of going home, but of his dying. I simply couldn't believe that time had come. To this day, I'm haunted by the possibility Jim heard me and thought I meant I didn't want to bring him home--which was all we wanted, because it was what he wanted and what we could still do for him.

By the time Jim's boss had disengaged from both of us, the ambulance crew looked at me--an undoubtedly pitiful sight, crying and holding the neon-pink paper anyone in that line of work can identify--and said, "You can go in back."

I sniffled indecorously into my sleeve. "No, that's okay, I can sit up front." Rule-compliant until the end.

They looked at me and spoke in unison. "*Please* get in back."

~~~~~~

For the first time among countless trips we'd made together on the same roads, we faced backward, our view of the familiar obscured by letters spelling AMBULANCE in mirrored reverse. The siren was off as we traveled back in time, far longer than the ride's twenty-five minutes.

We were taking Jim home.

I can't do this. I can't do this, I texted Bob, who'd gone ahead to the house. He texted back what I hadn't yet grasped: *You already have.*

Only since then have I imagined, when seeing a silent ambulance, that it might be bringing someone home.

Jim brought up two things, one wildly practical and one straight from his heart. His palate cleanser was a ministerial reminder to me, from his frugal side as the family financial planner who had in each child's infancy begun saving money for institutions of higher learning.

As the ambulance pulled away from a hospital where his chemo injections of vials of precious white blood cell boosters had been billed at roughly $86,000 each, he told me, "You need to remember to cancel my phone line, because it's a hundred dollars a month."

That out of the way, he paused said, "It's important to do something for Bob."

I'd have to think about that for several weeks before beginning to sew a nautical quilt for the captain of our team, designed around our shared family ocean adventures. It would take me another year to finish; every stitch soothed me.

~~~~~~

Jim's last ride covered the same stretch of road where he'd traveled to and from his work and our daughters' school. We had once taken a left onto the same minor highway when I was in early labor. I remembered how, after each of our children arrived, we'd complete the circle home with the overwhelming bounty of a new addition slouched into a backward-facing infant seat and swaddled in a sweater knit by Grandma Jackie. First white, then mint green, then pink, then yellow. In summer, spring, and twice in winter.

Never, until those moments in the ambulance, could I have imagined a subtraction at the end of a trip home.

I'd once been in an ambulance on the same stretch of road, its siren shrieking. Jim had calmly been waiting in another Emergency Room, close to the yellow house we hadn't then ever seen. Our son had fallen hard onto cement and had an ostrich egg-sized lump on his forehead. The ambulance crew gave him a green velvet teddy bear that provided him enduring comfort long afterwards.

When we first drove on that road there were two working dairy farms on its eastern side. Neither our children nor I ever tired of exclaiming "Moo cows!" every single time we saw the rural wonder of wandering cows, any more than beagles grow weary of the sound of the same food clattering like tiny pebbles into their bowls twice every day, and yearn to experience it again as soon as possible.

We passed a bakery where we'd picked up treats for family celebrations. I'd once stopped there with our daughter Emma on the way to a visit with her friend Sage, Randy and Judy's daughter. A well-weathered farmer standing in line had asked me if he could give our four-year-old a two-dollar bill he said was passed along to him for good luck when he'd been in a store at about her age.

"Has it worked for you?" I'd asked him.

"It has." He smiled, retrieving contentment from some vision of his past.

We next passed the Stratham SPCA, where our younger daughter would volunteer the second she was old enough, and had persuaded all of us to adopt Rufus and Brady.

We next passed the family farm where we'd picked out summer tomatoes, buttercup corn, fall pumpkins, and bumpy mottled gourds. Jim brought me wildflowers from there when we came home for the first time as a family of three.

We glided by fairgrounds we'd driven to almost every summer, where Noah deftly outmaneuvered the fiendish fair games' designers, and always brought stuffed animals back to his little sisters. Even before we had children, we'd driven up from Boston in summer to explore a park in the same spot. Just weeks before Sam's birth, my feet had been so swollen that I had to borrow huge tennis shoes from our friend Jon. He'd looked at me and tried not to laugh, endearingly dubbing me 'Preggo the Clown.'

The same road, a feeder to the main highway north from Boston to Maine, branched off toward Randy and Judy's house, which had been the siren call for our move to New Hampshire. Over the years we would drive along it in our increasingly commodious family vehicles. Sometimes they were loaded with sand toys and summer books, or ski equipment loaded into in an overhead rack I invariably forgot about before doing some degree of damage by parking without considering the towering overhead load. It can be easy to lose sight of impermanent changes in what we expect to be around us.

This time, the ambulance silently pulled into our driveway, just ahead of a van bearing bright tulips from California relatives. The yard and house were filled with friends and family who'd been helping ready the house for Jim.

Inside the yellow house, he would return to himself and to all of us. He would laugh again, and find complete peace and comfort among endless tender words and gestures.

We brought him home.

14

The Man who Lived

When my husband began reading aloud *Harry Potter and the Philosopher's Stone*'s first chapter, "The Boy Who Lived," our children had asked him what its title meant. As with all questions, he thought for as long as he needed before answering. He suggested they read the chapter and then talk about what they thought it meant to describe a boy that way. Jim and I had looked at each other and considered what the title likely meant about Harry and those he survived, and what mark their absence had left on him.

~~~~~

All the planning we'd done and advocacy we shouldn't have had to do came down to a handful of days we'll replay for the rest of our lives.

Jim was exhausted when we arrived, but already seemed much less disoriented. Improbably, he told me he thought he'd be able to walk inside. He held onto me as I helped him sit up. The wary ambulance crew helped him get to the ground. There, leaning on me and Randy, he took the two granite steps to the porch and opened
~~~~~

the green door into the hallway he'd sponge-painted in autumn's burnt orange.

The old farm table in the dining room on our right had been moved to make room for a hospital bed. Folding wooden doors opened from there into the front room where Samuel F. B. Morse had once painted portraits. Musical instruments and furniture had been moved aside and it had been transformed into Bob's on-call room. He was there, doing an inventory of needles, medications, gloves, and alcohol wipes, after assigning one of our children to design a spreadsheet she'd swiftly produced.

The space was marred only by the aggressive prior delivery of additional items I'd made clear Jim did not want and would not use. The most intrusive were large containers piled with IV fluid bags, and--far worse--two immense, missile-shaped cast-iron oxygen canisters covered in chipped forest-green paint and far too heavy for us to move out of sight or mind. Their presence in this sacred space seemed a particularly cowardly and wasteful reflection of that physician's narcissistic injury, at Jim's and our own enduring expense.

Being my husband's proxy and ensuring his wishes were carried out was a sacred trust. It was grotesque to defy his choices--apparently because I'd dared interrupt one physician's misbegotten certainty that such calls were *his* to make, and his ego's demand we be punished for disagreeing.

No one should have to fight to safeguard a patient's end-of-life choices, or require a trained courtroom advocate to ensure they are honored.

~~~~~~

We heard voices bubbling in the kitchen, through a closed door. I had no idea how many friends and family members were there; our doors were open for people who loved Jim.
~~~~~~

Bob retreated when he was certain Jim could safely navigate the handful of steps to the bed. In one of very few moments when we'd be alone together at home, I read my husband's eyes and could only ask, "What?"

Not, "Are we thinking the same unbearable thoughts?" I knew the answer to that.

We sat on the hospital bed and looked only at each other.

"It's just... coming home to die." His words had already begun to slow, and had a ragged timbre I hadn't heard before. Bob later explained that a medication had caused it.

Jim's words were the ones I hadn't been able to say when we saw his boss outside the hospital, by the ambulance. Not that I couldn't stand the thought of coming home, but that I couldn't bear the thought of him dying.

Any more than I ever will.

~~~~~~

Dress was casual.

Bob, having moved in for the duration, wore sweatpants appropriated from his sons and a bracing device for his back. Its white plastic halves met in an oval punctuated by three blue segments strongly resembling an *anime* panda head. None of Jim's sisters would fail to smile when they saw it. Bob, grinning, said we shouldn't laugh at him.

"We're not laughing at you. We're laughing *with* that adorable panda." I told him as he tended to Jim--"keeping ahead of things," as Bob put it, so he wouldn't be nauseated or in pain as a medication wore off.

Bob looked at Jim. "Tufts gets your body.... I was wondering, can I have your hair? I've gotta tell you, Jim, I've always loved your hair."

Jim ran his fingers through the lush 'Jim flip.'
~~~~~~

"Maybe we should let Tufts know, and rethink the open casket thing and the whole plan," my husband said, with the smile that had gone missing until finally we were home together again.

~~~~~~

Everything around us told a generational story. Countless gatherings had happened around the old wood table Jim's bed displaced. Birthday parties, Easter gatherings. Infuriating word games which had driven Uncle Daniel to distraction when he couldn't solve his wee nephews' and nieces' devilish logic puzzles. We'd once waited there for the abjectly unsuccessful tofurkey to join us at the first Thanksgiving following our daughters' announcement of nascent vegetarianism. Puzzle pieces had blossomed, conjoined into floating continents within each puzzle's outer edges. Each inner part was pressed into place with a soft crunch against the weathered pine, which danced with milky fissures where the ghosts of colonial woodworms shimmied.

I'd laid out dozens of quilts on the table, basting together backing and batting and hand-sewn tops before joining them with thousands of tiny stitches which would hold them together even as their edges frayed to spaghetti-thin cotton strips while their recipients ran their fingers over soft binding.

Jim's bed faced an autumn-hued quilt with an alphabet of fruits and vegetables inspired by one of our children's favorite picture books. It was surrounded by a series of Emma's paintings upon square canvases she'd built. Underneath them was an oval table Randy had made as a wedding gift and finished in a glossy nutmeg color. Atop it were cards our nieces and nephews had made for their uncle. The folding doors to Bob's on-call room had been the backdrop when Jim persuaded our children to pose for Mother's Day photos. They opened to the west-facing windows overlooking the stretch of fence we'd once seen struck by lightning. Between
~~~~~~

the rooms, someone had thought to position a love seat, so people could sit together by Jim's side. Suzannah had printed out photographs she'd helped her aunts arrange around the room.

Our friend and best man Jon had arrived from Peterborough with photos I'd never seen before, including pictures he'd taken of us the night before our wedding, against a vivid sunset over the Charles River. Even in silhouette, it was impossible to miss Jim's easy smile. Jon also brought framed photos he'd taken of Jim, fresh out of college, on a cross-country trip with him and Gary, who with his wife Elizabeth had hosted that last winter music session and supper.

So now the rest of us can carry with us his contented smile as he was just setting out into the world, facing backward in the bed of a red truck, open container in hand. Laughing with his friends somewhere in the country's vast middle, on his way from Jackson Hole to Salt Lake City near the Snake River Mountain Range. Savoring life as it was handed him each day.

All of it--everyone present or call from a distance; every surface of sanded wood; every stitch and letter and word and pixel and brushstroke--was love itself.

~~~~~~

A hospice nurse came inside just once, soon after we arrived, to set up a morphine pump. She snaked its black tubing around the far side of Jim's bed and suggested scheduling visits from nursing aides, beginning the following Thursday. Six days away. Bob and I looked at each other and simultaneously expressed a polite version of, "Thank you; we'll let you know if we need another visit."

Bob had told me a person can go weeks without food, but not when unable to drink water, and we didn't intend to avail ourselves of the services of even the kindest strangers. When hospice nurses called to check in, I'd hand the phone to Bob, who'd tell
~~~~~~

them we had everything under control. We needed only the medications Bob requested, which would arrive on the porch as Rufus and Brady nobly did their job, announcing deliveries with majestic two-tone howling. Rufus took the alto parts.

After the nurse left, Jim decided he didn't want the pump. He preferred injections of pain medication and didn't want to be tethered to any kind of machinery. It was connected to an electronic device reminiscent of an extra-large remote control, with a panel of unlabeled buttons of indeterminate purpose. Bob frowned as he stood at Jim's side and tried to disconnect it while Jim sat up in bed. Concentrating intently, Bob began pushing its buttons to make sure he'd disconnected it properly.

Jim jerked his head to the left, rolled his eyes back and stuck his tongue out, as if the button combination had caused him to have a seizure.

After a millisecond of stunned silence, we saw his smile. We laughed so hard that the people gathered in the kitchen must surely have thought we'd lost our minds.

~~~~~~

No tubes, no procedures, and no strangers would mar a minute of these days at home, where time rolled back to zero even as it became immeasurable and inconsequential.

Soon fewer and fewer people and sounds and scents and voices--and, ultimately, words--would made up Jim's world. It would shrink from our home to the dining room, and finally to his bed and us in a tight semi-circle around it. All next to the old windows which looked out on towering pines and silent stars and an incipient Worm Moon heralding spring.

~~~~~~

I soon better understood why Jim hadn't wanted to be anywhere but home, where his spirit returned. He was no longer a case or a patient. He was surrounded by love--past, present, and future--and stories he knew would continue to be told. He could glance at the taupe and royal blue rug, with its one ragged corner, and see stories he'd be handing off to us. These included the great Ficus over-watering, the rarest of premature endings among all that Jim had tended to. He could recall the lesson he'd codified when we briefly were parents to just one child: that we might continuously maintain only two of three categories at the same time: a baby, two professional careers, and a household. And one of the things we always had to maintain would be the baby. Some things might have to give.

He was within the same space where we'd gathered with lifelong friends just a few months earlier for a spirited celebration of what all of us understood would be his last birthday with us. To his right he could revisit our family's past Christmas Eves, listening to music he curated and decorating the tree. He could see Emma's easel, where she'd painted much of the art that surrounded him. Over the fireplace was a carved wood mirror shaped like a sun, its rays painted in gold leaf. He'd given it to me years earlier. The fireplace sill held the brightly painted wooden Danish ducks my mother gave us as a wedding present. She told us they could face away from each other, in our stead, should we have any serious and lasting disagreement.

They'd remained bill-to-bill.

He could see the room where he and each of our children created music, on everything from a piano and trombone and trumpet to bells, a piccolo, and a handful of harmonicas. A vase held a cluster of mallets, some tipped with oversized soft heads, like flowering summer daisies.

~~~~~~
~~~~~~

In January, after finishing her first semester's exams several states away, our daughter had told us she was going to take a leave and come home. I suspect her intuition may have led her to make that decision soon after I'd dropped her off at school in September. In early October she'd come home for the first time, and gone with her father on the walk she memorialized in a painting of him and Brady, both lit by crepuscular rays streaming from a vanishing point beyond the forest as they walked toward the light.

After she'd told us she wouldn't be returning to school, Jim had listened to my concerns about the disruptions for her after just arriving for her freshman year.

"But what if I die before the end of the semester?" he'd asked me.

What would I do when he wasn't with me, to gently make me face unvarnished truths?

~~~~~~

Bob and Jim had referred to our medical aim as a "double zero": no pain and no nausea. A level of comfort never once attained during or between emergency hospitalizations. I think what finally made this possible was a third and fourth zero: no inattention and no delay. The night before we brought him home, Bob had fortified me by forewarning: "There will be bumps."

There were not. For once in recent memory, the surprises were pleasant. The mountains moved by our family and friends ensured an immediate response to any harbinger of discomfort. Such end-of-life care cannot be improvised. It involves no medical machinery, but takes many hearts and hands. At home, we could read any sign from him. We could see it in his face and hear it in the way he breathed, even as he slept the sleep of the just.

~~~~~~

Not long after Jim came home, he lost the desire to listen to the music which had always been part of his days, even at the hospital. The sounds he preferred were those he couldn't have heard anywhere but home: our voices, the beagles' not-so-lyrical stylings, and laughter. No strangers' voices and no mechanical noise.

Bob shook his head as I talked to him in the kitchen while friends were visiting Jim in the next room.

"Pancreatic cancer has a 5% five-year survival, and I think that 5%'s misdiagnosed. I've talked to gasteroenterologists who've been practicing for decades, and they've never seen it." His tone was resigned. As calmly as he spoke, sometimes his words were infused with regret at what even he couldn't do.

"I thought it was a 5% percent two-year survival rate," I murmured, preoccupied with the pancreatic surgeon's memory and only tangentially registering his point.

Then I began to think about an element of the unsaid--that even if that "big deal" surgery and arduous recovery had been possible, there would have been no reasonable hope of long-term survival.

~~~~~~

Late that night, Emma sat on the opposite side of her father's bed while Bob and I hovered over him, trying to peel off the backing from a new, larger pain patch. She wordlessly held out her palm for the patch, then immediately and efficiently peeled off a narrow strip and handed it back to Bob. What we had assumed was backing had been the active part of the new patches. We hadn't been able to recognize a shift in what we'd grown, over a very short time, to expect to see.

Bob applied the new patch, noting the time and dosage on the spreadsheet she'd created. She waited a beat while I pulled the quilt back up over her father, then asked, "What about the old patch?"
~~~~~~

I checked his right side and found the exhausted old-style patch.

"I guess we better add that to the spreadsheet," Bob said, placing an asterisk on it and writing "remove old patch" at the bottom. Our *Checklist Manifesto* fan, who by then was asleep, surely approved.

~~~~~~

When our son Sam was one-and-a-half, we brought his brother home from the hospital and found an anonymous poem in our mailbox. The first lines mentioned a big brother's "great dismay/ that a baby was born on Patriot's Day." Although I never was able to secure a confession from the author, there were at least two clues to its provenance: a familial tendency to produce dubious poetry, and an assumption that rivalry between such closely spaced siblings would ensue. (There was supporting experimental evidence on the point: I am thirteen months younger than my older brother.) It did not. These brothers have always had quiet, steadfast devotion to and healing powers for each other. Sometimes they alone can make each other laugh. Perhaps it's something in their spacing, their biology, or the embedded influence of their father's disposition. He'd awaited the brother never delivered to the household where he grew up among bountiful sisters he loved very much, and for whom he would have done anything.

Had they not been brothers, I hope our sons would have found each other as friends--the kind of friends who became and will always remain brothers to my husband.

~~~~~~

I first visited the university where I would meet Jim during full-on cherry blossom season. I'd investigated another Gothic prospect during a late winter still weighted with the sullen, hulking aftermath of one of the Century's great New England storms. It was no contest. When my husband-to-be had visited the New Hampshire college he originally planned to attend, he was assigned for the weekend to a group of hard-drinking fraternity brothers. He decided it was not for him after all, and chose to go several states' south, where we ended up in the same Plant Biology lab class.

A simple twist of fate.

~~~~~~

The next days would straddle the seasons. Jim had arrived home on an oddly warm, sunny early evening as that endless winter's calendar days wound down. Within twenty-four hours our house would be cushioned in the reverential silence of newly fallen snow, more like fat miniature snowballs than structured crystals. Spring then visited one last time, such a sudden rift that it seemed like cherry blossoms could bloom once more for Jim before the next storm. On that last night and day it snowed again, not gingerly but in fast-falling sugar-cube flakes so bright they seemed like constellations. The glowed atop deep green pines standing vigil at the hill's crest outside the dining room windows.

In that handful of days, his body seemed to mirror those transformations. At first, he sought warmth under handmade quilts, but as the house grew colder he seemed to overheat. His temperature would begin to seesaw without regard to the evenly heated air around him, as his breaths eventually stretched out to one each twenty-five seconds, then twenty, then fewer, and his heart eventually slowed to a beat each minute, both so very long and so impossibly quickly before no beat came on the other side.

~~~~~~

At home Jim had all the tangible and intangible things we could still give him. His bed was covered with sheets our daughters picked out and the first quilt I'd made for him. For us. Underneath the bed was a jewel-colored patterned rug his father's mother had bought in an uncharacteristic splurge, and had treasured and passed down. The antique dining room table he bought for our first house had been shifted 180 degrees, where it became a repository for boxes of sterile needles to flush his port, blue nitrile gloves, alcohol swabs, and bags of mint-green foam swabs to wet his palate when he no longer could sip water.

To his immediate left was a small table where Bob laid out medications he might need to quickly administer from the designated 'special doctor's stool' from which he sometimes gently shooed me away. The stool was next to an immense brick fireplace with a built-in beehive oven in which Jim had popped real corn on cobs, to our young children's wonder and delight. A cousin of Jim's had recently traveled from Los Angeles and confirmed my intuition as to why Jim had been so drawn to this place. Luc said it reminded him of Jim's summer stay with their family, working with them on their colonial-era New Hampshire home.

"We are but stewards" of such places, I can still hear my neighbor Hobb merrily say about the even older colonial home he tended to three houses up the road.

~~~~~~

When our youngest child was even younger, I accompanied her to voice and piano lessons with our chanteuse friend Carrie, whose home studio overlooked a bay ringed by riotously blooming wildflowers and flurries of musical birds. Suzannah would choose her own super-sized songs and deliver them *a capella*. Sometimes Carrie would look at her intently, as if wondering how and why she chose them. After my daughter had run several times through Norah Jones' *Don't Know Why*, with feeling far beyond her years, she took a break and snapped back to her chronological age. She twirled around on a stool, conversing with Carrie's antique dog Sam and sipping water.
~~~~~~

Carrie tilted her head and asked her, "What's that song about?"

My little girl looked up and immediately said, "Regret." She added, "It was too late to fix." And she sang some more.

~~~~~~

We wouldn't have an instant's regret about insisting on bringing Jim home. He was completely coherent once we got him there and Bob took charge. His stubborn high fever disappeared. He even insisted on getting out of bed on his own, until his electrolytes began to waver from the absence of liquids beyond those in swabs to his palate. Bob convinced Jim to let him tag along behind him and hover--just in case the short distance to the tiny under-the-stairwell bathroom was more than halfway as far as Jim could go.

It occurred to me that such traits had been encoded in our fiercely independent daughters, one of whom barely had acquired fluency in the first of many languages when she began shaking off attempts at adult assistance and insisting, "I do it *myself*." And in our youngest, whose no-nonsense mantra as soon as she could form complete sentences was, "I don't *need* any help," followed closely by the occasionally alarming refrain, "I want to try *that*."

~~~~~~

The next morning, Jim ignored the foam swabs and sipped water from a cup. He was not conditioned by the same awful recent memories haunting me and Bob, of the waves of sickness which had followed every sip he tried in the hospital. His mind had been post-surgically fogged, and mercifully he didn't remember those terrible nights.

Bob and I anxiously watched each of his first well-spaced sips, then held our breath as he took several in quick succession, as if we were waiting for a quick-acting poison to take effect or a canary to exhale in a coal mine.

No sign of discomfort. Not a flicker of distress.

Victory.

As Dr. Gawande has emphasized, physicians need to know not only when they have failed, but also when they have succeeded.

~~~~~~

In the early morning hours, as winter edged into spring and blackness turned blue, Jim was fully alert. Suzannah had left for a day-long rehearsal, so I alerted her coaches that I needed to whisk her back to talk to her dad. I zipped to a brick elementary school in Portsmouth, festooned with icicles taller than I arranged in garlands of glittering stalactites. I drove her home so she and her father could talk. Although I was in the room with them, I either couldn't process what he said, or else my mind wouldn't allow me to retain it. Otherwise, I might not have been able to do what I needed to do next, and the next thing after that, beginning with maintaining enough composure to safely drive her back to rehearsal.

When we returned to the school, my head still buzzing with the absence of the words Jim had needed to tell her, I followed her to the doorway of the practice room where her teammates were spinning and dancing on mats while swirling oversized scarlet and crimson flags. Their hues registered on me as fresh and dried blood.

I misheard the routine's music as an ironic Mondegreen: *The Dark Days are Over* (rather than dog days). The last time her father had been able to go out to a place of his choice, and take the last photographs he would ever take, we'd gone with her brothers to her performance of the same routine.

I stood behind her and put my arms around her, though I could feel she wanted to move forward just as much as I resisted letting go. She gently broke away and said, "Mom, you have to leave now."
~~~~~~

She sprinted away, seamlessly rejoining her team. On my way out I could feel the tremors of their collective feet as they landed together, in order to leap as one again and again.

~~~~~~

By day our house was filled with people. The Glennon sisters, as holders of their name, had planned enough food for a long-term neighborhood lockdown. Unlike the last-minute foraging-for-a-semblance-of-a-meal family into which I was born, I married into a family in which planning and critiquing the preceding and ensuing day's food roster is underway while consuming what currently adorns one's plate. Every blue-black granite surface was crowded with the unaccustomed bounty. Had there been a liquor cabinet, it also would have been groaning.

Instead of their synchronized afternoon slumbering in the spot where the sun hit the slate floor south of the stove, Rufus and Brady were on quivering, highest alert. Their eyes were wide and bottomless, even for beagles, shining with equal parts astonished hope and relentless plotting--at least for comparatively more cerebral Rufus. They were prepared to seize the moment should anyone miscalculate what hounds are capable of in the presence of an inadequately supervised family-sized platter.

But soon the laden table had to be moved as far away in the kitchen as it could, because Jim didn't say, but we saw, that background noises were beginning to disturb him. He was recalibrating to a quieter space and needed more rest. By late afternoon, some of his oldest friends--including Gerard, Mike, and John--had driven up from Massachusetts and made shorter visits.

~~~~~~

That night, untethered, Jim, a student of the heavens, was able to stand upright and walk outside with us, past the birdfeeders, down the two granite steps from the porch, and to the top of the hill leading down to the pond. Standing with the support of our children at one shoulder and Randy at the other, Jim was the peak at the center of a line of family and friends.

Our miniaturized selves were fully silhouetted against an enormous orange super perigee full moon.

It was the biggest moon in nineteen years.

~~~~~

Very early Sunday morning Jim seemed to be asleep, eyes closed, breathing steady, yet also appeared to have "financial face." Randy sat on the floor next to me and we both looked up at him and perceived the same worried furrow.

"Tell him everything's under control," Randy said.

"Everything's under control," I said, only slightly more loudly.

Jim, eyes still closed, nodded his head infinitesimally. The furrow relaxed.

~~~~~

During lengthening periods of deep sleep, he still registered what we said. While hearing is the last sense to go, watching him convinced me that tone endures and matters even when someone can't process the content of what's said. As when Kurt Vonnegut's *Galápagos* widow ministered to her dying husband, "her tone alone would have delivered the same messages: 'We love you. You are not alone. Everything is going to be all right,' and so on."

I called Jim's boyhood friend Joe, a pilot based in Colorado. His wife--a hospice nurse who immediately knew what was happening when she heard my voice--told me Joe was flying. I said I'd get the phone to Jim if Joe was able to call back. I felt certain there would be one more chance for them to talk, and there was. It would be Jim's last call.

The last request Jim made was to a family member he wanted to make sure addressed another person's medical issue when he no longer could help find the right specialist. It seemed to me that my husband's successor as family touchstone and adviser, just like at his work, would have to be an entire committee.

Persistence of vision lets me see our friends, Dr. Bob and Dr. Mike, sitting in the adjoining room doing data entry in our makeshift pharmacy, reading up-to-the-minute medical journal articles, making and remaking a careful inventory of incoming express deliveries, and always keeping an ear and eye out should one of us beckon from Jim's side.

Later, but still early that Sunday morning in ordinary time, on Mike's way home from an overnight shift he'd insisted on taking so Bob could go home for the first time to sleep, Mike called me and told me to look outside, where the vast orange moon still hung low in the sky. I told Jim, who gingerly walked, leaning on me, to the front window to watch it dip below the towering trees by the church across the street.

~~~~~

When Suzannah was not quite three, she and I connected between her sprints around the same Portsmouth playground where, years later, just after Jim's diagnosis, we'd all sit with the Battyes, an entire family of friends who'd moved back to New Hampshire the day before Jim's diagnosis. We'd watched July 4th fireworks together for the last time.

I saw in her eyes, green-amber in the sun, an effort to think through some concept that was new to her.

It turned out to be death.

At the end of this internal process, she cheerfully announced: "So, Daddy will die first, then you, then Sam, then Noah, then Emma, then me!"

As with so much in her toddler repertoire, this was not a question, but an announcement. She'd settled the matter. And then she
~~~~~

continued happily cooking up twig spaghetti with leaf sauce and serving it to her siblings. That was the order of things. I don't know at what age casual acceptance of such concepts comes undone. Of course, it is not in the order of things for a parent to outlive a child as Jim's parents did, and as mine outlived their only son-in-law.

In reconsidering our daughter's earliest grasp of life and death I think I better understood what Jim had meant by saying this would be harder for us than for him. Having lived "this life," as he said, with us, he could let go. He could be entirely satisfied with the shape of it, though he knew I'd be incapable of letting go of him. When he said other people had it much harder and "lots of people" get through the death of a spouse, he meant not only that it isn't a singular event, but that someone else could have lost a child, or faced some other burden which might have been more than even he could bear.

~~~~~~

Every kind of love in this world begets love.

On Sunday afternoon, the last time Jim walked into another room, he slowly made his way into the kitchen. The room was filled with longtime friends, including Elizabeth, who'd inspired us to take that vacation from cancer, and her husband Gary, who had learned our household's pickier eaters loved pasta above all other sustenance. He'd brought with him his grandmother's table-sized wooden rolling board and valiantly attempted to teach me the alchemy of turning dough into gnocchi. Two huge pots of family-secret-recipe sauce--one for the carnivores and one for the vegetarians--simmered on the stove.

Rufus and Brady, whose eyes gave away that they knew something marvelous was afoot, were beside themselves with joy. They madly circled him as a friend got a chair for him, then sat at identical alert on each side of their hero as if he were an ancient Egyptian
~~~~~~

God. Their tails swished on the sun-warmed floor as they looked protectively up at him and improbably showed no interest in the food preparation festivities just feet away.

Jim graced himself with a last favorite flavor, asking me to soak just one of the green swabs in water with lemon added to it.

That would be good enough for him.

Our dancer daughter had just arrived home from a competition, magenta and gold and blue make-up still sparkling. He asked her about the show he would never in other circumstances have missed.

After a few minutes, he was ready to go back to bed.

I mentioned to Randy that Jim was having difficulty with the sound level from the adjoining room where people continued to gather. By late Sunday afternoon Randy had enlisted other friends and improvised and constructed an elaborate sound-insulating barrier between the dining room and kitchen.

~~~~~~

Jim's periods of consciousness dwindled. By Monday morning his focus had narrowed to what mattered most: writing notes for and talking to our children.

It would soon be three seasons since that late June day when we heard the words, "This is your tumor." It was the first day of spring and the final day of our younger daughter's school break. A friend's mother had picked her up for a four-hour rehearsal. Just after 8:00 that night, Bob drew me aside.

"I think he's going to die tonight."

"Should I get Suzannah back here?" Rehearsal would last another hour.

"He may not last until 9:00." Bob explained Jim's pulse was thready and other vital signs were weak. I frantically arranged to have another parent pick her up and bring her home. When she
~~~~~~

arrived, the house was dark except for the porch light and a soft light in the dining room. Randy met her at the porch door and brought her to the doorway by her father's bed, where she would have seen him unconscious in a way almost indistinguishable from sleep. Her siblings and I were around him, all touching some part of the quilt that covered him as he lay still between extended, punctuated breaths.

"What's going on?" she asked, both warily and with a fortitude I cannot describe.

Because, of course, she knew.

~~~~~~

Noah later described to me a phenomenon in quantum physics where time stretches by imperceptible increments, but in accordance with a precisely measurable equation.

In court, we prosecutors sometimes reenact a measure of time as it stands still when perceptions are altered by trauma. The nature of what happens in a moment, as opposed to a minute, can alter one's senses and seem to change the pace and passage of time itself. Thirty seconds facing a loaded gun may be an interminable time in which to fix in one's mind the features of a stranger who wields it. Three-and-a-half minutes with an assailant's hands wrapped around a victim's throat may have seemed eternal.

Time seemed to stop between each breath Jim took, as we waited in silence to see if his most recent breath would be his last.

~~~~~~

That final night, as spring slipped back into the harshest of winters, was a carousel of pictures and sensations. Our children and I switching off places on the bed where their father slept. Emma and Noah talking on the floor, foot-to-foot while two of their aunts comforted their brother and sister on the love seat next to them. Jim's sister Elizabeth saying she thought Jim seemed worried, then talking to him softly but intently, as if he were awake, as we watched his face relax. The feel of someone gently tugging at the bottom of the bright blue dress I'd borrowed from a daughter when I realized my own laundry had gone undone for far too long; it helped. It helped me maintain some modesty as I inelegantly scampered over my husband to whisper in his ear. His hearing, in the traditional sense, must have been gone by then as well.

Unlike in the hospital, there was reverential quiet, broken only by those startling intakes of breath. There was no medical equipment in our home except for the awful metal oxygen tanks lurking in this sacred space against Jim's wishes. The unwanted IV bags could be moved out of sight, but the immovable tanks slightly obscured the view of some of Emma's paintings, another offense I'm unable to forgive.

~~~~~~

Voice and vision persist across time and space. I can still hear not only what Jim said, but what he would have said if he could. And I continue to hear other voices, including the calming tone Bob used with Jim and our children, a soothing soundtrack and counterpoint to visceral visual memories. Bob knew how to speak to our children when I did not. He knew exactly how to get Jim to that double-zero. I don't think another soul could have done either. How I wish everyone in such a situation could have a Dr. Bob. Of the countless people Jim spent time with during his illness, I think Bob and Randy were among the only ones whose presence never unsettled him in any way--possibly because he knew he never needed to shield them from anything.

It must have been exhausting for him to try to protect the rest of us from knowing the depth of his physical pain before he came home. We could see his psychic pain--for us, not himself--in having to leave us when he spoke for the last time to his children and
~~~~~~

his friends. And he had told me, in two words, that he lacked the words to say goodbye to me. We'd been alone together for the last time, on the hospital bed next to the old fireplace where his copper pot held kindling.

"Have you told me everything you want to say to me?" I struggled to get the question out.

"Not nearly," my husband said in one long exhaled breath, eyes locked on mine.

He didn't need to say anything more.

~~~~~~

It was among the unique gifts of Jim's friendship with Bob that they could communicate with just a look, when a look was all Jim had the strength to muster. And, like my poor little brother, whom I burdened with delivering much bad news, Bob did endless duty communicating what our extended families needed to know. He talked to me and each of our children about the things few of us could have been entirely ready to hear. He was there for each of them, explaining the inexplicable and answering their questions when all I could do was stroke the hair on their downturned heads and tell them we couldn't make their dad not die, but we could and would make sure he did not suffer.

~~~~~~

Glennon family lore suggests that when my mother-in-law was in labor with the first of her children, my father-in-law drove her to Bethesda Naval Hospital and she refused to go inside. As I would learn, a first labor can be harrowing.

Like laboring to bring a child into this world, there was no going back from the turns the physical processes at life's other end took. It proceeded at its pace and contained vast swaths of silence. I found it was not true that one forgets labor's pain, but true that the memory of the process in the aggregate can be an undifferentiated fog.

The experience of watching someone I love die imprinted much differently in my memory. Moments within it are indelible.

My kind of memory is both a curse and a blessing. I relive, sometimes even as I sleep, details of awful moments of my husband's illness, and every moment he spent in pain until finally we brought him home. But I can also remember every moment he was surrounded by nothing but love, at home and in Ecuador and with his friends and family. I revisit all that he did live to experience in this cruel and sublime and unfair and dazzling world.

~~~~~~

By Monday, Jim's world had dwindled, in one sense, to the size of the room he occupied.

Earlier that day, one by one, our children had talked to him. He'd written something for each of them, so they could always have words from his heart within their reach.

Bob checked on him the old-fashioned and non-intrusive way, by the touch of a hand.

On Monday afternoon, Jim seemed to grow restless. He began to sit up, as if he wanted to get out of bed but was unsure what he wanted to do or where he wanted to go.

Bob asked, "Jim, can you tell me if you need anything right now? Are you having any pain?" There seemed to be a long pause. "Are you feeling confused at all, Jim?"

"I'm a little confused." His voice had weakened and was choppy from medication, but his words were merely descriptive, not anxious or upset.

"That's okay, we're fine." Bob managed to maintain the same even, cheerful voice every time he spoke to Jim--with the possible exception of the time I left them alone together to say goodbye.
~~~~~~

"We've got it all under control," he assured as Jim drifted back to sleep.

These were the moments they'd talked about. It was the vow Bob had made to his friend and Jim knew he would keep: Bob would make sure he had exactly what he wanted, and nothing he did not want, when the time came.

Bob sat on the stool next to Jim and nodded very slightly at me, as if telling me it was time.

All that night, when not checking on Jim, Bob quietly withdrew to the connecting room while we took turns arranging ourselves on Jim's bed and on the floor around him, lying or sitting or curled up on the loveseat between the two rooms. We talked as we sat around him.

"You can still have great lives." I said from the bed at one point, as our children were all within touching distance.

Emma was stretched out, lying on the floor at a right angle to me. She looked up and asked me, "Can *you* still have a great life?"

I paused. "I already have."

She looked at me, with no intention of letting me give up at that. "You're not *that* old."

~~~~~~

Somehow, Jim kept drawing breaths through that night and into Tuesday morning. When he did not have enough time left to allow any infection to take hold, Bob still carefully used alcohol wipes to keep the site clean before injecting any medication. By mid-morning, Myra and Patty had come to help.

The imprint encircling Jim's ring finger had entered its third decade in the making, and I hadn't been able to bring myself to ask him to take off his wedding band while he was conscious. When I understood he wouldn't wake up again, I tried to ease the ring from his finger. It wouldn't budge.
~~~~~~

"It's okay, it's appropriate to take it," Bob said, reading my face.

"I don't want to hurt him." It was a ridiculous thought in the circumstances, but no one pointed this out to me.

Emma gently applied soap and water to her father's ring, as I fruitlessly had tried with more jittery hands. She slipped off the gold band and handed it to me. It was too big even for my thumb, so I held it tightly in my palm.

~~~~~~

I was alarmed when Jim's right arm began moving upward, his fingers curling as if making a fist and fending something off.

"This is called posturing, and it's a perfectly normal part of the dying process," Bob explained as he tended to his friend for yet another unbroken day.

None of this information had been in that awful hospice binder.

~~~~~~

The church bells across the street struck noon.

Every time Jim took a breath, his Adam's apple rose sharply just above the "V" of his soft lavender cotton shirt. His face beaded with perspiration, and I leaned against him and wrapped my arm around him to touch his cheek. His other systems would shut down, and his heart would be the last to stop.

How could it be otherwise?

~~~~~~

Another hour passed; He was still exhaling. Our children wouldn't leave the room. Bob later told me that he was used to adult family members fleeing in moments like these, and how extraordinary it was for our children to have stayed to watch over and take care of their father.
~~~~~~

He explained the death rattle we were hearing, which didn't didn't sound like rattling at all. It was more of a repeating measure of a deep, sustained ghostly musical hum.

I stood with my hand on his cheek. Our children were all at his side with me. Stalwart friends stood in complete silence against the far wall. More for my own processing of the information than anything else, I repeated what Bob had just said: "It's just air being expelled."

"I *know*," Suzannah said, next to me, in that tone that reminded me how achingly young she was. I much preferred concentrating on her annoyance with me for the mindless repetition of what she'd just heard to my own rising fear of the sound.

~~~~~~

When Bob told me Jim had almost no pulse and his brain had stopped functioning, I asked if his heart had stopped. Overnight, he'd taken sharp breaths about fifteen seconds apart, an interval that had grown irregular and stretched out to nearly twice as long by morning. At that point he already seemed to be elsewhere and everywhere.

As soon as Bob told me his brain was no longer functioning, I saw that the recent, tiny furrows in his otherwise unlined face had completely disappeared. I knew he was pain-free and had no more worries. It was as if I could see the catalogue of what he held in his astonishing mind--the music, words, medicine, technology-- evaporating in earthly form, dissolving into black like the pinpoint pixels in a deleted digital image. But I never thought of them disappearing from him as he remains with us, in his way, just as his essential qualities could never disappear. His kindness and love, his wisdom and wit, his compassion, his soul. They're all still here.

A character in Primo Levi's story, *In the Park*, settled in among a host of fictional companions and eventually noticed that when
~~~~~~

he raised his hands, "the light filtered through them as if they were wax." When light began to come to and through him from every direction, he "understood that his time had come... and sat under an oak to wait for his flesh and his spirit to dissolve into light and wind." As I think it was with my husband, he "felt sadness, but neither fear nor anguish" when that time came.

As in Emma's painting of her father and Brady, I always saw more of an expanding and inviting light and lightness than impinging darkness whenever I looked at him. And when I see him now.

~~~~~~

The omniscient but admittedly not entirely reliable narrator of José Saramago's *The Stone Raft* noted the "risky acrobatics" involved in writing about a continuous process, and the absolute impossibility of writing about two or more events which take place at the same time. But I know that in the world outside the room in which we were cocooned in cushioned silence as snow began to fall again, my younger brother and our parents were waiting in Massachusetts for the phone to ring. My big brother had returned to his children in Chicago and waited there.

Jim's parents were at their New Hampshire home with two of my brothers-in-law. His youngest sister was in Massachusetts with her three young children. I didn't find out until long afterward that her protective big brother had somehow known to tell her not to come to our house on that last night and day because he wanted her "to stay whole."

In a coffee shop in Pennsylvania, Jim's eldest sister sat at a table with her phone at the ready, feeling in her heart that this would be the day she got the call.
~~~~~~

Jim's other sisters were in our kitchen, one newly soundproofed door away, cooking in the hope they could coax our children and me to eat something that day.

~~~~~

Jim's heart was still beating. Bob said he'd never seen a heart withstand so much for so long, and continued quietly choreographing what he wanted Patty and Myra to help him with. He used both hands to signal and point, summoning resources as if he were conducting an ensemble.

Eventually, after hours had passed, Patty turned to Bob and quietly said, "He's not going to do this in front of his kids."

I knew she was right.

Their father's heart kept beating, beyond all reason, until just moments after the five of us ultimately turned our faces away.

At the very end, hardly any of us spoke out loud, even to whisper. And afterward, during the only time I was completely alone with my husband after his final breath, I held onto him and whispered into his unhearing ear an unwitting haiku.

When his heart did not beat again, Rufus and Brady were outside in the yard. For the first time in his comparatively relaxed life with us, Rufus joined Brady in frantically howling and jumping and scratching at the door to get back inside. We could all hear them wailing from the other side of the newly soundproofed door.

~~~~~

The last time I was alone in the room with my husband, the hospice nurse came inside our house for only the second time, to pronounce him dead. I don't know who called her. She spoke to him gently, respectfully, telling him what she was doing.

"I'm going to check your pulse now, Dr. Glennon."

I sat in a chair at his side, crying. When she'd finished, she told me she was sorry and held her hand to her heart. She treated him with more dignity and kindness than some physicians had when he was alive. I was so grateful to her.

~~~~~~

I would still see the body that had been his, in the phantom hospital bed, every time I reached the third-from-the-bottom stair that turned and opened into the dining room's landing, long after the old table had reclaimed its rightful place and the bed was long gone. I would see him, and somehow also see myself in my daughter's blue dress, next to the body he no longer occupied. But eventually I would be able to see him in every other room in that house. His house. On ordinary days, with our children as they grew, and on the birthday we knew would be his last, still enjoying the fellowship of food and music and laughter among this world's best and truest friends and family.

~~~~~~

Jim broke up with me in college, for just two weeks, when both of us were teenagers. Perhaps it goes without saying that, after weighing the available data, he reconsidered. He never thought it was too late to think something through and, where possible, do what it took to undo any meaningful mistake.

Like most people, I didn't relish being the dumpee, and conveyed my puzzlement to him. He said, with as much emotive frustration as he tended to show (that is to say, hardly any), "Did you think at our age it would last forever?" I didn't see why it couldn't, although admittedly it was improbable given that I was his first girlfriend.

How, indeed, could anyone have expected this to last forever?

And then it did. The Reverend told our children when he arrived at our house that day that it was a gift for them to have seen their parents live out their vows. He didn't know they had also seen our friends live out their vows to their father, including Bob's promise he would be with him through the end.

The fact that half of marriages end in divorce and half in death does not mean all marriages end badly. I don't even think of our marriage as having ended.

~~~~~

An important concept in evidentiary law is anchored in the impossibility of "unseeing" things. A trial judge has considerable discretion to admit evidence so long as its probative value outweighs its prejudicial effect. A defense lawyer may jump up and object when, for example, a prosecutor moves to introduce crime scene and autopsy photographs. It has been my observation that people blessed with unfamiliarity with such sights may alert to and become extra-attentive to whatever it is that someone does not want them to see.

When I was in law school, back in the days when antique professors used overhead projectors, my Evidence professor introduced this concept by displaying a crime scene photograph of a young, long-haired brunette shot in the head and chest and splayed on an office chair. The hole in her forehead was neat, and a discrete stream of blood had dripped down her eggshell button-down collared sweater. An arc of blood spray had attached itself to the open drawer of a ransacked gunmetal gray filing cabinet behind her, centered slightly to her left, on which the lighting cast a sickly green tint.

As mild as that photograph was, considering what I've since seen, I obviously cannot "unsee" it.

I don't know what imprinted on our children from their youngest years, but I've seen how their father's grace and courage and humor took shape within each of their beings. I hope the joy
~~~~~

they had with him will vastly outweigh the searing images of those last days.

After he died, and after all our children had kissed him and said goodbye, I babbled about how I wished they could remember how their father was with them when they were born, and how lucky he considered himself for every moment he spent with them. I wished I could somehow give them the parts of their lives when they were so young they might not hold what I still carry--the sacred quotidian moments of each day. They must know they always were profoundly loved. But I wished they could also see and hear what I always will, from before they were able to consciously collect memories. Their father, the young doctor, coming home from work to our firstborn, each day with the same question, "How's my boy?" The response--"He's perfect"--would be followed by a description of the day's dazzling ordinariness. The way he sat on our first blue couch reading to our one and two-year-old sons, and how Noah leapt off his father's lap every time his infant sister made a noise in her Moses basket. He would make sure her receiving blanket was tucked around her, then give the same pre-verbal benediction: *Aemmaababyayayou* (which translated to "Emma the baby, I love you"). The way they held their youngest sister's hand when she exhibited any distress, and held up colored objects and carefully watched her reaction to discern what her favorite color was. They decided it was buttercup yellow, a near match for the velvet lining of the Les Paul guitar case that she and I in tandem told her father it was out of the question to sell when he briefly let us glimpse his financial concerns.

~~~~~~

While his only son was alive, Jim's father's voice never even wavered in my presence. I would hear it catch only once, as he read Psalm 23 at his son's Closing Ceremonies and the rest of us,
~~~~~~

numbering in the high hundreds, promptly dissolved. And only once, on a parental frequency that lifted my body from the couch where I sat stroking my younger daughter's hair, did I hear what he worked so hard to contain while remaining strong for the rest of us. My children and I were in our living room, next to the room in which my husband's body still lay, when two of my brothers-in-law solemnly accompanied my father-in-law to see him. All three were wearing deep blue jackets and ties.

If Dvořák's *Stabat Mater* were distilled to a single sustained note of abject grief, that was the sound.

But the note had evaporated by the time I was fully standing. My brother-in-law later told me they had soon gone from the dining room out onto the porch, where my father-in-law was himself again, talking in his measured baritone, which was also Jim's, and certain his son was in no pain and was with God.

~~~~~~

Randy must have gone to man the porch door after the children and I had retreated to the crimson couch. He'd opened the door and beckoned me out into the office space, where I saw my younger brother. Randy must have called him so he could drive up from Massachusetts. Neither of us could speak.

~~~~~~

From that day on I couldn't bear to look inside the dining room, although Randy made sure every vestige of palliative care was removed as quickly as possible. For me death lingered there. The room held what José Donoso described in *The Obscene Bird of Night* as "the particular imprint of" his "dying hour." I would see the room itself, on a continuous loop, as the place he died. And when I was inside the house, I remained stuck in that day as if I were losing my husband over and over again. Our children, however, seemed able to see the yellow house not as the place where their father died, but the place he lived and loved and was loved.

I was not meant to be its steward. Jim had told me I might decide not to stay there, giving me permission to accept the thought when it rose to the surface over the following months. Or perhaps I'd always known I couldn't live there without him, ever since the late June Sunday when my body had carried me to the overheated attic and I'd begun very slowly and tentatively to take stock of the artifacts of all our younger selves.

~~~~~

There were still moments of lightness, even that afternoon.

The hospice grief counselor came by just after the Reverend left, while we remained numbed and spent, leaning on each other on the long couch. I asked my children if they wanted to talk to him.

One responded, "Well, he does do this for a living. He *probably* knows what he's doing."

Randy internally translated this as something like, "Okay, we'll give him five minutes as long as he's come all this way," and ushered him into the room. Randy looked at my daughter, who shares with him an iron, no nonsense core and was sitting on the couch arm closest to him. He apologetically turned to the unsuspecting visitor, shook his head, and said, "I hope you brought your 'A' game, dude."

We couldn't help but laugh--not at the counselor, but at the impossible situation into which he'd been dropped. It was exactly the kind of thing my children's father would have said.

~~~~~

A few hours later, Suzannah's teammate's mother drove up to the porch to pick her up for rehearsal. No one had thought to call off the trip. I asked my daughter if she wanted me to let them know she couldn't come.

"No," she said. "I'll go."

I watched as she seemed visibly to gather the full strength of her balletic soul and pick up her gear. The rehearsal would go on.

At 2:00 a.m. I sent a message to hundreds of our friends, letting them know Jim had been home, where he wanted to be, thanks to the loving kindness of the immense circle of people who treasured him.

The next mail delivery brought an announcement of my husband's 25th medical school reunion at Tufts, to which his body had been spirited away to help future physicians learn their craft.

He was already there.

Part II: Ghost Company

Without End

Photograph by James Glennon

15

Off the Clock

The newer ghosts moved in right away.

After 1:20 on that March afternoon, I could measure days only by ambient light and its waxing and waning absences. When the sun next appeared, or at least registered on me, a single luminous red cardinal lingered at the bird-feeder anchoring the apex among Jim's ordinarily hectic feeding stations.

As soon as Rufus and Brady blasted inside, chased by a gust of sunlight through the open door from the barn, they began feverishly snort-sniffing anything on their map of the world that reminded them of Jim, including me. They nuzzled my hands and sweater and blue dress's hem as I sat on the kitchen floor after his body was shepherded back to his medical school in Boston.

The five of us had returned to the crimson couch as the sky darkened halfway between the longest and shortest of the year's increments of daylight and its absence. Across the room, beyond the carpet's frayed edge, the printer Jim had acquired so he could give away prints of his Galápagos photos revved itself up unbidden. It groaned into gear with a deep metallic hum, flashing green and blue and red lights as it seemed to undergo some inner turmoil.

This so deeply unsettled one of my children that I had to pull its plug. I would give the almost new, but already haunted printer to a landscape photographer friend, as I know Jim would have wanted.

~~~~~

When Brady insisted I take him back outside, he threw the surprising force of his twenty-two pounds of flesh and sinew into a full stop by Jim's truck. He lifted his front paws toward the driver's seat door and looked in every direction, a whine catching in his throat.

I told the beagles he loved them, too, and that they were always good boys for him, even if the latter was not strictly true. They always intended to. They wanted him to be proud of them, and they did their imperfect best. He never asked more of anyone.

~~~~~

That night, in a darkness outside time, Judy walked with me upstairs, past the spot at the landing where Jim ultimately had sunk in pain only a week earlier and handed me the phone to talk to Bob when he couldn't. We rounded the corner into my bedroom-- the singular possessive, which had not otherwise changed.

Half-past winter solstice's blistering early blackness, the new snow reflected just enough moonlight to allow me to take in every colorless aspect of the room without turning on either of the bedside reading lamps.

Jim's table held tomes and journals he would not finish; the reading glasses he'd had little time to use, and an oversized travel catalogue with page after page describing parts of the world he hadn't yet had a chance to occupy. A wastebasket overflowed with ripped square packets from alcohol wipes and discarded wrappers from injections I'd made into his port, hands shaking every time he talked me through the choreography of capping and uncapping vials and needles.

When Judy left the room, it would be the first time I'd been alone that day. Death day.

I stared at the tiger maple bed. It is king-sized; I assuredly am not. The mattress is set at a height where Jim could sit, feet firmly anchored to the floor, facing the church across the street. He would adjust his vivid patterned ties and well-worn work shoes, drawing their laces so tightly that they made a soft zipping sound, then took in a sharp breath as he knotted them.

More recently, after his work clothes had been put aside and out of view, he would lean forward in the same spot instead of sitting upright. My fingers trembled and my stomach lurched as I bit bit my lip and followed his instructions for the three-step infusions into the port. None had been nearly enough to help him.

I must still have been studying the very recent incarnations of the two of us at the bed's opposite horizon.

"Are we going to need to get you a new bed?" Judy gently asked.

~~~~~

In the swirl of the next few days, as countless people wandered into the house and we prepared for Jim's Closing Ceremonies, I sometimes had to suppress the urge to run upstairs to be alone with the same ghosts I initially fled from: mine and his, but mostly ours together.

~~~~~

My parents sent wildflowers much like the ones Jim brought me after our first child's birth. I desperately wanted the violet and garnet and yellow-orange buds never to lose their color and shape and scent. The lilacs gave it their all, but even they couldn't trick capricious time and destiny.

I resisted opening our black mailbox because I knew how empty I would be the day it carried no handwritten and heartfelt note about Jim. Only more bills and paperwork I wasn't ready to face or manage.

I didn't want our older children to go back to their schools even as I wanted them to be able to.

The yellow house did not even feel like home to me that first night.

When eventually I began taking photographs, I couldn't bring myself to push the 'delete' button on even headache-inducing fuzzy images. To do so would be to see the screen turn black by bits and then disappear altogether, a glimpse of this world lost forever even if no one would have revisited the image. When it was preserved, at least someone still could.

I could not bear even incremental additional subtraction, not so much because of the nature of the nominal loss, but because it would make something else irretrievable.

16

The Flattened Penny and
the Fly Ball

Weltlichen Güter. My husband's wedding band is the only jewelry he ever wore, and among few things he carried. His worldly goods were easily catalogued: the Les Paul electric guitar in its butterscotch velvet-lined case, his photography equipment, and the telescope he used to survey the heavens he knew so well. He no longer needed the hammock he would carry into woods to suspend himself weightlessly among trees, where he would drift into the sleep of the just as he looked up through the filigree of each forest's infinitely interlocking bones.

Still, during the weeks after his death, every drawer I opened contained objects which stopped me cold--even when I'd recently opened the same drawer. I found a discrete jumble in his top bureau drawer. I realized as I stared at it that he must have emptied his pockets before the last time I brought him to the hospital. I deduced this from the lone key. Only two days before that last hospital admission, he'd been outside in the barn, showing our sons how to retrieve everyone's ski gear, including his own. Even then, he was convinced he'd be well enough to ski with our children during the upcoming school vacation week.

He had ten days left.

Our sons were home from school to watch their sister's Saturday night performance. I drove us all to South Berwick, Maine, where we sat on bleachers with insufficient leg room even for me as Jim watched our daughter dance. In the last photograph he would ever take, she stood and stretched her arms skyward, holding her palms aloft and looking up as if the gym's ceiling harbored true light. Her fellow dancers arranged themselves around her like fallen rays of sunlight.

I could tell Jim was in pain by the way he held himself upright. By the time our sons had helped him back to the truck, he'd doubled over and was violently sick. He didn't want to go back to the hospital. I injected medication through his port before he slept on his back, lying on top of our quilt despite freezing high winds for which our walls' horsehair plaster was no match. I lay awake next to him, my hand slightly above his left arm as he slept because I was afraid its weight somehow might hurt him. I still could sense his pulse.

Exactly two weeks later we would be at his Closing Ceremonies at Phillips Church.

He must have emptied his pockets' contents into his bureau's drawer between that night and our final trip to the hospital a few days later, knowing he wouldn't need them again, but that I'd find them before long. He'd given me his wallet and remaining keys weeks earlier. In the drawer, along with the tiny key, he'd left behind his medical insurance card; a cobalt blue hospital card bearing the name of the Boston hospital where he had not, after all, been examined; and a flat piece of navy plastic the size of a credit card with no external markings. I knew it was embedded with the coordinates by which radiation fruitlessly had been vectored toward his pancreatic tumor for seven weeks.

And he had carried a penny.

It was not just any penny, nor easily recognizable as ever having been a coin. It had been flattened into a thin, smooth oblong sheath, more deep gold than copper. During the summer after he graduated from high school, it was pulverized on railroad tracks near St. Froid Lake in far northern Maine. After Jim's diagnosis, his friend Gerard came to visit him. They'd grown up on Massachusetts' South Shore, Jim engulfed by sisters and Gerard toward the end among ten blue-eyed towheaded children of the most calmly attentive and good-humored mother I've beheld. He was the first childhood friend Jim had introduced me to. We'd walked at night along Nantasket Beach, past the looming skeleton of the wooden roller coaster that would also soon disappear.

Its silhouette called them back--at the time only by a few years--to mild high school high jinks at Paragon Park. Gerard said he'd chance any ride but a roller coaster. I was once afraid of those, too, but I caught Jim's smile. There was no ride either he or any of our children wouldn't try and try again. My memory of our walk that night is always enhanced by a layer of Richard Thompson's *Wall of Death*, part of the musical score superimposed somewhere along our way.

Decades later, as Gerard and Jim sat at our kitchen table, the intervening decades vaporized. Jim was serene, anchored in enduring friendship with another sterling soul among his chosen brothers. I left them alone together and wandered back into the kitchen as Jim later grew tired. Before Gerard left, he took the penny from his pocket and slid it across the kitchen table to Jim. I didn't at first see what my husband held in his hand. I wouldn't have known by its shape what it was or had once been. But as he ran it between his thumb and fingers, it was as if I could see what my husband saw in it. Its feel alone would have conjoined past and present.

Texture has its own subtext in the space of memory. The smoothness of worn satin as my child-sized fingers rubbed rhythmic ovals on a blanket's light blue satin binding while I steeled myself, trying to forestall each dreaded swallow's searing pain during perpetual bouts of strep throat. A rhododendron, once a living, blazing blue, transfigured into a brittle sepia tumbleweed, its corolla faintly *clacking* against each other like tiny ivory beads. A moth's chalky wings, so insubstantial they might crumble to white ash with too close a breath, and with them the ghosts of our younger selves telling stories by flashlight about what most frightened us then.

I knew that in addition to ordinary high school adventures and misadventures (in which I gathered my husband had always been the designated driver in a core group of five friends), he'd introduced Gerard and Joe to 'The Camp' the summer after their high school graduation. Jim's mother's family camp was not of the tenting variety; it was a cabin built by a half-dozen of his mother's brothers, who included three Catholic priests. Of multitudinous siblings, nine had reached adulthood, including its heavenly complement: two Diocesan priests and one Franciscan, one Dominican sister, and one Daughter of Wisdom. The latter had been Christened Jeanne D'Arc, lending some support to the confluence of given names and destiny. She would spend a quarter-century providing nursing care to women and children in Malawi. The rest stayed closer to home. Throughout and beyond their nephew's life, the Fathers Nicknair would remain triangulated within the 1.5 latitudinal degrees which separate Lewiston and Montreal. In rotation they'd conduct the marriage ceremonies of dozens of nieces and nephews, beginning in our branch of this very fruitful tree when Jim, at 24, married me.

Jim had told me how he, Gerard, and Joe had driven more than ten hours, from south of Boston to Saint Froid Lake, just shy of Fort Kent. Most small towns in the Great State of Maine have considerably larger populations than Aroostook County, where my mother-in-law grew up in Winterville (current population 321, a density of 5 1/2 people per square mile). During their trip's second half they'd dodged heavily weighted southbound logging trucks, their loads tethered with varying degrees of insouciance to flatbeds as they careened around hairpin turns en route to commercial ports. My husband had been on high alert for moose who might venture out and collide with the insufficiently vigilant. Sheer moose tonnage always prevailed. From his own boyhood summer journeys north with his family, Jim knew additional hazards abounded. They included poisonous berries which may have been consumed by young Valére, who was among the children who did not grow up to be Jim's uncle.

As with every other part of the world and its heavens, it was the everyday wonders which held my husband and called him back there. During that trip they'd seen Northern Lights for the first time. I considered possible cause and effect: my husband loved to study night skies, and Joe went on to be a pilot. They'd procured a dubious grade of canned beer, and liberated some before paddling a canoe into Eagle Lake's dark waters, where they glided perilously close to an immense black-eyed moose standing by in water by the far shore. I hadn't known Gerard and Joe when they were seventeen, but I could and can still hear their voices since, rendered in two degrees and intensities of Boston accents. Gerard's voice is always cushioned in a good-natured smile. Joe has a pilot's directness and economy, and was the last voice Jim heard by phone.

Running his fingers over that penny, Jim could revisit the early years of those unending friendships. Holding it, he could again see the Aurora Borealis and the baleful gaze of a moose standing thigh-high in St. Froid Lake. He could remember how he'd exercised relatively newfound beer-drinking skills--but only after turning Mother Mary's statue so she faced away from them in the cabin's roughly hewed stone fireplace, lest she be offended by witnessing such debauchery.

And they had put a penny on nearby railroad tracks, which Gerard had retrieved and held onto for all the years and in all the places he'd landed since then.

~~~~~

Jim had so treasured his memories of the family camp that he took us all there for several summers so we could carry it with us, too. He coaxed even the most reluctant among us out onto the lake, in gently rocking canoes and atop inflated tubes pulled behind a boat in a heart-pumping rush. He sprinted to honeybee symphonies in fields of never-cut grass, helping usher our children's bright green and blue kites aloft. He introduced us to culinary atrocities like rubber donuts and so-called hot dogs with the color and sheen of a scarlet candied apple.

He pointed out birds by species, showed us insects and plants, and waded where our children and their clustered cousins gathered clouds of tiny silverfish in buckets of green water to promptly release in a rush back into the lake. He plucked a lake leech from our toddler daughter's pink toe and convinced her she should not let that first taste of this place deter her from sampling whatever was around her: it would almost always be weighted more heavily with surprises of the good kind.

I realized that, just as Jim's wedding ring is a talisman for me-- something I can touch to transport me back to him and to us--
~~~~~

he must have kept the flattened penny in his pocket during the months he endured treatment and as his symptoms worsened and the pain took over. By touching its smooth sides, he could have heard the lapping lake water and Gerard's and Joe's voices. Now that I have the penny, I can, too, even though I wasn't with them then.

He would have been reminded of lifelong friendships, of wonder at nature, and of the ways our younger selves experience adventure and weigh risks. Of firsts rather than lasts.

He knew I would want to hold onto the penny.

Trying to discern what he wanted me to let go of seems much more complicated.

~~~~~

Downstairs on my husband's desk, around the corner from the dining room I could no longer bear to see, a lightly scuffed baseball sat alone in a cobalt mug inscribed with a school motto: "Truth, Even Unto its Innermost Parts." Jim had plucked the ball from the rarefied air atop the Green Monster, on a Father's Day I had no conscious inkling would be his last with us. Through a complicated interstate series of events and exchanges, it was decreed that one precious ticket would go to my younger brother and the other was all mine, to use or bestow upon any person worthy of it.

Jim may have been selfless, but he had a talent for inveigling certain important things. He used it sparingly, as one should, and had gently lobbied me: "You know, you're still young, but I've been around for fifty years. This could be my only chance."

And he looked at me with those eyes, in the light of that day between dark green and russet. He tilted his head with as much of a pleading grin as he could offer without either of us laughing outright. It was not unlike the irresistible faces beagles make, cocking their heads and looking deeply at us, unblinking. As if we were
~~~~~

their entire world and lone repositories of their bottomless love and devotion--whenever they simply want to negotiate another t-r-e-a-t.

I couldn't help but relent. I told him it was going to be his Father's Day present and he was lucky to have a wife who'd give up such a treasure. He brought me back a fly that has no wings. A fly ball, lightly scuffed, as if with cocoa powder and not desultory city dust.

~~~~~

I have not been atop the Green Monster, but I hold this memento, the shagged Fenway fly. I am not alone.

Our children aren't old enough to be weighted by the loss of hope that attended such endings as that of game 6 of the 1986 World Series. There would be a game 7, but conditioned unbelievers knew how it would end. And so it did.

But in 2004, a mere infant-to-young adult life span later, after we held our collective breath through the playoffs and the Red Sox at very long last prevailed, intergenerational joy erupted. It united the living and not a few of those who were no longer with us to see the day. A riot of baseball souvenirs appeared in more and less sacred places. Jim wasn't the only internist who marveled as patients of advanced age and complex chronic conditions appeared in his office, seemingly occupying a heady space outside their earthly vessels.

It was as if that single season's remarkable ending had left them at peace with the shape of their lives. I wouldn't have been surprised if lab results and vital signs suddenly reverted to evidence of shining health. If scans suddenly had divested themselves of worrisome images as radiologists chuckled and shook their heads, convinced dire diagnoses must have been mistakes all around.

"No problem, doc, these things happen."
~~~~~

I would have understood if non-elective surgeries and long-term therapeutic journeys had been canceled, with no hard feelings, among mass spontaneous restoration of patients' less scarred younger selves--the people they'd been before decades of laboring forward under The Curse, and its compounding effects on other albatross-like encumbrances we carry.

These ruddy, well-oxygenated older patients would have announced to their surprised physicians that living to see the Sox win the World Series was good enough for them.

New England's graveyards fluttered with tiny pennants. In untouched pixels they would have been rendered in white and red and a touch of navy blue felt. But to true fans they would have registered as seas of scarlet, bright cardinals among late autumn grasses and fallen leaves beginning to decay into another winter. Properly reared young fans brought championship memorabilia to resting places of forebears who had not, after lives of yearning, lived to see this particular miracle. But that Pentecost red would have been easy to spot from far higher than 37' 2" above left field.

~~~~~

When we brought our young sons to Fenway Park for the first time, they already could call a pitch better than I. They weren't old enough to have stayed up even until the Seventh Inning stretch, but fate had handed us four golden tickets and we did not protest. We witnessed our sons' sublime first Fenway moments, as the pitch of the rising cement stairs and the descending tiered stands beyond them formed a diamond-shaped frame around the field's crosshatched Kelly-green grass. Our sons proceeded ahead of us up the stairs as if in a sacred processional to the bright lights ahead. We took our seats and watched them stare as the Shortstop ticked off his ritualistic glove checks. Our future math majors were far
~~~~~

more interested in analyzing his patterns than in watching the typical warm-ups playing out elsewhere on the field.

While they were thus mesmerized, an already abundantly hy-
drated stranger spilled an entire cup of beer on me, emitting emotive frustration only at having to pay for another. At least my
toddlers didn't reek of brew, part of the still-wafting aura attending that night as it lives on with me.

Questionable sobriquets for the opposing team and their sparse
(and for the most part wisely incognito) on-site fans tumbled at
increasing volume from the bleachers as innings accrued. Fiercely
surging wind seized and lifted discarded paper, gathering shards of
priceless tickets and shreds of flotsam into an impromptu ticker-
tape parade. Bony fingers of thin blue plastic--the kind newspapers
were wrapped in when *The Boston Globe* still left ink stains--drifted
in a maelstrom around us and fell onto the field. Our boys watched
in wonder.

<p style="text-align:center">~~~~~</p>

In a silent house, I found myself alone watching a game, far
from Fenway and at an unquantifiable distance from my husband
and that late September night. I wasn't nearly as invested in either
the game's or season's outcome; 2004 alone probably would have
been enough for me.

Then there was an obstruction call, a pinch runner pick-off, and
the pièce de résistance: a Keystone Cops rundown. It could only
have been more entertaining had it ended with the old hidden ball
trick.

What a view Jim must have had this time.

I wandered back to the visible northern hemisphere of the
once-hit baseball Jim gave me. Somewhat less than half its whole,
its ballast out of sight below the mug's rim. One hit had been
enough. To call its marking--not quite deep enough to scar it--a

frisson of Fenway would have been far too delicate for fans who'd recently urged New Englanders to "Cowboy Up" (much less the hard-core bleacher crowds who, well before *Sweet Caroline* sallied forth, had me barely suppressing the urge to cover our young sons' ears). Perhaps more to the point, to feel a frisson of anything would have gave felt inherently forward-looking. But this swath of ball-park detritus will always take me back.

And it would have seemed dispirited to label as a "smear" the lingering imprint where a Red Sox batter made contact, possibly after tapping his bat to the ground, golden particles spraying up-ward in the setting sunlight that escaped through the surrounding city blocks' seams as the air cooled.

So I think of it as a dusting of Fenway, residing forever under raised double stitches. Like the dusting of stars over hammocks which sway more gently than canoes on still water. The sprinkled stars beyond violet, green, and lemon Northern Lights which break the black night over St. Froid Lake. Like the stardust of wizards and fairies and magic. Of fathers and mothers and daughters and sons on diamond fields and quiet shores. Of come-from-behind victories after heartbreaking losses, and gold-copper pennies like messages in bottles, floating back to us again. Of persistent hope and curses broken and wishes which still sometimes come true af-ter being crushed once, and again, and more.

~~~~~

When I later left the yellow house for the last time, the final thing I spotted--and had missed on countless cleaning-out trips--was an unopened box of baseballs. Relics of Jim's many Little League coaching years, they'd been set back on a high shelf in the barn. Like the flattened penny and the fly ball, they rekindled each sense. The *thwacks* of hits and the loud swishing vacuum of miss-ing. The acrid smell and taste of fried food lifted from sometimes
~~~~~

seasons'-old oil. The faces on both teams' players as, in a game-win-ning play, a catcher leapt and clenched and opened a weathered glove both when it was empty and when it was not.

It would be spring again, somehow, in the wake of another sum-mer and fall, and a winter neither ready to let go of me, or I of it.

~~~~~

No one, but no one--with the possible exception of Lin-Manuel Miranda--wrote love like Pablo Neruda. Neruda didn't merely write "of" love. His words are indistinguishable from the emotion itself. His poem, *If You Forget Me*, lingers over an extinguished fire's remains. They transport a surviving partner to the woman he out-lived.

Both the flames and their lingering ash.

Sultry summer's torrent and autumn's cool unrolling.

A smooth bright perigee moon and the desolate landscape of a burnt log.

The song, before and during and forever after.

Every sense, every moment our minds retain in the madness of the methods by which we navigate profound loss, carries us, like Tralfamadorians, back and provisionally forward, but always to and from and with those we love and have loved, and who have loved us.

Hard butterscotch candies wrapped too tightly in red-gold cel-lophane twisted at both ends, carrying a hint of the scent of the soft saffron leather handbag from which my grandmother Helen--whose closely held secrets kept her from smiling, but not from loving us--would fish them out as her signature treat. Grandma Jackie's cheese triangles. August tomatoes and tiny dried rosemary branches. Purple cauliflower and a *Dulce de Leche* birthday cake on a boat at the equator. A final taste of lemon on a mint-green swab.
~~~~~

The sweet pea and rose soaps in hospital rooms where we held our swaddled newborns as we introduced them to their not much older siblings. Other hospitals, emergency rooms, stifling heat and stinging chemicals. Linen and immodest threadbare johnnies with sprays of what was not quite missing--paler dots of hushed pink blood that may or may not actually have been embedded there, had I looked longer and harder at the time.

Voices I still hear long after they fell silent. The spaces between my father's thoughtful pauses, now echoed by one of my sons as he translates the mathematical universe for me. My father-in-law, who did not sing even in church, making up songs for our young children. The piercing sorrow of the single sustained note that escaped him when he saw his only son's stilled body. My lifetime best friend's mother's Danish-accented English. The laughs of sons before their voices grew deep. The change in pitch and pacing I thought I heard in my daughters' voices as they grieved, when it seemed impossible any of us would laugh again. My own voice when it faltered. My husband's, as it never did, still greeting calls on our children's phones.

How it felt to hold my children's hands at every age as they grew. The absence of the steady hand holding mine as our flights took off, when I was still afraid of flying.

The things we carry are rarely things, after all.

17

Homer Nods

A grieving character in Andre Dubus's *Dancing After Hours* wonders how others fail to see "in her eyes and at the corners of her lips the dark glisten and static quiver of stored tears." Sometimes the sensation of grief isn't outwardly palpable, yet makes one wary of those living their lives and performing daily tasks in apparent normalcy. It faults them for not knowing or seeing what is unknowable and unseeable.

But even audible and visible tears can be far from cleansing.

Elif Batuman's *The Possessed* apprised me that Persian has only one word for crying, while Old Uzbek had dozens, including words for sobbing "ceaselessly in a high voice...in hiccups," and "while uttering the sound *hay hay*." While hiccuping is not my forté, my repertoire already incorporated most of the salty menu. I don't know if it also included the audible angst occasioned by infuriating bureaucratic insults to those already hollowed out by loss.

After losing his wife, C. S. Lewis noted he had not been forewarned "that grief felt so like fear." Only the grief preceding death had struck me as fear--the high-octane fear that prompts fight or flight or freezing in place. (The less frequently noted fourth reaction to intense fear is much rarer: an impetus toward annihilation, inward or outward.)

No one ever told me grief felt so physically, viscerally painful. No one told me grief feels so much like bodily injury--damage that gives no sign of healing, and about which there is no helpful data to be gleaned. It's all unquantifiable *feeling*, idiosyncratic and unpredictable and exhausting.

Both anticipatory grief, anchored in fear of what lay ahead, and its new incarnation after death felt like a physical entity, and a sharp-edged one at that. As Dubus described a sister's grief for her brother, it "lay beside her, hovered behind her. Shards of it stayed in her body; she could touch the places they pierced in her brain and heart."

It was like that, too, for much longer than I would have imagined.

~~~~~

Everything ached, physically and psychically. I sat downstairs in the room that had been a communal workspace for six and stared into its emptiness. Only one of my daughters was home with me at the time. I'd thought no one else could see what was in my mind's eye.

"Are you back in the room?" my daughter asked, divining where my mind had relocated me, just around the corner and in the recent past.

'The room,' it was understood, is the room where her father had died a week earlier.

I'd had the mirror-opposite experience during a second day of active labor. I had asked Jim why a woman in a nearby room was screaming, puzzled that I had no urge to do so with searing contractions, and had instead retreated into sustained quiet.
~~~~~

Jim had gently said, "Stay in the room." Everything I needed to focus on was right there in my reach. Nothing outside it mattered.

~~~~~

The cues which set off raging bursts of grief were wide-ranging. There was no way to guard against them. One child was undone by coming across XL gym clothes. Another suddenly stopped eating, fork raised, and couldn't stop crying; Rufus and Brady awakened and hastened that way to offer comfort. It was constant, but changed hour by hour. It could be launched simply by setting eyes on something we'd seen hundreds of times before. I looked inside a black bag Jim had kept hanging on a rarely used doorknob. I thought it had been an overnight bag for when he was on call, but instead found binoculars inside it. I realized he'd kept them at the ready in case he heard an unusual bird or animal sound.

Who would tell the birds?

~~~~~

As April began, winter revisited us for a single day. Inches of fresh snow replaced the interregnum's gray slush. Gingerly, I ventured out on my own. I found myself silently weeping as I walked grocery store aisles, past items only Jim had enjoyed and I wouldn't bring home again.

By our son's graduation day, exactly two months after his father's death, I'd lost track of enough ATM cards and slips of paper with scrawled contact numbers to carpet a small room. I constantly misplaced my phone. I returned to the therapist we'd spoken to together in January and walked past the couch at his office's rear brick wall, which Jim now had all to himself. Before I sat in a chair for one, I looked Jim's way. He sat quietly on the couch's far left side, where I'd welded myself under his arm three months earlier. I fished through my bag in vain hope I'd find my most recently replaced credit card.

"I'm losing everything," I said out loud.

My psyche might not have proved a hard nut to crack.

~~~~~

Until Jim's illness I'd been afraid of so much: flying, highway driving, balancing a checkbook. Dentists, technology, brown recluse spiders, and indoor daytime bats. Dark lacquered wood furniture that reminded me of the first funeral parlor room I'd steeled myself to enter. I'd even maintained an unhealthy dose of apprehension about public speaking, notwithstanding my line of work.

At first, irrational fears came flooding back, and then some. Even thinking about the room where he died filled me with dread. For months I experienced an intense new fear that something equally disastrous soon would strike me, too, and my children would lose both their parents while struggling to navigate their father's loss.

But already many of these former frights had ebbed--especially, given our children's logistical needs, the added highway driving. I'd never to my knowledge encountered indoor brown recluse spiders, so I thought I might as well cross that off my list. And when Noah cleared his throat and nodded in the direction of a panoramic photo canvas his father had printed after his final hiking trip, asking if I was aware a bat was right above me, only a light scream escaped me as I observed an undernourished-looking bat hanging from the the canvas's edge, upside-down among Baxter State Park's mountains. I'm proud to say I did not continue screaming as I dove to quietly cower under the desk while Noah ushered the wee fellow outside to echo-locate his family.

~~~~~

During those first days and weeks and months, I tried to navigate the peculiar bureaucratic flotsam of death that often falls to survivors. I was required to disgorge lacerating raw information to disinterested and curt strangers. I made notifications to Social Security on behalf of our minor children; canceled Jim's DEA prescription number; and, for an obscene amount of money, ensured our family's health insurance continued. Corporate errors spontaneously regenerated. (Take heart, Lamarckians). I refilled the same Groundhog Day forms. I felt like the quarry in an endless game of 'gotcha' in which powerful institutions had calculated that, after several rounds, most people would give up from the additional incremental weight on already bowed shoulders. I am not that person.

Metaphorically, at least, each mail delivery brought to mind a particular character in Nikolai Gogol's *The Overcoat*, who possessed "a peculiar knack, as he walked along the street, of arriving beneath a window just as all sorts of rubbish were being flung out of it." Opening mail continued to enable me to practice my lingering Old Uzbek-style sighs. I received scolding missives for not having supplied my dead husband's signature on forms sent only after I'd canceled and paid off the phone line in his name, as I'd promised him in the ambulance. I assured the carrier's representatives that they would have had cause for complaint (including a report to law enforcement) if I *had* produced his signature following his demise.

I finally relinquished the landline, so its electronic voice would stop announcing my children's father was calling, having seen the looks on their faces when a sibling called in on the old-school phone as we aimlessly opened and reopened the refrigerator, looking for something tasty that might magically have appeared within it. I began to navigate many years of overlapping financial aid documentation, along with all the rest of the paperwork Jim had always spared me.

I discovered that, from a hospital bed, he'd done our tax returns by hand and filed them eleven days before he died.

It was a leaden world punctuated by unpleasant surprises along a spectrum between merely irritating and heart-stopping. A billing representative called two days after her own hospital's Chief Medical Officer's death to ask to speak to him about a $30 co-payment mistakenly recorded as not having been collected. An all-out shakedown letter arrived on the letterhead of a purported Massachusetts "subrogation specialist," which I happened to know could not in any way have been implicated in our medical bills. I responded in detail and in the tone its author deserved.

Most of the time it was easier for me to be furious at such faceless, disingenuous, and larcenous demands than all-out bereft at every minute of every day. But it was additional ceaseless negative emotion. These chores were not just annoying but also viscerally unsettling, because the people with whom I was forced to deal didn't know my husband. He mattered nothing to them, but for me was ever-present in every piece of paper, every conversation, every eternal wait through an insidiously crafted menu of numbered buttons to push to direct my call to another sub-menu equally beside the point of my call. I felt I'd let him down with every task I couldn't complete. And I felt the much greater weight of everything I couldn't do for our children.

~~~~~

I cannot describe what it was like to see my husband's death certificate. Until I read it I hadn't known his precise time of death. That day had not been made of the usual complement of minutes and hours. When I holed myself up inside, I sometimes could imagine that he wasn't absent from the world outside our house. I sometimes caught myself pretending he was simply away at work. And a peculiar digital life endured. His voice continued to greets callers
~~~~~

on more than one child's cell phone--characteristically, with a pun. As a formerly hard-drinking ex-cop in Lawrence Block's *A Drop of the Hard Stuff* mused after hearing a murder victim's recorded phone message, there are ways in which we no longer "die all at once."

There were few people whose calls I had the energy to take. I stopped looking at my husband's minimal social media, which within weeks of his absence began to send him messages urging him to get back online. Missives to my own computer inquired whether I wished to "reconnect" with my husband. Algorithms must have detected a disruption within one realm among our contacts.

Oh, how I wish it were that easy.

That has not been the way he keeps in touch with us.

~~~~~

For eight months I tried to straighten out a single phone bill. We were owed $71.38. Not that I was fixated on it. I spent untold lawyer hours with "customer service" representatives, re-explaining that in fact I had *overpaid* my husband's bill, having absorbed from him the understanding that, one fine day, a refund almost always would be yielded back to us. When the overlords did eventually come to see their error, they began issuing refund checks in my husband's name, notwithstanding having identified his death as their reason for unilaterally and without notice canceling all six family lines. The persistently non-negotiable checks were followed by renewed and aggressive bills for the initial line that had forever gone cold, which I again assured them he had not used since his date of death. I suggested they consult their own carrier records and counsel to solidify the point.

Had it been a $30 bill, I might not have bothered, but by then it was a point of honor. Stubborn, costly honor. I'd sent them a $25
~~~~~

certified copy of Jim's death certificate, bared for these strangers our documentation that I was indeed the one privileged to be paying the bills, and after each of these conversations had been treated to a spritely, "You have a great rest of your day!"

I was on the phone again after opening a letter chiding me for not having deposited a *third* refund check made out to a person whose departure from this mortal coil would have made my doing so at least a light felony. I had questions.

No doubt inspired by my tone, "escalation" again proceeded apace on their end.

"Let me get the account information again and talk to my supervisor. Middle initial 'N'?"

"No, middle initial 'M,' as in '*mayhem*,' '*murder*,' '*mandible*.'" I seethed, grinding my teeth.

"Okay, and last name 'Clennon'?"

"No, *Glennon*, 'G,' as in '*grotesque*,' '*gash*,' '*gurgle*.'" (If I'd given it any thought, I would have added "garroting.")

"Oh. Okay, got it."

"Great."

"I've got to say, ma'am, most people only give me one word, and it's not usually any of those."

~~~~~

Then, one day, Homer nodded.

Not the Homer who advised his son Bart, "You tried your best and you failed miserably. The lesson is, never try."

Instead, I drew a federal civil servant who alluded to *Ars Poetica* after swiftly resolving a nagging problem. When I expressed surprise and thanked him, after an arch aside about laughably incorrect advice I'd received from his agency's brethren at the local level, he said, "Even Homer nods."
~~~~~

It isn't just that I finally hadn't drawn the institutional representative with the highest inverse correlation of cluelessness to combativeness, but that I finally encountered a *listening* person. His effortless response was the kind Jim would have offered, understanding that not everyone who causes needless work is a villain, and not every mistake is a personal affront.

"Cut them a little slack" might be the more current version of *quandoque bonus dormitat Homerus.*

And while you're at it, Steph, cut yourself some slack, Jim would have added. This, too, would pass. And it was only money.

~~~~~

I realized only as the pace and depth of bureaucratic insults finally began to taper off that these nameless people had provided a convenient outlet for my diffuse, directionless anger. When cancer left me without a villain capable of pursuit, human and institutional provocations gave me a way of venting. But faceless exchanges were an inadequate substitute even for my highly adversarial work life, much less the cushioning camaraderie of my work family. They helped me appreciate those bonds and shared purpose all the more once I returned. I missed having a purpose--something I felt I did well and at its best can help people in great pain find some measure of justice, if not solace.

It is much easier to channel rage toward things which don't as deeply matter when they disappear. It's less stressful to engage emotively with anonymous voices, and discuss questions with definitive answers, than to risk falling apart in deep conversation with someone truly willing to listen and hear.

~~~~~

A stranger waited for a car repair with a copy of *The Last Lecture* in hand. I sat in a nearby chair staring at nothing, hoping that Nellie the mom van would pass one more inspection. For no apparent reason, the woman looked up from her book and turned to me and said, "You know, only one in a hundred people gets pancreatic cancer."

"No, no," I reflexively began to argue (as certain lawyers do). "It's *much* rarer. Only 13% of pancreatic cancer is diagnosed in people under sixty, and 25-to-30% percent of primary pancreatic tumors are accounted for by smoking...." I trailed off, looking down at my own reading, and therefore was not treated to whatever look may have been dispatched in my direction as she speed-walked to collect her keys from Bill, the mechanic who would teach my youngest how to check her tire pressure--a skill never imparted to me because Jim took care of all those things.

Snippets of meaningless statistics still sloshed like inky waves. My brain apparently had held them in reserve to cut off at the pass any discussion with a stranger that threatens to go deeper than numbers.

"I mean, what are the odds, actually?" I'd once mused aloud in front of one of my children, who immediately intuited exactly what inner thoughts prompted my question as I'd transported another stack of medical insurance paperwork to my desk from my husband's.

My daughter sensibly deadpanned. "Well, at this point, 100%."

18

When the Word has Broken

My husband had made only one request about his Closing Ceremonies. He left the content entirely to us, but asked that we have his service exactly four days after his death. It seemed an easy assurance to give and a puzzling request to make. Perhaps he'd sensed the four-day mark would fall on a weekend, when far-flung friends and family could travel to be with us. Or that the early Spring day would prove perfect--never a sure bet in New England.

It was sublime. The music; the hymns; the words sung and spoken, the moments when sunlight launched itself through an enormous stained-glass window and adorned the church's somber dark wood with jeweled ribbons. Our son Sam, wearing one of his father's ties, its loops perfected by Randy, read Amy Gerstler's poem about perpetual spring. Our daughter Emma read Louis Untermeyer's ode to a father who did not allow barriers to form between him and the world's grace and beauty. None of us wore black.

Given my through-the-roof tension before the service, his reasoning likely encompassed how well he knew me. I hadn't told him I'd want to speak, because I knew he'd have tried to spare me the distress of believing anything I said would be inadequate. He would have foreseen what swiftly overcame me, including the visceral intensity of emotion inside our house in those days' maelstrom. He knew one of our children would take on the task of making a playlist for him, and that if we had more time to fret over what any of us would say or do, at least one of--we all knew who--would fill that time with ever more expansive fretting. I'd never have stopped second-guessing myself.

Knowing us as he did, he didn't want to add to our stress. Knowing him as we did, we knew he would have felt anything that came from our hearts was more than enough.

~~~~~

Jim had told me, "This is for you. I won't be here." It may have been the only thing he was wrong about.

He was there, so palpably that people who hadn't been lucky enough to know him could see the man he was and were attentive to Reverend Thompson's exhortation to "live your lives as though you knew this man."

One of his colleagues told me that during the drive home she told her husband she "couldn't come to terms with how unfair his disease was." Why Jim, and why so young? Her husband, who hadn't met him, had absorbed from the service how complete his life had been despite its brevity: "It seems like he was always the smartest guy in the room. Maybe he's just the guy who always finishes the test first while the rest of us are still working to figure out the questions or second-guessing our answers."

~~~~~

I was told I might find myself wanting to scream at times, but I never did. The rich variety of occasions for tears always prevailed. Before I returned to work full-time, I found a more constructive way to channel the component of grief comprising my fury with those who failed to show compassion for my husband. I traveled to dozens of hospitals to speak to health care professionals about our experiences with devastating illness and end-of-life care. I stressed that after patients die--sometimes very quickly and brutally--those who love them will still carry, for better and worse, how they were treated. I told them what it felt like when my dying spouse was told that fulfilling the only wish we could make come true for him would be an unreasonable imposition upon the people he loved, and what it was like to finally come home to unwanted and unwelcome oxygen tanks and IV fluid bags.

I discussed possible unintentional effects of even well-meaning words. It could be something as simple as the bruised silence in which families in oncology waiting rooms absorb postings addressed only to patients who will live--like photographs of smiling families at 'Survivors' Banquets,' and calendars listing survivors' meetings and other events for nearly every beribboned, color-coded category of cancer except our family members' statistically far more deadly ones. I shared my deep guilt for not immediately noticing my husband's pained reaction when a certain physician described a particular hospice house as "Shangri-La," and said he should go there because he would "not want to be a burden" to us.

It's among the things I'll never forgive that hospice physician.

After speaking, I repeatedly was approached by hospital staff who told me some version of: "I've said that to patients, that sometimes patients chose one option so they won't be a burden to their families. I had no idea that's how they'd hear it, that *they* would be a burden if they made a different choice." But I always made sure to tell each audience that if it were Jim standing there, they'd have heard a different story, more focused on the compassion he *was* shown.

I believe compassion often counts at very least as much as clinical skill, and that it is a rare thing to find the two qualities combined in such abundance as we saw in some practitioners, or as absent as it was among others. With all the compassion we were graced with, the shock of its absences carries the weight of superfluous trauma. Health care providers may be taught to introduce themselves to all the people in their presence. They can be trained at very least to count to ten if that is what it takes to avoid egregiously flippant remarks. And, if they're willing to listen, they can hear what their words sound like from the perspective of a critically ill patient or that patient's family and friends. But I do not think true compassion can be taught any more than one can teach someone perfect pitch, or to enjoy eggplant's undisguised taste and texture.

Physicians, not unlike lawyers in my field, can be compassionate without giving false hope, and realistic about what may lay ahead without being heartless. They can assist patients in understanding that entering hospice care isn't giving up hope, but acknowledging the reality that hope is no longer for a cure. They can even admit this is difficult to talk about, as I will always be grateful more than one of my husband's colleagues and treating physicians told me.

~~~~~

By the time I fully returned to work, I'd spoken at hospitals in several states. I traveled to a Martha's Vineyard hospital where I spoke to eight people and took the next ferry back, closing my eyes in summer sun, feeling the water's movement beneath my feet, and picturing the last time I'd made the same trip. Jim and I had biked all the way around the island when I was eight-and-a-half months pregnant with Noah; I must have had formidable balance back then.
~~~~~

I had the great privilege of speaking at Carney Hospital, where Jim had once done a rotation in internal medicine. It had been a few minutes' walk from our first house, and was the only place there were no questions at the hour's end. Then a physician who may well have helped train my husband stood and said it did not seem right to talk yet. He asked if I'd be willing to come back for a second day so we could all talk then. The tiered auditorium overflowed again when I did. It is no small thing when people are willing to listen and ask to sit with what they hear.

~~~~~

Even after those first dazed months, it was impossible to predict which ordinary tasks would undo me--speaking, walking, driving, shopping, re-titling a vehicle by the legal construct of 'survivorship.' I would walk store aisles, see parents shopping for toddlers, and remember how unremittingly exhausted and dizzily happy we'd been during those years. I'd make it all the way to the checkout counter only to stare at my own hand as I lifted from a shopping cart a food or drink my muscle memory had picked up for Jim. I'd release it, as if the item not only had cajoled me into picking it up, but had betrayed me.

~~~~~

"And how does a body break bread with the word when the word has broken"? Poet C. D. Wright asked the question in *More Blues and the Abstract Truth*. At first, I'd misread the last phrase as "when the *world* has broken." After a beloved person's death, I felt the world itself had broken for us, while its concrete tasks lingered. Wright's poem begins with unsettling physical images from a dream. The young speaker segues into visions of decay, of bodies and inanimate objects alike, and seeks answers from a grandmother who "used to grow so many things." How, following the death of someone soul-loved, does one keep doing what one used to? Thunderous loss stays with us, leaving a trail of questions which boil down to "What do I do now?"

How do we keep plowing through tasks which persist as if the world were the same--tending to dogs, making dental appointments, baking or breaking bread? How do I inhabit a still-spinning world when it's steeped in black and blue? The details and demands of daily life ultimately have changed very little, and the unanswerable questions haven't changed at all. Death remains as abstract as it ever was because I've only witnessed it. Faced with the immutable but unimaginable--death, which Wright describes as "none other"--it may be all we can do to persist, sometimes robotically, until we again can find grace in the extravagant and beautiful within the ordinary. Like bread and like water. Like the understanding of those willing to listen and sit with our words and our silences.

<h1 style="text-align:center">19</h1>

Punctuated Disequilibrium

Retreating into the past often was the only way I could navigate the present.

In Lois Lowry's *The Giver*, a single child designated the "Receiver" is selected and trained to become the community's sole steward of memories. Good and bad, exhilarating and devastating. Only the Receiver feels empathy and pain and happiness; sees color; and hears music. I would vastly prefer to have been the person who feels immense pain as well as joy than one of the many who feels nothing.

Even my own memory isn't populated only--or even primarily-- by searing moments. I would have relinquished all hope if it were. Over time, those terrible memories haven't become less intense, but they're more contained, like a deep wound that heals to an increasingly inconspicuous scar. The living man I can still see and hear in pain does not himself continue to suffer, any more than I continue to suffer the labor pain I won't forgot.

I have startlingly beautiful memories within the same awful months, like the soothing words our child spoke to her father about how glad she was that he was coming home. She couldn't have known he'd just been exposed to the offhand inhumanity of being told that doing just that would make him a "burden" to us. Every loving touch and thought expressed to him, and to all of us, continues to accompany us as we inhabit a world of hurt and betrayal and beauty and love.

~~~~~

I hope our children will always remember how they've loved each other and always been loved. I hope they retain what once was magical for them as children, and find ways to continue calling upon those memories as adults. Our exuberant, extroverted animal lover retains early memories of creatures she met. Her sister has always been called to faraway places and their inhabitants. Our outdoor adventurer Scout, like his father, felt at home in the endless outdoors; his memories of pre-verbal life always dwell in what he and his father discovered outside, from tiny pine cones on a felled tree's stump to fluorescent orange lizards. His brother was fascinated by what often lies outside our sight and grasp, like the magic of numbers and of the known universe we inhabit. Our children also remember moments of startled fright: an attack upon a cousin by swarming hornets, a son who fell from a dock and remembers my handing off a baby to his grandmother as I leapt into the water to scoop him up.

I remember from my own toddler years the wondrous and the terrible, and how they sometimes intersected. I'm glad for what both teach me. I can see my very young self in Turkey experiencing pure awe, pulling my hand from my mother's, and dashing ahead of her up narrow white stone steps and into an immense building where I watched birds fly in and out of open windows, circling a dome as high as heaven and surrounded by jeweled mosaics. And I'm accompanied by long ago moments which gather force when they surface to join a new hurt. Like my first memory of grief,
~~~~~

when a school classmate whose face I still see, frozen in time, died of pneumonia. I'd walked home from school, where our teacher told us what had happened, and stood on the slanted green bulkhead at home on a warm fall day, crying and asking an almost cloudless sky, "Will I ever be less sad?"

I try to exhale, but my breath catches along the way.

~~~~~

A ship's wheelhouse, or pilothouse, is the protected above-deck enclosure situated so a captain can see approaching obstacles, take in what needs to be known, and navigate and issue commands accordingly. In baseball terms, a wheelhouse is the portion of a hitter's swinging range optimal for contact with a ball. It's the sweet spot where one does the best at whatever one does. That's what I knew I needed to find and *feel* again after so many months of helplessness and despair. Sometimes I felt I was no longer equipped to occupy my own life, and had lost track of my core skills.

As I drove my daughter to school, she asked, "How do I spot an unmarked police car?"

This happened to be at least on the periphery of my expertise, so I launched into a treatise on common makes and models; the regalia a legitimate unmarked car might display; and the places one would be most likely to find such vehicles were they to contain authentic members of the constabulary. In keeping with my lineage of unseemly pre-worry, which unfortunately had solidified and been buttressed by my professional experience, I added that once she had a driver's license, she should not pull over for an unmarked car with flashing lights. Any miscreant can order those. Instead, she should call 911 to confirm the person's provenance while carefully proceeding to the nearest police station.

A normal parent might have paused to consider why her child would have posed that question. Of course, a normal parent prob-
~~~~~

ably wouldn't have a cluster of neurons dedicated to maintaining a menu of unmarked police cars' characteristics. But given my life in crime--or, more specifically, criminal law--I was delighted to feel that smidgen of a return to mastery in one part of my life.

~~~~~

Well before sunrise, when the beagles slept so solidly they didn't harken to footsteps signaling the possibility of breakfast, I'd stood in the dark after we returned from Ecuador. Jim and our children slept in the risen warmth of the floor above me. My cold bare feet were anchored to our yellow home's floorboards, logged centuries ago among brethren bound for ships' masts on voyages around this world. Jim's desk remained piled with paperwork he continued to handle. It was the last day of December and he'd celebrated the last birthday he would reach.

I dreaded New Year's Day, because the new year would be devastating.

I didn't even want to lose the rocking sensation that persisted long after we'd left the boat. My sea legs' echoes persisted for weeks, gradually evaporating like a star's red shift or a siren's receding Doppler waves. I didn't notice their absence until after the strangely comforting sensation was gone forever.

As I stood months later in the same spot, behind a desk upon which paperwork had grown gravely disordered under my tutelage, the room was no different. I remained bare footed on solid ground over a fortified foundation, as I had for much of my life while subject to gravity. But I suddenly realized I could only recapture snippets of the physical memory of being on a boat a hemisphere and a world away. The gentle rocking had been a perseveration, shades lighter than what we'd felt at sea. It echoed the way I still sometimes find myself swaying lightly from side to side whenever someone cradles an infant in my presence. I stand with my mind in the
~~~~~

past, a baby in my arms and the off-kilter phantom weight of a toddler or two on my hip.

~~~~~

Grief isn't simply a matter of mind or body, or of conscious or muscle memory. One need not even be awake to experience it.

Until that last winter I'd thought it was ambient noise that prevented me from sleeping like a normal human, and jarred me awake into continuing darkness whenever I eventually did make it into the arms of Morpheus. But on that small boat in Ecuador, where I'd been more at peace than at any other time since my husband's diagnosis, I awakened even earlier, when there was no man-ufactured noise at all. The sounds were subtle and indirect. Like waves tickling the underside of the boat they held aloft, and just a shadow of the *shoosh* of wings above me.

I would feel my way, barefooted, up narrow stairs to the bow, and listen to and watch the darkness. Once I saw a soundless light-house beacon, cycling itself awake every four seconds. At other times I saw nothing but black water and sky. Only natural sounds registered: unfamiliar birds' calls, sea lions' comical bark-belches. Unfurling waves which would break at their surfaces when manta rays flew through and above them like ascending fireworks and danced. I choose to believe they sing only to themselves and each other, in their way, as they fly.

~~~~~

Back home, on the rare occasions I reached deep sleep, grief's sensory curiosities seemed to coalesce in dreams impenetrable only to me. I dreamed of adorable Pomeranians suddenly turning on and attacking us, and of finding and bringing home babies aban-doned by New York City subway turnstiles. My children readily translated my subconscious for me. Fluffy small dogs suddenly turning homicidal? To my daughter this was a glaring example of my undercurrent of fear: even puppies suddenly could become aggressive, defy my expectations, turn the world upside-down. The babies? Anyone who knows me also understands I would have had more if I could.

Over the years since then, I've continued to remember my nightmares, but realize they've done some of the work of grieving for me, processing and casting off a procession of fears and helping me understand their eventual reductive distillation of what can still break me.

~~~~~

After neurologist Oliver Sacks underwent surgery to remove a tumor from his eye, he experienced what he described as "a persistence of vision." Medically, he explained, there are two distinct forms of "visual perseveration": one in time and one in space. Macdonald Critchley's research referred to them as "paliopsia" and "illusory visual spread." Dr. Sacks experienced both. He could look at what was in front of him, close his eyes, and see the scene again precisely as he'd viewed it, rather than as an artifact of filling in what was missing. In one instance he found that with his eyes closed he could see people still moving, as if he were watching a continuing loop within "an arrested fragment of the past." Adapting to the new way he saw what surrounded him required significant shifts for a man with such mastery in multiple fields; it literally required new ways of looking at the world.

Sacks' physical optical manifestations, it struck me, are similar to how we see not only the people whose deaths we grieve, but also the younger incarnations of those we love, along with our own past selves. What I see seems more than visual perseveration--more even than visual animation. I see both still and moving images of my husband everywhere. He is larger than life, as he was even when he was here. I see the rest of us, too, as we are and were and have
~~~~~

been all along and since. But I also began to see Jim without us, in places neither he nor we had ever been. It's as if he's superimposed on all landscapes. Out of my reach but within my sight, almost always in an outside space far above and beyond me. Healthy and in motion. Communicating even when he doesn't speak. He is always, always there.

I believe this is how healthy haunting works, too.

2 0

In and Out of the Woods

I n *The Cave*, José Saramago wrote, "I don't doubt that a man can live perfectly well on his own, but I'm convinced that he begins to die as soon as he closes the door of his house behind him."

Jim asked almost nothing of us, in the before and in the end, but expressed his wish we all be attentive to the curative power of movement. Even just steps outside into each day, and especially those days we wouldn't feel ready to face. Perhaps he sought for us some visible assurance that the world still spins. And although I'd find him in dreams and otherwise empty chairs, I knew that no matter how vividly he materialized, I'd never again truly find him in any inside space. He was at heart and soul a wanderer even when he was here. Untethered by gravity, I knew I'd more readily find him beyond the doors.

We want our wanderers to return to us, but perhaps we need to go to them.

<div style="text-align:center">~~~~~</div>

Marilynne Robinson's *Home* captures the distinct yearning pull of each memory of the missing as "loss pulls us after it." I think the mechanism remains the same when there is almost too much to re-

194

member of someone. People with Hyperthymestic Syndrome recall every bland autobiographical detail of each day of their lives. Ordinarily, more intense and traumatic memories are accompanied by a rush of stress hormones that fix them distinctively in the brain. My brain seems to hoard both kinds of memories.

If memory itself is made of what is lost, then I have lost very little. There is no end to the anecdotes and conversations I carry or my visual memories of him and the words he spoke and those I saw him keep to himself. My dreams sometimes seem a cruel trick of memory because my subconscious tills and turns those memories and lets him return to me, but only briefly, and in such vivid detail that my mind seems to be manufacturing new memories of him. Then, when I fully awaken, he's taken away all over again.

What I didn't grasp for quite some time was that my husband isn't a wanderer looking to come home to a place we'd shared, but that I'd need to venture out farther to more fully find him, and what he might want for me and for us.

At first, I didn't wander far.

~~~~~

A sinking sun had glowed white beyond a copse of pine trees, but both the sun and horizon had been swallowed by navy-gray mist by the time I arrived at New Hampshire's rocky shore. Sam Smith's *Stay With Me* was playing on the radio when I parked near Odiorne Point, a place filled with memories of our children's summer days, along with the sub-zero day when we were entirely alone there, excitedly waiting to report to an operating room for our third child's birth.

Those more attentive to weather forecasts than I wisely had stayed home. Not another soul was in sight when I began hiking toward the Drowned Forest, which emerges only at low tide, when
~~~~~

the ocean recedes far enough to reveal a snake nest of coniferous trees' roots.

In a stretch of deep green forest to my left I caught a glimmer of movement as the path rounded its first corner. When I looked more closely, a deer with enormous black eyes stepped out onto the path immediately in front of me. She looked directly at me, tilting her head to one side. We searched each other's eyes, but when I infinitesimally raised my camera she fled into the woods and disappeared.

I stood in thickening fog, beseeching. *Please don't go. Please come back.*

Her departure made me inexplicably sad.

~~~~~

I trudged on toward an even larger nest of naked trees from which all color had seeped. They'd steeped in salt water until their branches gleamed like whale bones even in the absence of sunlight or moonlight.

More softly, then soundlessly, *please come back.*

But the deer was gone. I ventured down every path that honey-combed off the one I'd entered, eventually realizing I was lost. At about the same time, I discovered I'd accidentally flipped on the wrong setting for my new camera. The few fuzzy pictures I'd taken would likely make me seasick on review.

I adjusted it and began following the ocean's sounds. Finally, soaked, I emerged close to where I'd started, by a path framed with short stone walls. It was exactly where Jim had squatted with his camera to take photos the final time we'd walked there, when he'd carried the portable chemo pump during his final infusion.

By then it was fully dark, but for sudden, close lightning strikes as the night's ordinary notes began to sound overhead. I thought I saw bats' movements overhead. I heard the light hiccuping *rat-a-*
~~~~~

tat-tat of their swishing efforts to locate each other among the high trees. I saw something else, which I'd never noticed before: a small sculpture just across from the rocky stretch of shoreline where Jim had rested during his final September, in noon sun and cool wind. He'd taken a photograph and paused before he took another, looking out over the rocks toward Whaleback Lighthouse.

He'd run his right hand through his suddenly salt-white hair and said, "I think it's getting thinner." Or perhaps he'd said *he* was getting thinner, although I saw neither. Sometimes winds alter what floats along them. Then he was quiet until he stood, more slowly than usual, and began taking pictures again. This time I wondered if he'd slowed because he was already in great pain and didn't want to tell me.

But if this sculpture had been there then--a beautifully rendered doe, just feet beyond the low stone wall bordering the path we'd taken, then surely he would have taken a picture of it.

Then the sculpture moved toward me.

This time the doe didn't flee when I gingerly held up my camera and took a picture, the downpour silver-plating its image as if it were underwater. The rain seeped through my jeans as I knelt in the grass. Before stilling itself again, the doe moved closer to me in a posture Brady often used: he'd bow his head toward me as if to tuck his head under my hand when he sensed I was upset and would benefit from the solace of petting him.

The doe remained lightly bowed and just beyond my reach, looking at me with no sign of fear until I was ready to go.

~~~~~

Another overnight storm had left lasting scars at our yellow house. A hit-and-run driver had skidded off the road and toppled our mailbox, sending it sailing away from the granite post that had long anchored it. Tracks revealed the driver then swerved and
~~~~~

crashed through the same pre-disastered stretch of sturdy white fence that Jim had rebuilt after the lightning strike.

What were the odds?

The new snowfall was so dense it clumped on overhead wires like chunky beads. It lay so heavily on every branch and evergreen needle that the trees seemed to glare at us, lined up like a squadron of Black Forest hunters. It suffocated the rhododendron bushes by our porch, crushing them in wavy layers, dejected furrows in their crumpled faces. The tiny white Christmas lights my husband had braided through the same bushes, which had sparkled through every season's depths until then and greeted me during the silent wee hours every time I'd returned home by myself, had gone out for good. Replacing them would have seemed too festive.

~~~~~

I began venturing out into the woods farther from home. Several miles up the road, I could climb a watchtower and see night coming from every direction. On my first sub-zero trek there, I waded through thigh-high snow in knee-high boots. Without evident pattern, one foot would merely skim a soft powder surface and the next would crunch heavily down through a layer of ice glazed by a setting sun. I quickly grew tired. As the sun dropped, it cast snowdrifts into the gold of kraken-guarded treasure.

From atop the tower's platform, it was nearly impossible to distinguish boundaries among striated reflected sun, sky, snow-covered fields, and distant mountains. The speck that was me stood on the watchtower, not always crying.

~~~~~

Winter soldiered on. When I accidentally injured myself so seriously that I couldn't get myself to a hospital, or had a medical procedure requiring blissful sedation, I realized there would be times I'd likely have to ask my own children for assistance. And it unnerved me every time I had to list my oldest child as being my next of kin.

I tried to be certain that I at least had the same routine medical care that had failed to help my husband, because I knew he wanted that, and more, for me. I took my formerly needle-phobic self to get blood drawn, if only because I'd briefly developed an irrational fear of imminently orphaning my children. Until then I'd carefully guarded other family members' lab slips and prescriptions, but left my own to languish in the disorder of my van until they were long out of mind and frequently out of date.

Determined to do better, I carefully set aside a lab slip on my dashboard, dutifully fasted, dropped my daughter off at school, and reported straight to the Path Lab at Jim's hospital. I signed in at the bend between the radiology and oncology suites in the same space where a flotilla of vials had been filled with his still renewing blood.

I handed over my insurance card, which listed one less name. The person doing intake took the card, tapped on some keys, then handed it back.

"Other than that, has anything changed?" A rote question. She didn't look up.

Other than that, everything's changed. My husband's gone. My children and I have grieved every minute and somehow made it through many of the first holidays and birthdays without him, including his. Trees which stood for hundreds of years, higher than the church steeple across the street, collapsed in an unearthly October blizzard, onto and through the roof of the old house he loved. They left behind holes which bitter winds will wail through at least until spring.

Every unreachable light bulb in every arcane size and wattage has burned out and I can't find where he kept their replacements. I hobbled in here after weeks in a cast and on crutches. Now I sense rain coming in my foot and in the fingers I shut inside a solid wood door because my mind is never fully concentrated in the present. The beagles will happen upon something with his scent and I'll watch them sniff and search for him. Sometimes they seem even more woebegone now. And how can I know if they wonder whether they did something wrong? Why he didn't come back, why he doesn't run with them anymore, because I want them to know it wasn't that he chose not to. And if they dream of him like I do, does it hurt their hearts every time they wake up and he's not there?

"No." I said. "Nothing else has changed."

~~~~~

After my own lab results failed to deliver unpleasant surprises, and as winter stood fast and ferocious into February, I drove to New Jersey one morning (by then a mere half-day trip for me) to accompany my daughter to an annual Service of Remembrance. The day began with sunshine and a bright, clear New Hampshire sky, while snow squalls simultaneously were battering my daughter's claustrophobic dormitory window six hours south of me. By the time I arrived, the day had cleared to pure blue, but swiftly again turned gunmetal gray as soon as I opened my car door. Snow began to fall, and wind gusted so fiercely it was difficult to stand upright as we walked her bike uphill to the University Chapel.

The service's program listed the names of missing alumni and classmates, including her father and a student who'd entered with our daughter's class. Reconfigured into a bell curve, the list's great middle would have been occupied by those who'd lived long lives in which they welcomed the children and grandchildren--and even great-grandchildren--in pews around us.

Other people are allowed to get older. I heard Jim's voice again.

Representatives of each class walked to the front of the chapel, where they unpinned flowers from their lapels and added them to a wreath.
~~~~~

"*Another throng shall breathe our song*," we sang.

Students read prayers: El Maleih Rachamin, Surah Al-Fatihah, and Bhagavad Gita.

"Did you understand that?" I whispered to my daughter after a student wearing bright turquoise spoke the latter.

"That's Sanskrit, not Hindi," she educated me. She did not yet speak Sanskrit.

The program was punctuated with directives to *Please stand if able*. I was reminded of the afternoon when Reverend Thompson came to our house as my children and I were collapsed on the couch, and asked me, rhetorically, "How can we get you to where you don't have to lean?"

I still needed to be restored to less wavering verticality.

We sat with our friends Joe and Diane, who'd helped me move our daughter into her dorm, and driven all the way from Pennsylvania to New Hampshire in an ice storm to move her back home during her father's last months and to visit with him one last time. Jim and I had known and loved them since Joe was his chief resident.

Mist shrouded the chapel for well over an hour. Copper leaves rose from the ground and audibly whipped against the high windows' jeweled glass. Even indoors, two plump snowflakes still clung to my daughter's hair.

The last words everyone sang, facing the altar, were from Beethoven's *Hymn to Joy*.

Joyful, joyful, we adore you, God of glory, God of love; Hearts unfold like flowers before you, opening to the sun above....

As we sang the last five words, it was as if something had tapped us on our collective shoulders, beckoning us to turn and face the Chapel's front windows.

Melt the clouds of sin and sadness, drive the storms of doubt away; Giver of immortal gladness, fill us with the light of day.

At "*fill us with the light of day*," sun filled the Chapel from the front. Nearly everyone inside, having felt the shift as the first rays poked through, by then had turned around to look far up into the heavens beyond the stained-glass windows and marvel as the colors streamed inside.

Diane hugged me and my daughter.

"How did they do that?" I asked her, meaning those who'd organized the service.

"*They* didn't," she smiled.

Well done, Jim, I thought.

~~~~~

The day before Jim lapsed into peaceful unconsciousness and died, Bob told him how knowing him had changed him. Bob and Myra's daughter Becca would sing *For Good* at his Closing Ceremonies.

Jim told Bob, "The part of me that others take with them and the part of them I take with me, that's my concept of the afterlife."

On the long return drive, alone, to New Hampshire, I caught a flash of light in the rearview mirror, from a cartoon cloud outline of brilliant coral light as the sun set in an otherwise gray sky. At that moment, after numerous misbegotten detours, I'd finally reached a part of western Massachusetts where a favorite radio station abruptly re-assumed the identity I sought: 92.5, The River.

Music had always accompanied every family car trip. During a road trip to Cooperstown three years earlier, I'd been unable to name a group. Corrections sometimes were made. "No, mom, it's not 'Butcher Block for Babes.' It's 'Death Cab for Cutie.'" Miles later I'd bowdlerize another song title or group name.
~~~~~

As I drove back north and caught the sinking sun's orange-pink light, the first song played: *I'll Follow You into the Dark.*

Lyrics--like nearly everything else--continued to be tinged not only with grief's prism, but also the subset of sorrow populated by those who've lost a longtime partner. A recent medical study--not reading I'd have recommended to bereaved spouses--had tracked extraordinary medical perils people face in the immediate aftermath of a spouse's death. I'd already given myself ample reason to wonder how I possibly could sustain myself even physically. I'd at first heard this song in a more clinical way, as expressing the intersection of the shock of an overwhelming loss with a wish, born of grief, to disappear into a shared void. This time I heard it in the way I think Jim intended when he last spoke to Bob. My husband knew as much as a mortal can about whatever lies beyond. Whether it's dark or light, I'm with him there. But he's also still here with me.

21

A Swath of Sepia

Jim's birdfeeder's scarlet visitor sported the only pure color I remember seeing on the day he died.

Grief, like mid-winter, can be wrought in black and white. It distorts and strips away color. Beyond the barn door, the land at 43 degrees North was divided more like old-school prison stripes than early spring's emerging blended colors. Partnered and alone. Linear and wavering. Dead and alive. Here and not here.

But if I found myself outside at just the right time, the cardinal might swoop in for an encore, always solo, his feathers back-lit in the true red of lushly leafed ripe strawberries shining with quenched thirst. Bright red stippled with seeds and ringed round by green. When I no longer caught sight of him, it seemed the world turned monochromatic.

~~~~~

By the calendar, winter had grudgingly given way to spring, lingering not in white but in solemn grays and absent colors. Jim's garden's threshold was rendered in solemn sepia, touched with sickly yellow. The hue of iodine swabbed onto an abdomen before emergency surgery. Of compromised livers and the anti-emetic my
~~~~~

mother would push in a tiny spoon through my furiously pursed lips before my father sped down highways, his progeny untethered in the back of a station wagon; for someone so highly attuned to the catastrophic forces the universe exerts on more and less precious earthly cargo, he was a shockingly terrible--but lucky--driver. A menace even at a bicycle's handlebars. He'd never have been able to sustain a garden.

~~~~~

Known best for his love poems, Pablo Neruda also had something to say about inscrutable chickens. In *Cierto Cansancio*, he was weary and wary of them: "they look at us with dry eyes/ and consider us unimportant."

"And they do... and we are," Greg Brown observed while picking away at a guitar after describing the poem's gist to a live audience. "It's just hard to take it from a damn chicken."

While any fowl could have enlightened me about my own lament's insignificance in the scheme of things, I wasn't prepared for grief's shearing-off aspects; the density of what remains in its confined spaces; or its exhausting cumulative weight over time. And after the terror-fueled despair of imagining my husband surrounded by blackness even when he was still here, I felt a certain weariness. It was beyond sleeplessness, and more like numbed purposelessness.

Others moved forward, as it should be. The daily tasks so many friends heroically helped us with fell back upon me as our children resumed school schedules. It seemed not only that I was unable to experience joy in any moment, but that I couldn't feel anything outside a colorless band of grief, spiced far too intensely with anger at all I couldn't control or contain.

I became weary of weariness itself--of the absence of plateaus and zest. There were ranges of positive feelings I could no longer
~~~~~

muster, languages I'd likely never again master after being out of practice for so long. I couldn't imagine how people endure years of the fear and trials and uncertainty that had been compressed into Jim's not quite nine-month ordeal.

I saw fluent speakers engaging effortlessly in equanimity, and even overt happiness. I could remember feeling joy. But I couldn't remember what it *felt* like, and I remember almost everything.

I had no trouble feeling pain, loss, and profound loneliness. I sometimes felt physically ill with worry about my children. And I felt much love, still. But joy as I'd remembered it went missing, and I missed it.

~~~~~

It wasn't until summer began making its incursions into spring that I began to appreciate the ways color itself had changed. Until then I'd felt, but didn't register actually having seen, a beagle-wide dry swath separating Jim's garden's gated area from a bright row of flowering pink trees and hydrangea bushes he'd planted closer to the house. Across the neutral divide were vibrant yellow-green leaf carpets and peonies so ready to burst at the seams that they obscured the twisting branches of fruit trees he'd planted beyond them. Buttercup dandelions had sprouted and scattered around them like stars in the constellations he'd surveyed.

I could not pull the lovely weeds.

The midline between the trees and blooming garden remained the color and prickly texture of hay. It solemnly hosted the watered-down ghosts of bushes which had in previous years burst into bright magenta and lilac-blue by then. Several times a day I would cross this strange colorless strip of land with Rufus and Brady. Had I taken them out front, toward the sidewalk and gazebo, I likely would have had to encounter people engaging in normalcy I was not nearly ready to rejoin. Snow had receded like
~~~~~

the outer layers of a topographical map, eventually disappearing from sun-crisped hydrangeas' clamshell petals, denizens of a tea-died world without Jim.

One morning, Brady lurched to a stop as we began to pass them. I looked where he was sniffing: a single bright lavender hydrangea had erupted into a heart shape aloft on the shoulders of somber companions.

A solitary starling--and they rarely travel solo--with a shimmer of gold-violet dancing through its rich black feathers touched down just above the blooming heart.

Had this space always mediated between winter and what follows? Or did I notice its reticence only when I wasn't ready for flowers in full conjoined bloom, or a murmuration of starlings rather than a single flight-ready soul?

At the antique-linen swath's edge, I saw that a plum tree Jim planted when he was sick had burst into full royal purple blossom. A riot of lemon-orange daffodils whose bulbs he must have buried had emerged and were bobbing not far from his quince tree. Its sturdy trunk was bent like a horseshoe under the weight of incipient armored fruit.

~~~~~

The barren strip might have been just an artifact of underwatering and absent rain, or my lack of skill in maintaining growing things at the perilous and complicated stages when rooted shoots venture above ground and become open to capricious fate. But evidence suggested otherwise: the grass on both sides of the sepia strip remained uniformly green and all too high and lush, splashed with tiny violet and yellow sprouts.

Perhaps the formerly colorless stretch had been more exquisitely susceptible to to sea-sawing temperatures. Or could it have been a trick of my perception, and therefore my memory? Maybe
~~~~~

these particular clusters had never bloomed as early as their neighbors. or my thumb was even more leaden than I'd thought. But until I saw it had happened, I wouldn't have believed straw stalks could reanimate in purple and lime, any more than that they could be spun into gold. Their drooping rice paper shells had seemed incapable of reviving. As if they'd been pressed for a century between the pages of books put aside as their readers wandered and never returned.

~~~~~

By true summer, Jim's garden's full color spectrum had reconstituted itself, and perhaps even overcompensated for a shaky start. There had been a series of thunderstorms like the ones he'd watched at his final conference. As I watched Rufus and Brady during one such wet afternoon, I looked downhill to the pond, knowing I'd never be able to properly maintain all that Jim had created and nurtured.

A double rainbow appeared over the water and tapped me on both shoulders.

Frederick Buechner, far better situated than I to take liberties with the original Noah--the "old sailor" he described in *Wishful Thinking* as "an expert in hoping against hope"--understood the considerable nuances of even the greatest blessings. Within his relief upon finally beholding a rainbow after 40 days and nights was a kernel of concern that God could have required such a conspicuous reminder of what He'd promised. It occurred to Noah that God had a lot on His mind. Thus the need for a symbolic reminder might mean His promise otherwise could have gone by the wayside, given all on His plate. And if God's promise could be forgotten, the flood's horror and trauma could be unleashed again.

That twinge of doubt compounded itself, as such feelings do, especially when conditioned by harsh experience. So even as Noah
~~~~~

forged ahead with the work of beginning anew, rebuilding and re-planting once the floodwaters receded, he was haunted by intrusive thoughts of the past and all the animals left behind. Although many had been saved, a world of beings had vanished. What had been lost was vast, and the dazzling new world had arisen from the suffering of innocents, including animals Noah might otherwise have saved, but instead went unnamed.

~~~~~

When I first sat on a runway without Jim, our Noah would be beside me. By name as well as nature and nurture, he may be particularly alert to rainbows. He looked out the rounded window as we taxied away from Logan and saw an unusual rainbow, rendered not in bright regimented planes of color, but in muted pastels bleeding into one another. It was far wider and more acutely arched than any I'd seen. But in the second it took me to touch his brother's arm across the aisle to point it out to him, the rainbow had vanished, although the plane hadn't moved. If Noah and I hadn't seen it, I would have doubted it had been there, as I now sometimes wonder whether the world really was monochromatic while we tried to navigate out of that winter's depths and back into the growing seasons.

~~~~~

I'd crossed the dead space outside our house every day, until I noticed it had blended back into a seamless whole with what it had been cleaved from.

Unlike pain, death can be described by nothing *but* metaphor: crossing over, pushing up daisies. *Fermer le parapluie.* Escaping "parca's creaking scissors" (if only during the Reaper's vacation break in *Death with Interruptions*). One's pet parrot might appear to be pining for the fjords while in fact its "metabolic processes are now 'istory'": "'e's off the twig" and already has "joined the bleedin' choir invisible." All of it reduces to blackness. It's impossible to know how much of a stretch each metaphor may be until after Death's violet envelope has been delivered.

I know my husband didn't want me to be stuck in the space I occupied, or to have a cemetery marker exert its pull on me. He knew I wouldn't have been able *not* to stop at a grave, taking root there rather than letting myself be pulled away into light and growing green.

You'll get through this. I hear him again, as if I'd been the one afflicted.

I hear a ghost's voice in *The Poisonwood Bible*, which he'd read first, and beckoned a grieving mother back to the living and growing spaces which make up the enduring counterweight to a mamba snake's poison: "Listen. Slide the weight from your shoulders and move forward. You are afraid you might forget, but you never will....Think of the vine that curls from the small square plot that was once my heart. This is the only marker you need."

Eventually, he must have known I'd need more than one push to walk back into color. Into the presence of the living and the dead and the earthly present our senses can absorb. More steps, no matter how unsteady, one at a time.

<h1 style="text-align:center">22</h1>

Ghosts on the Wires

After I'd misjudged yet another step's distance from the earth and broken my ankle for a second (and not last) time, I couldn't get our torque-rich dogs out of the house without having my crutches pulled out from under me. My brother drove up and installed a sturdy wire line on which I could watch them as they chased scents on a sliding lead.

A single black bird with just a shimmer of green would stand sentinel on the wire, watching but not joining the birds who flocked to Jim's nearby feeders. He didn't even startle when Rufus and Brady rushed out, vigorously shaking his makeshift perch. Soon cardinals and blue jays began appearing at the feeders, which were just a few feet away from the forest green hammock where Jim rested and read during treatment. It was suspended between two towering trees, one of which had since been substantially diminished by a hurricane. Unmoved even by the same kind of suet cakes I'd found in Jim's truck, the black bird would remain alone on the wire.

One day Noah, who even as a toddler had such a discerning eye for birds that he could identify them by silhouette, pointed out two red-tailed hawks over the empty hammock. I hadn't seen a sin-gle raptor in all the time we'd lived there. Red-tailed hawks inhabit a John Hiatt song my husband knew I loved in the Before--when its reference to reaching "the other side" meant only the far side of a canyon.

These two hawks were soaring and spinning in an intricate dance, one hovering high but within a small range, not venturing far from trees which had stood for hundreds of years. The other's range was far broader. He'd fly away and return to engage the other, as if trying to coax her away from the tree. The pair re-minded me of two scarlet macaws and their mating dance, which I hadn't seen but was preserved for me in my husband's and daugh-ter' photographs. I'd stayed home with the excuse of tending to newly adopted Brady and ferrying the boys to school, but in truth I'd long feared flying, and knew my absence would free Jim and our daughters to delight in what would turn out to be their final father-daughter trip. They would ride horses, zip-line from dizzy-ing heights, careen around mountains' sharp curves, and lean out of rickety boats to snap pictures of birds.

~~~~~

Other winged things began to appear in my path, or perhaps I just became more attuned to their presence. A large moth landed and dawdled in tattered grass. One wing, dotted with tiny white hearts, was lightly broken in a tributary scar slightly above a per-fect single heart shape. The other wing was pinked clean through, sheared off in a zigzag underneath another cluster of hearts. I won-dered how it kept aloft with such a large piece missing.

Butterflies seemed to appear everywhere as mid-summer ap-proached. There were more than I'd remembered ever seeing. Nor had I considered how quiet they are, a counterpoint to their loud
~~~~~

colors. They serenely went about their business, only occasionally glancing back at me with opaque black matte eyes.

~~~~~

Far less typical winged things appeared in our backyard that summer, including formations of Blue Angels whose wakes left parallel white curlicues on pure cyan skies. Sometimes a single plane would veer off ahead of its companions and out of sight. As they practiced at nearby Pease Air Force Base, we needed only enter Jim's garden for a 360-degree view of their perfectly synchronous flights.

I began religiously using my camera to preserve what I saw while alone, from angles I'd rarely explored. I would slide under outdoor sculptures and parse the particulars of posted warnings for colorable loopholes. Underneath a feasting butterfly's magnificent wings might be the spectacle of me getting the close-up, wriggling backward on pollen-riddled ground, camera in hand, grinding allergenic flotsam into dresses my daughters began handing down to me. My children understandably tended to keep their distance as I angled to capture the quotidian and omnipresent, flinging myself onto a dirty sidewalk, one arm tilted to shoot up through a flowerbed for the illusion that dancing tulips dwarfed the North Church's spire beyond them.

In less-than-waterproof boots, I would wade into the frigid Atlantic for a better view of steep isosceles cloud formations. Teeth chattering, I darted up on rusted metal bars to record the glorious scalene buffet of Old Ironsides' masts and rigging at sunset. More than one of my offspring would pull me out of harm's way with a drawn-out *Moooommm* as I dawdled in the middle of city streets, pointing my lens to catch a tower framed by anthropomorphic clouds or bisected by a bright jet stream. The intricacy of detail I could get by pressing a button--especially when I finally gifted my-
~~~~~

self with a phone with an exquisite camera it pained me Jim hadn't lived to enjoy--gave me a sense of connection in a changed world.

~~~~~

Of course, my subjects were uninterested in me. But I was wildly interested in every shot and each missed or blurred one: talons' perfectly symmetrical grasp on flower stems; softly swooping cilia trailing down a leaf; birds guiltily looking away as they hoarded more berries than they could consume. And I found, at least in retrospect, that I was always on the lookout for broken things: headless parking meters, askew fence posts, goldenrod glowing within branching fissures in a Mt. Auburn Cemetery headstone on which a single red cardinal perched and gazed back at me.

At the same time I was exploring such up-close wonders, I developed an obsessive quest to photograph unreachable vistas. I spent nearly every black pre-dawn at the ocean, staring out even while the beagles still slept, until there was either a glimmer of what kind of light might be coming or a bank of gray swallowed the sun.

Sometimes we're drawn to the close-up and sometimes we do everything we can to maintain the space between us and what lies not far ahead. Grief occupies its own swirling vortex, and can cause some people to keep their distance from the grieving. But the intimate inside view yields its own insights, and sometimes a strange solitary beauty.

~~~~~

Along with Brady's extraordinary emotional intelligence, he had a highly specific talent for escaping into torrential rain. I'd trudge through woods in whatever out-sized footwear I found nearest the door, my calls to him disappearing in the deluge. Eventually, sometimes hours later, I'd catch his throaty howl in the wind and follow it to wherever he believed he'd ferociously treed some taunting squirrel. He would ignore me as I approached him from behind and leapt to put my arms around him. Despite the inelegant scent of soaked fur, I would hug him closely and tell him how deeply worried I'd been that I would never see him again. He'd turn his lovely maple eyes to me, his nose dotted with raindrops which resettled on his tongue as he bark-howled. He'd cast his eyes heavenward, without regard to any still-chortling squirrel, as if wondering what further unusual treats the heavens might dispense.

Hiking back from one such extended misadventure in the woods, we passed piled leaves, soaked only at their top layers over waves of variegated brown that dulled into umber and crackled and curled like arthritic paws. I wondered how I could possibly hope to rake them. On my periphery, closer to the house, I saw what looked like an undulating blanket of deep brown flecked with yellow, spread over the unmowed grass.

It began to move on its own, breaking apart.

Not recalling any opportunity accidentally to have ingested hallucinogenic mushrooms while wandering in the woods, I realized it was alive: a living sea of thousands of small birds. We were surrounded by twittering, frantic banter not unlike a chorus of feet treading heavily upon squeaky puppy toys. The birds rose in a collective thundering *flap* and flew away over our heads. We watched them settle as one across the street, where they covered every inch of a leafless tree next to the church.

A fan of terms of venery, I've possessed (and possibly coined) an accord of Hondas, a distress of court dates, and a howl of beagles. But over the years I'd entirely missed naturally occurring wonders right outside our doors, including tens of thousands of in sync monochromatic starlings. I hadn't noticed their shape-shifting clouds, which I've chased ever since Brady and I saw them that day. I hadn't known to listen for their whispering collective wings before they come into view. Like an embrace, which would be incomplete without a beating heart's melody, such offerings are richer when more than one sense is engaged.

~~~~~

It wasn't only wings. In so much time alone and in one-sided conversation, I learned to listen as I lingered where other voices might carry. A slight rustle in marsh grasses led me to my first muskrat sighting. Two rotund, hilariously wobbly fellows with puddle-slicked fur suspiciously surveyed me from behind reeds in an enclave the size of a half-bathtub. I learned the rhythms of outdoor spaces, like a trail where one red-winged blackbird's call would be echoed back, and I soon would find myself surrounded by bright orange epaulets as others strained forward to reply. They held tightly to the tops of reeds taller than I, which swayed and bowed but did not break from their weight.

I became attuned to woodpeckers' tricky acoustics in different densities of surrounding woods as seasons passed. Once I inexplicably felt drawn to a stretch of Rye beach well before sunrise. I sat on a bench facing deep black-blue when I heard sounds approximating the rustle of a six-foot human in tall, dry beach grass behind me. I turned and could barely make out a man with a camera lens so enormous it could have offered a view of the Wolf Moon two weeks hence. He held one finger to his lips in the universal *shusshing* stance and his other forefinger pointed to my right. I glanced there, finding a gold-eyed snowy owl perched on the railing at my right, companionably waiting with me for the sun to rise.

I'd never photographed birds before, when they were among Jim's most frequent and favorite subjects. He left me so many images of what I'd missed while he was here. Memories are like that, too. It's not just the lone wolf; it's the pack. I may seek out the
~~~~~

sweet single songbird, but the deluge can arrive unbidden, sometimes before we're ready to contemplate it, and risk overwhelming us. And like thousands of undulating starlings--or a handful of Blue Angels in flight, or two rare dancing birds--the shape of the whole shifts with no attention to us. Sometimes all I could do was watch the unreeling and regrouping. It would hold me in place until the messengers moved away, on their own terms and time, animating a covey of clouds.

23

Surprise Me

Grief is an edge and a rounding and a punctuated, unending sigh. It takes deep breaths to settle, and sometimes almost nothing to fuel. At first, time seemed to pass not in minutes or hours or in one direction, but in the measure of each improbable intake of air. Those breaths would fuel tasks my body insisted must still be addressed, without input from the real me: the sleepless shadow others somehow still didn't see I'd become.

My husband and son had originated a two-part family catch phrase that begins with "Surprise me." It applies to almost any question, from "What should we have for dinner?" to "Where do you think I should I go to college?" The universal rejoinder is rhetorical: "Pleasantly, or unpleasantly?"

English might benefit from more words for permutations of the word 'surprise.' Perhaps one for the kind of surprise that freezes one in place for upwards of a count of ten, or causes one to scour a room for a sufficient source of tissues. Surprise that causes one's heart to fibrillate so emphatically that those within six feet must hear it; or creates a pallor not of seasickness, but of certitude the world's stopped turning. That makes one reflective or wistful or ca-

218

pable of only a quarter-smile, or launches a migraine. Or the kind of surprise that one is 95% certain the heart at hand cannot withstand.

I've never fared well with unpleasant surprises, even the milder ones which accumulated once we began a family of our own. "You mean morning sickness can last 24/7 for *seven months*?" "Tossing just one little red dress into the laundry did *that*?" "An epidural doesn't always take?" "Did I forget to enter that in the checkbook?"

"How did I get to be *thirty*?" I'd wondered aloud, well into marriage and parenthood.

"The inexorable march of time?" Jim immediately offered.

He wouldn't be there for my next Birthday of Significance, when my children and friends indulged my wish for a pirate party suitable to my then most recent injuries. I was down to a single crutch and lower leg cast, which made an excellent peg leg.

~~~~~

I couldn't locate even a German or Old Uzbeck word for surprises encountered during the early cleaning-out phase of grief. What word might capture clearing a pile from a chair and seeing discharge instructions listing dozens of medications and ending in bold type: 'VAD accessible'--as if my husband himself were a device to be plugged in? Or lifting his books from the bedside table and seeing a medical journal dated the month he died, opened to his notes on an article about how to become a better medical leader? Or finding button-down shirts he'd purchased--on sale, because he was frugal only with money--when convinced he'd return to work after successful surgery in Boston? The shirts were in cheerful shades of blue and pink, folded inside crinkly cellophane in a drawer beneath suit jackets I'd need to clean out and donate, too. The rack with his trademark patterned ties was undisturbed, at a
~~~~~

height beyond my reach, but I could run my hand along the accordion of silk triangles at the bottom, which carried an evocative hint of their cedar wood lair.

I'd been frozen by the aching surprise of coming across medications unrelated to his cancer, which I realized he must have abandoned when he knew guarding against long-term health issues had became too tenuous a bet. And what word captures finding a spill kit underneath the bed in case toxic chemo drugs had escaped the tubing in the portable pump attached to his port? It contained sky blue surgical garb, presumably for me to apply in a mid-infusion emergency, along with a packet sealing a sterile scalpel whose purpose in a civilian setting I didn't care to imagine but nonetheless envisioned. I'd never been instructed about its existence or use. Among under-the-bed dust bunnies and elephants, I found another item that must have been meant to soak up a toxic spill: a pillow-sized package of shredded bluetranslucent material, like the makings of a bridal bird's nest.

In a drawer formerly dedicated to socks I found emerald medicine bottles resembling old-school film canisters, set aside when their contents had failed to help during Jim's treatment, and a prescription pad bearing the DEA authorization number I'd been startled to learn I was expected immediately to advise the federal government to extinguish when he died. I found his Boy Scout leader clothing and patches, and one of many sets of running gear. Still hanging on one of the house's only two closet doors was the deep-piled green and blue robe with thin crimson stripes which he'd been wearing when he came downstairs the morning after his diagnosis. He'd told me he knew how hard his likely treatment would be--not for him, but for me. My selfless husband said he knew how *I* felt about nausea and vomiting, which had beset entire pregnancies and reduced me well below featherweight and fighting form.

Just touching the robe returned me to a sea of synesthesia, none of it soothing. I could hear high-pitched beeps in hospital rooms as each fluid bag's contents entered his veins; the *zippppp* as adhesive tape was stripped away from IVs; the *whoosh* of constant infusion as he slept and I watched him breathe. I could smell the unsettling amalgam in the oncology pod's overheated air. Burnt coffee grounds and something as pungent and searing as ammonia on a fresh cut. I could feel his feverish skin; the outline of his port's circular ridge; the smooth surfaces of the oncology waiting room puzzle pieces with which we rebuilt Baroque feathered angels. I could taste an allergic prickle in my throat from the whisper of wool that always hovered too closely, within a basket of hand-knit hats for patients who'd lost their hair. I see every detail of every room my husband occupied because of his affliction. But I can never recapture the memory of being able to touch him.

<p style="text-align:center">~~~~~</p>

For many reasons having little to do with my attic cache, I knew I couldn't stay in the yellow house, where I'd continued to scatter unfinished books and sewing projects in various stages, like the trails my mother would leave of partially emptied Danish Modern coffee cups and fabric scraps from unfinished collages.

Until Jim's diagnosis, I'd always read books straight through. I'd since developed a habit of starting several, then putting them indefinitely aside and beginning new ones which might better temper my constant distraction. I came across Fernando Pessoa's *The Book of Disquiet,* which I'd put down at the point the narrator described art as providing him "relief from life without relieving [him] of living." The novel's title had called to me--or to who I was when I'd picked it up--but I remained unready to continue probing such confluence between life and fiction. The novel had been posthumously published, and created a world in which the lost continue to appear before the living and grieving. Pessoa's own ghost would appear as a character in a novel I had also put aside, written by a countryman I hadn't realized had in real life been Pessoa's own grieving friend. There should be more words for connections beyond coincidence.

I'd learned enough already to understand Pessoa also was describing ways in which the lost selves of both the living and the dead, interwoven, are retained by us even if we cannot recreate a perished loved one's words. A character could still "describe, in four photographic words, the facial muscles he used to say what I don't recall, or the way he listened with his eyes to the words I don't remember telling him. I'm two, and both keep their distance – Siamese twins that aren't attached."

~~~~~

I'd perfected the thousand-yard stare shortly after Jim's diagnosis, a barrier to the world beyond the two of us that remained impossible for me to navigate.

Deep sorrow alters--not necessarily always for the worse--the meaning of almost every word and lyric. It distills combinations of words and silences, and sometimes redefines a single word. Goodbye. Love. Grace. Compassion. Friendship. Kindness. Cruelty.

Missing.

Words are felt and read differently within grief's hold, even--or perhaps especially--when one is largely surrounded by other seemingly unafflicted people. I've dwelled in the shadows of words no other living person has heard. Things we said only to each other. All the things I wish I'd told him when I could have been certain he heard them. The unbreachable distance extends to my fellow living
~~~~~

humans who don't share--at least, not yet--this strange twinned, intertwined, sacred space.

~~~~~

Pessoa's friend José Saramago's oeuvre encompasses the poetic and the onomatopoetic. *The Elephant's Journey*'s narrator broke third and fourth walls, addressing readers-to-be in the voice of a character he explains is long gone: he "went *plof* and vanished.... Imagine if we'd had to provide a detailed description of someone disappearing. It would have taken us at least ten pages. *Plof.*"

Grief has its own sounds as it breaths through us. After weeks of startling myself by seeding our home's silences with heavy sighs, I discovered that the audible *hhhhhhhhhuuuhhhh* is considered a physiological hallmark of the grieving process. It is a sound as certain to emanate from the bereaved as is the impulse to touch the smooth surface of glass over a photograph of a beloved person's face. The random quick, deep, near-humming intake of air--a *hmmmmhhhhhh* more like a frightened gasp than a sigh--marks a similarly universal symptom: a sudden catch in the throat, a racing heart, an abrupt full stop during the great middle of any ongoing activity, when, all over again, I simply could not believe my husband would never come home to us.

Even before his death, my own senses began changing. When, as a side effect of chemo, he began to describe scents I didn't detect in our shared air, perhaps it was my perceptions, not his, that had become untrustworthy. I heard things he did not, like a high-frequency buzzing in electric cables on a pole across the street. Maybe he was the one who correctly read the world around us. Or perhaps there was more than one accurate way of reading it. But I eventually realized I didn't hear only unpleasantly evocative sounds. I began to listen for the measure of my husband's voice when my children spoke and when, lost in their own thoughts, they did not.
~~~~~

I listened for the music he loved as my daughters listened to his collection and gathered new music he would have enjoyed. I heard his love of quirky, wide-ranging music as my children settled among different musical smorgasbords when I drove them to and from school. On long highway drives from which I would have been absent had their father still been here, my daughters valiantly tried to educate me about hip-hop music, just as they began to make inroads into the foundations of some of my overly entrenched thoughts about blame and injustice. My older daughter's playlists bounced around distant parts of the world she'd begun to inhabit, collecting everything from German techno pop to Bollywood music when residing in countries I'd never seen. I heard their father's passions echoed as our children considered how and where they would spend their time as they grew into adults. Over time, my own senses continued to change, but not always unpleasantly and in one bleak direction. Some surprised me by reappearing, reconfigured and richer. It was never a net loss to try to pay closer attention to both what had changed and what remained.

24

A Beach Bouquet

Awhisper less than a full year had passed when I followed my husband's suggestion to mark the first anniversary of his death. He was not prone to bad ideas. My sub-optimal portion of the plan was to try to trick time by flying across multiple zones, technically allowing us not to be earthbound for the fathomless actual date and time that would mark one year's passage. But first, a day earlier, we would gather on a southern Maine beach.

On Jim's last day, we'd been surrounded by fresh snow. On this day, time had sprung ahead and it somehow was summer on the rocky shore. The sun was so strong that giddy black flies had hatched and begun feasting three months early. The five of us, still and always etched into my mind as six, met Randy and Judy and Bob and Myra at the Marginal Way. When we arrived at the narrow strip of beach that had called to me, at the hour upon which my subconscious insisted, it was empty except for a family that included a dog whose honeyed curls and eyes echoed those of my youngest child. With the Labradoodle's humans' nodded assent, Suzannah knelt on pebbled sand and held her gaze as she ran her

225

hands through her fur. Emma shed her white sandals and tested the water.

My back to the ocean, my children stood in a half-circle in front of me and our friends formed an arc behind them. I read Mary Oliver's poem about a turtle leading her children as they were "dangling their pretty feet" in a pond, knowing that a "murky splash" would soon come. Exactly when I read the last two words, feeling a catch in my voice and the need to regroup before I continued, a wave advanced far enough to lap at the back of my feet. It tickled my heels with its own splash. A nudge and a wink. I looked up, over my shoulder, at the clear blue sky. My unsteadiness evaporated.

So often, I noticed, signs had begun to come from the unending ocean as well as from above it.

Thanks, Jim.

We held red-rimmed coral roses unwilling as yet to entrust their unfolding to the unseasonable warmth. Emma, in a bright white cotton dress with splashes of printed roses and deep green leaves, planted her rose in the sand. Each sibling and friend planted another. As we retreated from the water to explore limestone rocks, I looked back and saw a young child with her father, who crouched by the roses, snapping photographs with a camera like the one Jim had used.

It was exactly what he would have done, had he happened upon a bouquet of roses on the beach on a sunny March Sunday.

~~~~~

That night I felt something had lightened and lifted. Our children had devised a game and were laughing as they played it. Sam described it as being "like Survivor--if everyone was on the jury *and* arguing at the final tribal council, and also has to vote someone else out." It was a delightful medley of probability, social in-
~~~~~

veigling, mini-tests, and outright bribery. I heard Noah issuing a challenge to his siblings, evidently to give them a chance at bonus points: "Whoever can say 'Irish wristwatch' fastest the most times..."

I remembered how Reverend Thompson had observed that everyone who spoke at Jim's service had captured some facet of his humor and made the mourners laugh. (He'd let forth his own wonderful booming laugh when I observed I'd been the first girlfriend, and had reason to believe I was the last.)

This night's laughter was magical. I learned how healing it was to listen for Jim's wit, channeled through our children. I noticed the way they'd sometimes hand off the set-up, to give me a chance to utter the words their dad would have spoken.

"Can you take the cannoli, mom?" Noah asked me at *Breaking New Grounds*, a local gathering place still visible to its past denizens, but not those who've only known what's since taken its place. In air that carried the sublime smells of an industrial-sized vat of coffee beans being ground, Noah held out a a bakery box with a wink as he shrugged into his jacket.

I paused the beat his father would have; he had exquisite timing.

"Should I leave the gun?"

~~~~~

All of us, at different paces, reached a point where we sometimes didn't crumble at the thought of who wasn't there. We did not always have to steel ourselves at a phrase, a thought, a memory, a picture--in our hands or minds.

"Laughter will come," the Reverend had said at Jim's service, "and it's a good thing."

And it is, and always shall be.

~~~~~

In the wee hours of the true first anniversary date, three of us fled New Hampshire and launched ourselves back in time, north by northwest to Seattle, then hurtled across the heavens with the eerie sense of suspended stillness within a plane speeding through the indeterminate darkness of black skies over black sea. We emerged 13 ½ hours ahead of ourselves in Osaka, and took a train to meet Emma, who'd traveled ahead of us to present a paper at a conference in Kyoto.

On the hour that marked a year after her father's death, it was already the next day in Japan.

Perhaps I'm at heart an aspiring Tralfamadorian, as are so many people who contend with unpredictable repercussions of death and other traumas. "And so it goes," in context, always follows death. It emphatically is not easygoing resignation or capitulation to what one is a witness to in this life. Mine was also a fool's errand: there is no escaping the heart's experience of such a day and hour. It's a fixed scar not confined to clock or calendar. We would have felt it wherever we found ourselves in the world. But we had endured a year, and I knew how pleased Jim would be that our daughter had coaxed us so far beyond my own comfort zone.

We saw a bird whisperer in a park by early-budding cherry trees; paper prayer scrolls aloft on strings above sculpted sand; and botanical gardens and bamboo forests. We wandered among thousands of vermilion pi-shaped Torii gates tipped with black at a Shinto shrine on Mount Inari, where they were set inside each other and arranged in gradually decreasing sizes, like a never-ending Escher drawing.

We were told it's more common in modern times to wish for business success than for rice and saké at local shrines, but that one can wish for anything by way of those endless Torii gates. I strongly felt Jim's presence as we climbed the mountain paths in the rain, but was unaware at the time that 'Torii' translates to "where the birds rest." Already, so many messages and messengers from our devoted caretaker of birds had come to me in flight, theirs and ours, outside our home and across the world.

I made wishes for my children, as I think their father would have, feeling peace in a way I hadn't remembered I could.

25

Table for Two

On another solo wedding anniversary, my best woman and I had an only slightly margarita-fueled discussion about the nature of ghosts and my groom's constant presence with me. We considered how I might introduce him to newcomers to my situation and psyche. I didn't plan to remove my wedding ring, and his remained on a chain around my neck. I still couldn't use the words "my late husband," let alone any variation of the 'd' word. This seemed occasionally to confuse people as I began to encounter more of them. Tineke considered whether less jarring alternatives could be used--perhaps my 'ghost hubby'? Tineke couldn't help noticing what I did not: whenever we met, I behaved as if he were seated to my right.

Particularly after losing his wife, José Saramago populated his novels with an intriguing variety of ghosts. The ghost of one of his friends lives on in *The Year of the Death of Ricardo Reis*, a story that lingers with me in at least one unresolved riddle: how many senses do ghosts have in common with their living selves? In a meta-metaphorical digression, a character describes ghosts as having four senses, but leaves us to wonder which has gone missing once a soul occupies another dimension. In life, as traditionally defined, the friends shared an understanding of the spirit. The ghost of the friend Saramago lived to grieve explained, "We mourn the man whom death takes from us, and the loss of his miraculous talent and the grace of his human presence, but only the man," because his essence remains in our world as "a mysterious beauty that cannot perish." (It may go without saying that my literary tangents trailed some minutes behind the margaritas.)

But back to our table for two... or at very least three.

Tineke seemed to scan the room for concerned countenances when my enthusiasm went unsuppressed. I pointed to a dessert display: "Look! Flourless chocolate cake!"

At our wedding, just a hop and skip across the Square, a friend of my mother's had made a rich flourless cake that miraculously held itself together until being reduced to a delicious memory. Despite a record-breaking 99° recorded at Boston Harbor just as the ceremony began, it hadn't melted into dense dark chocolate puddles (as would my spectacularly failed *unintentionally* flour-deprived cookies for Santa years down the road).

Tineke considered offering our waiter the explanation that we were there because it was my anniversary. She decided this might invite more questions than it answered, given that no spouse occupied the empty chair to which I directed my sustained attention. She is by occupation a therapist, but only recreationally that with me. She looked at me in that way therapists do, and agreed that even in Cambridge, bystanders might be puzzled by my engagement with someone who technically wasn't there. It did not take her long to reconsider "ghost hubby," a suggestion to which I'd begun to warm, although that might have been due to the July heat and the rarity of a dollop of alcohol in my system,

"But he's here all the time with me," I said, gesturing at the chair next to mine. "Is that insanity?"

"No, that's love." She said.

~~~~~

"The wind was a torrent of darkness among the gusty trees/ The moon was a ghostly galleon tossed upon cloudy seas/ The road was a ribbon of moonlight over the purple moor.... "

The Highwayman came riding up to the old inn door, but too late to reach his sweetheart while she was alive on the other side. Phil Ochs set Alfred Noyes' poem to haunting acoustics best listened to when autumn skies darken in New England. Similarly, the sun's terminal plunge at the end of a shortening day pairs perfectly with Richard Thompson's 1952 *Vincent Black Lightning*. Both are about doomed couples. Three of four star-crossed lovers emerge in ghost form, including a strangely sympathetic bandit named James. Beloved partners are outlined in shades of red--motorcycle-riding, red-headed Molly and the young woman who braids a dark red love knot into her long dark hair.

Both songs are about hauntings. They feature dying words and deeds of people loved unconditionally despite some considerable foibles. Of the four, two are done in by musket and one by shotgun blast. Only the love of young James' life remains on this side of the *olam* of Leviticus. He leaves to her his keys to the only tangible thing he treasures, a symbol of his own freedom in this world. The other young man, whose name we do not learn, haunts the night roads, trying to keep his promise to return to the woman he loves. But she is a ghost, too, apart from and eternally looking for him. We're left to wonder whether she occupies a different moonlit darkness, or perhaps a different light.

I'd listened to both songs for decades. Of course, the songs hadn't changed; the way I listened to and heard them did. They
~~~~~

remain stories of epic and infinite love that endures in the good kind of haunting. They aren't needling ghosts who linger to perform some task, or answer questions we couldn't bring ourselves to ask in life, or perhaps didn't understand we'd want answered. Such couples do not require intermediaries. They remain forever bound to each other, still holding the full measure of the love that "bears all things, believes all things, hopes all things, endures all things," and never ends.

<h1 style="text-align:center">26</h1>

Deep Storage

nne Stevenson's *Sonnets for Five Seasons* considers September "The wisest time." It took the rhythms of many transitional months, and at least the first season of autumnal spirits in a different home, to truly appreciate my relationship with ghosts. Eventually I understood that many gentle such companions had accompanied me all along. I initially may have made myself unapproachable, or perhaps they hadn't know quite what to make of me.

Moving had been an extended, aching experience. I'd never lived anywhere entirely on my own. Despite having been the in-house lawyer, I also hadn't ever signed such onerous paperwork by myself. I'd always scrawled my signature next to colorful arrow-shaped sticky notes Jim had affixed in order to guide me. This time, I signed on the left and the partnered signature line stayed empty. I flashed back to the lawyer's office we'd hastened to after Jim's diagnosis to make sure our advance directives and guardianship choices would be memorialized. We'd sat at the conference table, synchronously suspending our pens after each paragraph and dispassionately dissecting each provision in clinical detail. Would we want antibiotics in one condition or another, or supplemental oxygen, or to be intubated?

"No couple I've ever had in here has talked about any of these sections," the lawyer evenly had observed.

It was as easy to discuss and record those decisions about what we *both* wanted as it was horrifying for me to picture those things soon coming to pass for my husband alone. In fact, it was strangely comforting to think I might somehow still go first. It was much harder for me to be objective about financial decisions. Jim had saved not only for our children's care and education, but for his retirement, and ours together. It wasn't just the unfairness of his never having the years and decades he should have had to slow down and enjoy life in this world once our children were on their own, but my sorrow that I, alone, might.

"Let me put it this way," the lawyer said when I cringed at the financial paperwork. "Would you have any concerns that the person you make your executor would mismanage what you leave to your children? Do you trust them with everything you have?"

"Completely," we said in unison, and signed.

~~~~~

Selling the yellow house and moving to a new one overlapped summer and fall, leaving months in which I wasn't settled in either home or season. I went back and forth, bringing pieces of the past with me. The new home was on a tiny, fence-free corner lot in a densely settled neighborhood a few blocks from a downtown waterfront. The location would make it impossible for me to keep myself confined indoors, or escape seeing and walking among people--even during our first winter there, when ten-and-a-half feet of snow would pile up and into its second story.

At first, a confused and clingy Brady would whimper at the disorientation and disconnection from what he expected to see
~~~~~

when the door opened, especially after dark, when even in the new house, Jim didn't come home to run with him and Rufus. On more temperate days, I could walk them past the Harbor and all the way to the ocean and a strip of rocky shoreline. I hoped the view, and the abundance of dogs we'd encounter, would cheer them.

Most people in our new home city would not know me as 'the widow,' although some did. I soon discovered quite a few had known Jim, sometimes as a physician and often as a coach and Boy Scout Troop leader. The first time I took Rufus and Brady out the door, keeping them on sidewalks instead of walking through fields and forests, I ran into a woman whose son my husband had coached in Little League. She told me how sorry she was, what a wonderful man he was, and the mark he'd made in her family's life. As I continued past a corner house, I saw someone gardening outside. I recognized her as the spouse of the obstetrician who'd delivered our youngest child.

"Say hi to Jim for us," she said.

I looked up into a clear sky. "I will," I was able to say without tears.

~~~~~

When we were about to make our final trip from the yellow house, Emma was ten hours ahead of us and across the globe, with only a backpack to hold her worldly belongings for a semester.

On a penultimate sweep, each of the rest of us chose and carried from it something too special to be entrusted to others' hands. From the silver-flecked dark granite kitchen counter his father had selected when a less enduring one had given up the ghost, Noah picked up a clear vase filled with cobalt glass marbles. It held sprays of dried wildflowers and baby's breath from flowers my parents had sent for his father's Closing Ceremonies. Sam's most treasured memento, I discovered, was a battered baseball--a game ball
~~~~~

signed by all of his baseball teammates when he'd been in a Boston hospital. Our son remembers the kindness, rather than the fear that had imprinted on me during his illness. I carried the blue mug with the Fenway fly ball Jim had caught for me and his flattened penny. Suzannah carried the Les Paul electric guitar her father has acquired with all his savings when he was not so very much older than she. I later learned it had provided the accompaniment when she dedicated a Jack Johnson song to her father, singing *Hey, Little Girl* inside the same church where his Closing Ceremonies had been.

~~~~~

Soon after the move, I realized my youngest also had something more sentient in mind for our new home, in which she'd spend far more time than her siblings were likely to. Down to one full-time resident student in the house to which I'd moved us from the only home she'd ever known, without complaint, I fell for the old, "Let's just take a look at the beagle puppy" trick.

I couldn't help myself, even had I foreseen that this little nugget, who even full-grown would be outweighed by any Sunday side-dish at Papa Dick's house, was possessed (not a word I use lightly) of a nascent personality that spelled T-R-O-U-B-L-E. He'd survey whatever towered around him, including massive German shepherds and his own medium-sized beagle brothers, and somehow still absolutely believe he was King of the Wolves incarnate.

I must have become unhinged. After drastically downsizing the house and its contents, I'd left us full-time residents outnumbered by tricolored companions whose tri-tonal howling neighbors were unlikely to appreciate. Scooter didn't appear to have emotional scars, but it soon became evident he was equally lacking in common sense. He had a heaping portion of guile, which did not promisingly mesh with his overblown self-confidence. It was he
~~~~~

who'd challenge looming, teeth-baring canines studded with silver points like those on a mace's business end. Or bears, had the neighborhood been less citified. I did not grow up a 'dog person,' although many of my friends and at least some of my children fear I'll become a crazy old dog lady once they settle far and wide. It may be some gauge of Jim's family's fondness for dogs that all he remembered of childhood family pets was a dog named Zero. It had taken years of careful advocacy for Suzannah to talk us into adopting Rufus.

Jeff Jarvis wrote that dogs are, in their own sensory way, time travelers. They re-sniff the past and detect what lies ahead, upwind. When I began to unfurl the carpet with the missing piece in the new house, in which it would exceed the size of the room it occupied, Rufus and Brady both immediately and uncharacteristically abandoned the adjoining kitchen's scents. They frantically began snort-sniffing the carpet. I'm certain they were looking for Jim. But Scooter was neither a prisoner of typical sad-eyed beagledom, nor freighted by any such angst.

~~~~~

On Jim's next birthday, in somewhat lopsided conversation with this triumvirate of velvety souls, I took it upon myself to introduce Scooter to our missing household member. I wasn't sure Rufus and Brady were up to the task; they seemed especially wistful. So I found myself conversing with a puppy Jim never knew, in a home he never saw, and who wasn't in a position to understand the hole in his brothers' map of the world. I talked everything over with Scooter, whose eyes are more of a bittersweet chocolate, and distinctly lighter on the eyeliner than those of the beagles who so loved Jim.
~~~~~

There is nothing one cannot tell or ask a puppy. Next to my husband, they're among the least judgmental and most forgiving beings I've encountered.

"If a person's not here anymore," I asked 5.6 pounds of puppy, "how do I introduce him to you?"

Never-to-be cerebral Scooter narrowed his eyes in a knowing way, as if he understood when I told him he'd have loved Jim, who would have held him in one strong hand as he did our children when they were of similar heft. I knew and agreed Jim rightly would have thought me unhinged to acquire a puppy. But he'd be glad for us to have this warm bundle to hold during the coming winter, to snuggle up with as we made our way without him, and to look at me in a way that made me think another sentient being relied on and loved me back. There's not much downside to having a dollop of bottomless trust and love added to one's life.

~~~~~

I'd returned to work in the same job I'd been so lucky to find when I graduated law school during our marriage's early years, when we both became certain our occupations were also our callings. Our professional lives coalesced in our understanding of service. The rigors of medical training and practice were vast, but Jim continued to sleep the replenishing sleep of the just.

We lived in a Dorchester neighborhood near Ashmont Station. Our neighbors Bill and Vanessa were a few years ahead of us on the one-two-three kid combination, were often outside and always ready to assist me when Jim was on call. Diagonally across the street, Larry and Becky provided another aspirational model: they had closely-spaced teenagers, fostered multiple children, and I'd never seen either of them without a smile. After the first few New Year's Eve open houses at their home, Larry poured a cup for Jim. Above the chatter and laughter from an overflowing crowd of
~~~~~

neighborhood families he said, "So, when do you think you two are going to have kids?"

Jim looked at me, as I swayed only slightly from the wracking nausea that accompanied any hint of the smell of sustenance. He quickly hid the grin I glimpsed and said, "We were thinking around the second week of August."

Becky and Larry, who were among the first to know, were far more overtly excited than our own immediate families. My mother, in particular, considered herself much too young to be a grandparent.

~~~~~

We left Dorchester two weeks before Sam's birth, when Jim joined Bob in an internal medicine practice. I would commute back to my work and return to gloriously open space surrounded by woods. I savored the quiet and the brief opportunity to nest. There were no longer neighbors in sight, but this did nothing to curtail our friendships, old and new. While I could be reticent, it was Jim's nature to invite people in. Without him, as we grieved, the woods around our next home had allowed me to tuck myself out of sight while wishing us back to each beginning and forward to somewhere short of any ending. I'd tried to seal myself off, but I understood, at least for my children's sake, that I'd need to rejoin their transformed world. And that I couldn't do that in a haunted yellow house.

Moving had begun in earnest with the deep, dark attic storage. While Emma was doing underwater research in another hemisphere, her boyfriend had assisted me not only with heavy lifting, but also my continuous technological issues. As moving day approached, he'd been helping me hoist haphazardly packed boxes, most of which I'd labeled DEEP STORAGE with any writing implement at hand or underfoot. Sinister broad Sharpies. Glittery
~~~~~

purple ink which commanded my hand to form dissonant curlicues. Ink-bereft pens I used to carve into cardboard boxes.

"What is *'DEEP STORAGE'?*" He'd asked me, with some trepidation.

He'd recently needed to break it to me that my catastrophic hard drive incident would require the restorative properties of a 'Clean Room,' which had conjured for me images of angelic fairy folk ministering to my device. I agreed this sounded a bit more foreboding, but had no specific memory of what I'd tossed into the boxes.

I'd been affixing the label to two broad categories of things I'd found while excavating the attic. One was items I wanted to keep, including an absurd amount of books and easily hundreds of yards of fabric. The second was far more daunting: belongings of Jim's and of the two of us together which likely would mean something only to me. I felt unable to part with them, but it was too painful to go through them or make a rational calculus. The diplomas which should have hung on his office walls for decades as he continued to do the work he loved. My wedding veil. The perfectly fitting second-hand tuxedo he'd picked up in Cambridge and worn to weddings and celebrations ever since, beginning with ours. Camera equipment not even Suzannah knew how to use, or what irreplaceable parts might be missing. The Boy Scout Troop leader shirt that should have adorned him at an Eagle Scout ceremony I attended in his place, next to an empty chair. The Scouts had been urged to go out into the woods and world and continue doing what he'd led them to do.

I suppose 'deep storage' was also a category of hope that someday we'd be able to look at and touch things without the tears, and pass them along to those who might use and treasure them in places they too would call home.

27

Another long December

Winter came around again. I stopped at a pharmacy where the staff had known Jim both as a prescribing physician and a patient. I'd taken note of the hush whenever I handed over a pile of his prescriptions before each of his days in the chemo pod. Rounding into another February without him, wearing the single glove I could find, I stepped out of freezing air into blinding fluorescence and Valentine's Day displays of carnation pink and red. It remained almost as unsettling as the first time I'd walked into a stationery store after his death, coming face-to-face with undeliverable Father's Day cards. I'd wheeled around and hastened back out the door as if the cards might swoop down and attack like Alfred Hitchcock's fowl--a murder of crows, an unkindness of ravens, a sedge of bitterns.

Such days' edges had softened enough that I didn't literally flee this time. I remembered that last Valentine's Day, when Jim had handed me a box wrapped in shiny Boston Celtics green. It matched the boxes I knew contained necklaces he'd carefully chosen for our two winter-born daughters' birthdays. We gave each other cards containing variations on the words that we didn't know where to begin. Both of us meant we did not know how to begin to end what we said to each other.

He made my card by printing a picture of the two of us in Ecuador. A few days earlier, two young nieces had visited him, sitting at our kitchen table with colored paper, glue, and plastic scissors with rounded blades shaped like bunny ears. Although crafting was not on any bucket list equivalent of his, it was a special enough occasion that he'd joined them. My card is adorned with pink and red and white foam letters glued in a merry rainbow arc over our picture.

I might very well panic if I ever were to misplace it.

~~~~~

Winter haltingly segued into spring again. The same calendar space where death had become a memory that had taken over the yellow house for me. The late winter sun burned so furiously before plummeting that I often had to look away. Until I had moved to another home and city, I wasn't often outside at sunset. I'd become inattentive not only to how it simmered, but also how it did so over time. Daylight rarely continuously receded. Sometimes the sky would burst back into bright technicolor half-an-hour after it had quietly retired in thinning dark plumes, lulling me into thinking the show had ended. Neon pink, purple, and orange would suddenly bubble back to stipple clouds already blended into a reduction of clotted plum. At dusk, clusters of geese testing whether it was time to resettle would continue dispatching small search parties, like musical notes in a never-ending score.

~~~~~

While unpacking yet another inadequately labeled box, I'd discovered that the last book Jim read was the same biography of Alexander Hamilton that Lin-Manuel Miranda had happened to pick up for a vacation trip, with epic results.

As time had passed, there already seemed so much on which to fill my husband in: "Now it's a *hip-hop musical!*" I'd exclaim, holding the book up to him in the fashion of an Executive Order. He would tilt his head and nod, smiling, as he ran through the immense internal musical catalogue he hadn't let go until his heart stopped beating--if he did even then. *Of course*, he would think, *what a wonderful idea.*

Miranda's Hamilton tells his wife he'll see her on the other side. She outlives him by a half-century. Until then she can catch a glimpse of him only in the eyes of the living, from whom she seeks out any story of him she didn't already know.

One line about death and memory appears in three different *Hamilton* songs, but never in the same simile's company. First, young Alexander wonders if his own death will be like a beat and not a melody; he questions what metaphor might capture it. He'd already experienced so much traumatic death--including his mother's--that he did not need to imagine death itself, any more than my children and I now need to imagine my husband's. It surpasses simile; it's all too vivid and concrete.

After Hamilton has witnessed still more death, and the means of his own seems likely to be of a piece with fellow soldiers', Miranda dispenses with metaphor and the line stands unadorned: death is only memory. But Hamilton survives battle and then survives his son, enduring what is to parents the indescribable but all too horrifyingly imaginable unimaginable.

Finally, from ten paces away, Hamilton realizes not only how he will die, but that his first simile was faulty: in death there is after all neither a melody nor a single beat.

During his last hours in our Hamilton-era home, I felt Jim's immense intelligence, including his vast knowledge of music and melody as it began to filter back into the vastness outside his vessel. Even then his heart kept beating until it slowed to a stop, while snow fell, as in James Joyce's *Dubliners*, "upon all the living and the dead."

Love is the melody and its absence, fire and ice and back again, all the songs and after.

28

Sixth Sense after Sundown

In a season of descent back into earth, we largely settled into the new neighborhood. My camera didn't seek out only displays of saturated color, but was drawn to desiccated, muddied, collapsed flora. It was always some aspect of light that arrested and pointed me to what surrounded it. The sun striking a lone circular pumpkin in a field of narrow ones shaped liked patrician Secretaries of State's furrowed noggins or reflected in a pinpoint star in a cedar waxwing's eye. A dropping moon reddening a sky dragon's cloudy breath at sunset, or turning a river into liquid gold and flowing fire.

When I ventured outside, I found not just people, but abundant ghosts. Sometimes it was my new neighbors who made the introductions, especially during Halloween season. Spirits occasionally solidified. My complicated and rich relationships with floating, flying things had commenced immediately when my husband was physically absent. It took some time and space to appreciate and welcome hauntings rendered not in darkness and fear and regret, but in the lovely bright copper of poet Vijay Seshadri's "diffident and polite" dead.

~~~~~

"Just because you don't believe in something doesn't mean it isn't true." The advice was dispensed at an Easter gathering by a strangely compelling *Boardwalk Empire* character, a World War I sharpshooter whose half-mask concealed only visible portions of his deep wounds as he carried skills not readily adaptable to civilian life into the moral complexities of life in New Jersey during Prohibition.

I hadn't believed in ghosts. I was vaguely aware of the jaunty residual hauntings celebrated during *el dios de la muerte*, but that was not the aura I'd experienced in the yellow house. It instead retained the black and white negative of my husband's body on the deathbed that quickly had been spirited away.

There, Jim had always had home projects underway, and sought to maintain and restore portions of it to the most faithful approximations of how they'd been built and meant to be. A massive such project was to have begun in early July. The contractor had appeared at our house in early July and was surprised to find us both at home on a weekday. Jim told him of his diagnosis with pancreatic cancer, and that it was perhaps not the ideal time to repair the old barn.

The contractor had looked at Jim, an outwardly robust, healthy man who betrayed no sign of illness, let alone such a devastating one. He blurted out, with a hint of the disbelief we all felt, "The good kind or the bad kind?"

My ever-unflappable husband replied, lightly, "I'm not sure there *is* a good kind of pancreatic cancer."

By the time I first moved, I'd begun to realize there are good and bad kinds of haunting, and only one of them is the stuff of nightmares.

~~~~~

The house I left was haunted for me by illness and pain and death.

Once I moved, I began to be haunted by Jim in another, welcome way--as he was in life, and somehow thereafter. My new neighborhood was splashed with black humor. An ersatz tombstone reading BACHELORHOOD appeared on a toy-scattered and leaf-strewn lawn. Freddy Krueger and his homicidal brethren were rendered as pumpkins, sitting on porch rocking chairs and reminiscing about the good old days. Yards were adorned with spiderweb-strewn headstones and black roses.

Vijay Seshadri's glittering poem, *Bright Copper Kettles*, describes the benevolent, loving, continuing presence of the dead who do not wish to frighten or supplant us. They're accompanied not by a slasher movie score, but by the dulcet tones of The Reverend Al Green. In such tender hauntings, I could watch a bird waiting patiently on a branch for me while his fellow fowl scattered.

What kind of bird is that, Jim?

I could listen to my children playing music trivia games and trying to name songs and bands from decades past.

Your dad would know. He'd know them all. Which one was that, Jim? It's on the tip of my tongue.

He'd come to me when I sobbed on my drive home alone in the dark from marching band finals on a field in Old Orchard Beach. Although I'd spent many nights with Jim there and on other frigid fields, I hadn't realized until the camera was in my hands how numb his fingers must have been as he calibrated the precise settings to capture sufficient light in those nights' early darkness.

I know you don't want me crying while I'm driving, I said out loud, looking safely ahead because he was no longer always confined to my undersized passenger seat. *But I can't do all of this alone without you, forever.*

It doesn't help to think in terms of forever, I hear in his deep voice. *And you're not alone.*

Immediately, on the radio, Chrissie Hyndes began singing *I'll Stand by You,* sent to me by the man who always will.

~~~~~

As another October neared its end, I found myself alone in my Victorian house. I spent most of my time downstairs, in a room with walls of the deepest blue--except for the one my daughters had painted in chalkboard black. There I regularly found delightful fleeting artifacts left by my children and their friends. Cartoons and riddles. Arabic and Bangla and Urdu notations. A running tally of poker winnings and Pokémon tournament scores, and re-minders to me of important tasks and appointments they didn't want me to forget.

Atop the black wall, I hung Emma's paintings of foods in each color of the rainbow (to the extent one can label as food a bright orange gummy bear and violet-foiled Hershey kiss). The same paintings had adorned her father's hospital bed faced when he fi-nally came home.

On the new house's large downstairs windows I'd sewn and hung aloft dense white canvas curtains resembling sails. At night sometimes I could imagine I was at sea, under a single bright streetlight that became a distant star filtered through midnight clouds.   .

~~~~~

When I was alone after dark with my beagles boys, I sometimes kept a noisy TV going, for the illusion of human company. While waiting for a World Series game to begin, I sat with Scooter on my lap on the cream-colored couch my daughters and I had picked out before I was aware we'd be acquiring a puppy for whom it was not a practical accessory. Already, the new cushions bore tiny tooth marks. I couldn't sleep after the game, so I kept a promise to a friend to check out *Long Island Medium*, and then caught almost all of *The Sixth Sense*. The spirits in both required an intermediary--a living, detached third-party. The medium conveyed a form of hearsay for which an exception had not to my knowledge yet been fashioned. The ghosts themselves, at least at first, were remarkably indirect even as they kept some promise, made an assurance, or answered a question still restlessly lodged among people they'd loved and left behind.

I didn't require an intermediary. Even if I had, I wouldn't have welcomed either the indirectness or involvement of strangers. I didn't find the show a good fit, possibly due to the degree to which I'd become jaded from reading people at work and play.

"*Of course. Any* month is going to be significant to someone inclined to speak to a psychic." I told Scooter, who seemed to nod sleepily in agreement. "No kidding. Someone in *every* family will have died after having a pain 'in front'," I growled at the unresponsive screen.

But *The Sixth Sense* was different. I'd seen it with Jim years earlier and remembered only the vivid, gory, frightening parts--the bad kind of haunting. This time it broke my heart. When a beloved doctor's ghost skips the middleman and directly revisits his young widow, she's fallen asleep on the couch while watching recorded moments from their past which bring her living husband back to her. I'd done this countless times. As she fitfully sleeps, she releases her grip on his gold wedding band. It clatters to the floor. Like me, she still wore her own wedding ring. In another scene, her ghost husband sits at a restaurant table with her. To observers, she's alone. A widow in a red dress signing the check for an anniversary dinner. I'd occupied similar spaces, in very close to the same dress.

She slumber-speaks with her husband's ghost, asking him what I've asked only while alone in the dark, although we widows understand there was no choice involved, and there's no answer to be had. *Why did you leave me?*

And her husband's ghost answers the distinct question that's haunted his wife and makes her unable to let him go.

I'd learned that even when we know what horror awaits, and how quickly it will arrive, we don't always know the questions to ask while we still can.

In the whirlwind of what arrives unbidden in our lives, we may have little idea what our newly configured and tentative selves will need to know or say or ask.

I still had two questions.

Perhaps the answers might still come to me some night, when the moon is a ghostly galleon, tossing and turning with me atop cloudy seas.

~~~~~

We cannot consciously summon thin spaces, but we know them when we feel them.

Intuitively, it seemed to me strange to call these spaces of weighty spiritual connection 'thin.' Even as an etymological matter, to characterize such moments and places that way seems off: it's the word 'thick' that connotes closeness and dense connection. A thin barrier implies relatively easy progress forward, while thickness suggests a tough slog, as though through molasses. So ancient is the metaphor of traveling through such contrasting spaces--"through thicket and thin wood"--that Chaucer assigned it a more contemporary shorthand of, roughly, "through thick and thin" in the 1300s.

A thin space or moment may be many things, but it does not strike me as a place or experience of easy passage.
~~~~~

At her father's service, one of our daughters selected and read *A Man*, a poem Louis Untermeyer wrote for his father. It begins by describing the kind of person who was his father's opposite: the type of man around whom one finds an atmosphere with a dark undertow, "thick with epigrams and smoke." The metaphorical layers of a conversation at the poem's beginning--the substrata underneath which "furtive things began to crawl"--are absent in a thin moment or place.

It occurred to me that "thin" is not simply the opposite of "thick," but conveys the absence of layers. The poem captured my children's father so well, fitting him perfectly but for a single word our daughter left out as she read: the more advanced but still far too premature age at which the poet's father had passed away. My husband's grace included the absence of dark layers--of pretense, posturing, harshness, deception, or guile. There was never any different person or persona hidden from view.

The air around him was thin. After he died, our daughter began to experience thin places around the world. I could feel them in her photographs and paintings, and in her voice as she spoke of her travels. I think grief makes one awash in time in a different sense--trying to slog through thick, or even seemingly impossible forward movement. 'Sticky' time, or even boomeranging time. I've lost track of time, day, date, and even year. In those thick spaces, not only have I felt I wasn't awash in time, but I felt I was running out of it--and that I'd fail to complete the many things which still needed to be done. But I knew I'd find thin spaces in the world outside whatever home I occupied, and that I could still share space with my husband there.

29

Making Friends with the Dark

When he was a young student, long before an ever-accessible interconnected cyberworld, composer Philip Glass regularly rode the old overnight B & O train that ran between Baltimore and Chicago. His trips preceded even the minimal distraction of being able to traverse the train for a snack or to encounter fellow travelers.

The lights went off at night.

Some of Glass's music, like guitar licks in John Hiatt's *Long Time Comin,'* carry what he heard during those long hours of silent contemplation in complete darkness, including the rhythmic contact of wheels on tracks and sustained exhalations. After decades as a musician, Glass said those sounds had become part of the way he experienced the world. He was able to hear how the long-gone notes and tones--assonant and dissonant, soft and harsh--echoed in his compositions and continued to reside with him.

My husband is built into the way I see and hear and listen and breathe in the world I still occupy.

~~~~~

When fighting the dark, it's difficult to overstate the envy with which long-term insomniacs regard those who can simply close their eyes and usher in solid, restorative sleep. My envy extends even to animals, like beagles who curl their warm bodies against each other and slumber in patches of sun. Cats snuggling into any available nook, cranny, or human appendage. I've never seen an animal wake up in a panic.

After seasons of rising well before dawn from woefully insufficient sleep, I began to learn to listen to night, which is never completely silent any more than it is purely black. Sometimes it's adorned with gradations of blue and violet, and filmy streaks of wavering silver. A brilliant white moon can soften night's silhouettes. While lights are off and others sleep, night has its own melodies and rhythms--none of which I would know if I weren't awake in the dark in the places my husband's death took me to.

~~~~~

Bird calls continued to signal the weather and seasons. Near my new home, two unusually melodic sets of wind chimes rang in even a light breeze. My ceramic Noah's Ark chimes tapped against the clapboards outside my window only when the wind moved northwest at a thunderous clip. The soundtrack was no longer smothered silence and the vistas weren't impenetrably dark. I realized they never had been.

In *Night*, Elie Wiesel contemplated how it is not light that appears first. Rather, the rising sun interrupts the already present dark. In Genesis, darkness did not follow light, but preceded it: "the Earth was astonishingly empty, and darkness was on the face of the deep." Only after bottomless darkness did God uncouple light from night.

Night pained me, but almost everything did, and darkness had its pluses. Paperwork, bills, and their mindless purveyors tended to intrude by day. At night, not always for the worse, there are no such distractions. We have an excuse to slow down, to lie down and still our souls even if we don't sleep. We have only ourselves to answer to. In daylight one can hardly ever escape as deeply into the loveliness of poetry or literature. In harsh daylight, the contrast between where we are and where we imagine or wish ourselves to be is too easily betrayed.

In darkness, we do not have to think in as focused a way. What floats to the surface unbidden and without distractions may reveal fragments of present or past beauty untouched by deep pain. I welcomed early nightfall and its ever-changing selections of color and pattern as they began to coalesce and restore the quiet I often paradoxically preferred.

Even night vision can delight us. When I close my eyes, I'm sometimes treated to kaleidoscope images of snippets of beauty I've only fleetingly seen by day: copper stone carvings; tapestry embroidery; tiny strokes of feathered blue paint rearranging themselves into endless pinwheels of tiny fledging birds.

~~~~~

I don't mind quiet, which often relieves me of finding myself surrounded by people whose sense of time and space I often feel I no longer share, any more than I share their normalcy and persistent bouts of happiness. When I finally returned full-time to work, I initially remained apart from the barrage of companionship in which others engage during daylight hours, like the convivial laughing and planning afoot at communal lunch tables when I slipped in and out to refill my bottomless coffee mug and take it back to my desk and close the door.
~~~~~

Outside the office and courthouses, people walked together, dined at shared tables, and leaned into each other conspiratorially. They smiled. On public ways, conspicuously partnered people gazed devotedly at companions who sometimes returned the look. They chatted in groups as they waited in lines and asked each other anodyne questions about their spouses and children. They whacked the snack machines, as I used to, after they'd gobbled their quarters but refused to disgorge their snacks. Not many people around me appeared to be persistently trying not to cry, but I remembered one stranger I'd seen crying alone on the Red Line many years earlier. I wish I'd said something to her. I can picture her still.

Of course, it was not companionship I thirsted for, but the companion I couldn't have with me, and whose presence I could feel even more strongly in quiet stillness, even if he sometimes returned only in a nightmare.

Grieving makes each morning seem at least mildly unreal, even unsettling, after night's non-linear tangle of time. I awaken; therefore I am still here. By the time I settled in a place that didn't itself hold the images and visceral experience of my husband's death, I developed another habit to contend with each approaching nightfall and daybreak. Even when a given day was too painful to face, I could stockpile its wondrous predawn and sunset moments, which I'd almost always missed in the long-ago days when I sometimes peacefully slumbered.

30

My Little Girl

Little concentrates demarcations in family life as much as the departure--if only for places of higher learning--of beings who once utterly depended on us. And the tables had turned. Even before their father died, I found I needed our children's help as I tried to manage tasks he'd always gladly undertaken. Especially when higher math or even low-level technology was involved.

The nest continued to empty, even as its beagle content expanded beyond reason.

Each of my children has always taught me far more than I could have hoped to teach them. As my youngest tested her roots and wings and prepared to graduate from high school, she illuminated life lessons which may be gleaned from those who channel non-earthlings and occupy non-linear time. She'd finished a school-specific rite of passage: a Senior Meditation. I knew little of this ritual, but was aware Scooter had consumed a good helping of fiber from her book of past Meditations. The evidence was compelling; it included Scooter palate-sized clumps of gummy pulp and shreds of paper in its distinctive Garamond font. My daughter, who'd learned over her still tender years not to give away nearly so much information as Scooter did, was willing to disclose only one tidbit about her own Meditation: it was about aliens.

"Did you get it done?" I was slightly afraid to ask, especially because she'd spent her winter term's final weeks with a horrible flu that turned her ethereal singing voice into a froggy, hacking mess. She nodded and unleashed a minor coughing fit.

"What was it about?"

"Aliens."

"Aliens?" I asked, sloshing coffee onto my suit, shoes and outgoing mail, as is my custom while heading out for work. "You don't mean, like, immigrants with documentation issues?"

"Tralfamadorians." She replied.

"Oh."

Enough said.

~~~~~

Tralfamadorians, as any Kurt Vonnegut fan knows, dispense pearls of wisdom and are not adherents to Earthlings' misconception "that once a moment is gone, it is gone forever." Grieving had reinforced that time is nothing like that.

A few weeks earlier, on the anniversary of the day we'd finally brought her father home from the hospital, I'd read Oliver Sacks' *Hallucinations.* Not unsurprisingly, Jim then dropped in on my dreams, but this time in a disturbing way that left me feeling there was something more I could have done. Time and time again, in the concentrated kaleidoscope of my rare REM sleep, Jim and I were racing to find the solutions to fiendish word puzzles. We would find the correct answers, but were always too late. In this dream world, governed by the strictest of linear time, only those who got the answers first prevailed.

When by day I consciously replayed the weeks and days leading up to my husband's death, I thought there must have been *some-*
~~~~~

thing more I could have done, some puzzle I could have solved in time to help him, and if not to spare him, then at least to alleviate his pain. To make anything easier for him. Some version of that searing self-doubt had persisted through each winter since then. The very feel of the air and light brought me back to those awful months. And every March, the memory of the moment his heart stopped beating and of the moments and days which swirled around it pulled me back into the same spiral of doubt and regret and pain. No new home could change that.

The anniversary of his last day with us had been weighted this time, again, with icy gray snow which smothered a tentatively budding floral vanguard. Just miles away, downhill from the yellow house I scrupulously avoided driving past, the same murky layer would be blanketing the now nameless pond we'd left behind. Descendants of fish never told of the pond-keeper's absence would be swimming in black water under ice made unsteady by freezing and refreezing in the tentative segue into another spring.

~~~~~

Within the same waking moments, I would have visions of taking a last walk with Jim around the hospital floor and also see our younger selves in an operating room in another hospital, as he held my hand and said, "It's a... *big*... girl." I'd peel back layers upon layers of moments among the years we spent together, never continuously back or forward, but rearranging themselves. Moments dusted in gold would sometimes toss themselves above the whole for my attention. The balance finally was beginning to shift away from the end and to each beginning and the vast lovely and exhausting and chaotic middle. The tripwires to devastating memories more frequently held.

As those initial years of grieving passed, my thoughts didn't always begin or dwell in the horrifying memories in which I relived
~~~~~

my husband's suffering long after he had been relieved of it him-self. Tralfamadorians understand the power of savoring memories even if we cannot control them, as did Billy Pilgrim: "If I am going to spend eternity visiting this moment and that, I'm grateful that so many of those moments are nice."

~~~~~

In what passed for the present, my sunny baby girl, whose favorite color was buttercup yellow, was also sweet sixteen, wearing a white cotton dress that luminesced in bright direct sun as she waited to receive her high school diploma. The sun also found the white-gold of the curls she'd been born with, creating the illusion of a wreathed crown above the deeper bronze waves which now reached well down the curve of her back. She held herself with a ballet dancer's weightless carriage even when she was not on a stage. She'd always moved as if she heard music and her arms were ready to be held aloft in the graceful equipoise in which her father's final photograph preserved her.

Three entire rows of folding chairs held her cousins and aunts and uncles and family friends, who'd showed up in merry bulk for her when her father could not take a seat. It had torrentially rained during every other graduation he'd missed, forcing each for the first time in decades into dreary, humid auditoriums. Her sister, at work in another hemisphere, had gifted the rest of us with detailed plans to leave the country in the wee morning hours.

In a preceding season's abject awfulness, when many of us were still encountering contemporaneous crises, I'd needed to know my children all had something they looked forward to.

"If we could go anywhere in the world, where do you want to go?" I'd asked.
~~~~~

The answer, from a child who for days had maintained a silence more painful to hear than the audible grief that preceded it, had been instantaneous.

"Giant's Causeway."

Siblings nodded.

Unsaid: *Dad would have wanted to see Giant's Causeway.*

"That's where we're going." I said.

Unsaid: *That's where we're going to be next Father's Day.*

Father's Day would fall a week after Suzannah's graduation.

I'd received her father's ashes back from his medical school.

~~~~~

First, we flew into Edinburgh. We climbed Arthur's Seat. The wind whipped a broadly smiling son who despite the cold was wearing a T-shirt--just as he had when we'd marked the first year after his father's death in Kyoto. I saw my doppelgänger, Lady Agnew, in the Scottish National Museum's Portrait Gallery. And I learned that most of us could have survived a solid week on a single authentic Scottish breakfast.

Our next destination was Belfast, where we encountered some paradoxes, like that embedded in the Titanic's motto. At a voluminously rainy juncture, we found ourselves on the waterfront, dwarfed by a glistening above-ground Delft Blue ceramic fish and in search of an afternoon plan. Suzannah suggested we take the Titanic Boat Tour. Not to put too fine a point on it, but *"What could go wrong?"* Jim would have shrugged, as Noah did, teeth chattering, not having packed any better for June in Belfast than I had for March in Japan.

We boarded a small boat, huddling for warmth. We were told that for decades the *Titanic*, built in and launched from Belfast's shipyard, was the Voldemorte of the sea: the Ship that Must Not be Named. Because of its fate, the ship that should have been a source
~~~~~

of enduring pride became a symbol of shame. Our tiny boat's captain told us Belfast had only recently reclaimed the *Titanic* and its engineering wizardry. According to him, no ship--not then, or even now--could withstand running at nearly 23 knots into a million-ton iceberg. The city had launched a campaign, reclaiming pride in its creation. Its new slogan: "She was alright when she left here."

It occurred to me that this captured many of my feelings about my children's graduations. I was so proud of them, and grateful to have had any role in nurturing the people they'd come to be. I will always be in awe of the way they handled what they had to navigate at such tender ages. I don't think I could have done what they did, staying at their father's side night and day as he was dying, then returning to school and all else that's since filled their lives. What happened from then on would be largely out of my sight. On any given journey they may encounter unimaginable beauty--and substantial, or even insurmountable, obstacles. Life largely is made up of joint enterprises, and fate can deal out opportunities and cooperation, grace and beauty, enduring friendships and every other kind of love. Along with the presence or sway of people who steer us hard a-starboard.

As a parent I'll never feel I've been good enough, but I've done some things right. Above all, I had a wonderful co-parent who lives on in all our children. In *Ways of Going Home*, Alejandro Zambra wrote, "Parents protect or forsake, but they always forsake. Children stay or they go but they always go." As much as they could be, my children were alright. They're unbelievably strong--more than I think they may know. I've needed too much of their practical help, but also have tried to be attentive to their direction and wisdom as I've trailed after them out into a wider world.

~~~~~
~~~~~

In Dublin, an abandoned home sits directly across the road from a bench overlooking the striated sea. It's just east of the spot where I scattered a small seashell of ashes into pastel seafoam barely distinguishable from pale cream sand and powder-blue sky. The empty house's front gate is secured by a salt-corroded chain with a hefty padlock that is conspicuously less worn. Where a window once allowed residents to look out to sea, Kelly green paint peels away from wood fencing and a teal-painted brick barrier. An archway over the front door appears to be missing, its peak sheared off to reveal a portion of skeletonized façade. A nautilus-shaped latch and iron *fleurs de lis* atop the gate--some tilting ever so slightly to starboard--are pocked with rough cinnamon patches of rust.

Unlike autumn's decay in New England, the most prominent visible undoing we saw in Ireland was of inorganic materials, including castle walls crumbling away from their immovable stone neighbors. Gorgeously looming disarray.

~~~~~

We forsook the Guinness tour and sought out the Broom Bridge, the stuff of mathematical legend. While crossing it, a professor bereft of a pencil carved into the stone bridge's side an equation that had visited him like a thunderclap, lest the epiphany be lost by the time he reached the other side. The cab driver who took us there said he was nearing retirement, had lived in Dublin all his life, and had never heard of the Broom Bridge. He eventually managed to find it, and we tagged after its ghost professor.

Ghosts are everywhere in Dublin. Some of them--unlike pencil-free mathematicians--are conspicuously celebrated. Among them is sweet Molly Malone, who rejoins her perished family's choir as she peddles bivalves freshly plucked from a salty stew of sand and sea. She eternally cycles in song as "her ghost wheels the barrow,/
~~~~~

Through streets broad and narrow,/ Crying 'Cockles and Mussels, Alive, alive Oh!'"

Her refrain makes a guest appearance in poet Carol Ann Duffy's *Midsummer Night,* which requires no close analysis to identify the prism through which I read an ode to the absent partner who is "[n]ot there to lie on the grass of our graves, both,/ alive alive oh."

~~~~~

Not long before our trip, I'd returned from work to my new home, driving a long distance on the same congested highways which had taken me to the yellow house when it was filled to the brim with family. I asked the not quite empty passenger seat, *What do you want me to do now?*

I got a musical response. Trusting but verifying, I switched stations. The same song immediately began. I hadn't heard it before: Michael Franti's, *I'm Alive (Life Sounds Like).* It was unusual, as far as my musical messages had evolved, because it was accompanied by merry whistling.

Usually you're not that heavy-handed, Jim, I observed.

Surely it is a hallmark of grief to continue to be startled one is "alive, alive," when someone you have loved is not. Not there to hear and see that strange bird overhead, or grass snowed over with feathers shed by Dublin cygnets intertwined under their parents' protective eyes. Not there to have skin warmed by the sun and stung by the season's buzzing creatures. Not there to leave a winding chevron of footprints beside mine on our way to the spot where we sprinkled a seashell of ashes into the water before noticing bright green algae that had arranged itself into a heart-shaped frame around a neighboring patch of infinite sand.

At a bright wishbone sunset over a cornflower swath of the Irish Sea, I watched our children, including our daughter half-a-world away, and knew their father was watching them too. I felt
~~~~~

the endlessly affirmative avowals of another Molly from Dublin with its fig trees and yellow houses and crimson sea and sunsets and let him know I'd received and understood his message.

You're alive, for better and worse. Stop wishing it could have been you instead and try to live, the same way you want them to.

I used a seashell to trace another heart in the sand, where it would soon disappear. I said, not loudly enough that my nearby children could hear, but enough that their father could, yes I said yes I will Yes.

31

A Forbidden Photograph

The task anchoring our trip came close to being thwarted--and to creating at least a minor international incident--after I snapped a single photo of an ornate blush-hued brick in downtown Belfast.

Sunday, Father's Day, was the one day during our travels when we needed to be awake and ready at a designated time--9:00 sharp--to travel up the coast of Northern Ireland in Paddy's cab. Emma had designed the entire trip around this day. We'd been off the grid for two days and I was unaware an international Summit was afoot until we'd breezed out of the landing area, passing a room brimming with disembarking forest-green clad police officers. It was the first clue something out-of-the-ordinary was going on. My master sleuth skills evidently had waned when we crossed time zones. An apparent official greeter smiled at Noah and asked, "Are you with Obama?"

Both perplexed and impressed (not to mention credulous), I blurted out, "You can tell a Democrat on sight?" She smiled even more broadly and pointed at my son's shirtsleeve, which bore an oval red, white and blue insignia not unlike a past campaign motif.

Still, I didn't compute that he'd then been expected until our cab driver mentioned he'd be speaking in Belfast the day after Father's Day.

~~~~~

When Jim had received the phone bill following our trip to Ecuador, I learned I'd benefit from a belt-and-suspenders approach to technology in any further travels. I needed not only to switch off my phone before I got near an international flight, but also remove its battery, so as not to accidentally accrue hundreds of dollars in charges. That also meant I'd not always have ready access to the correct time. Nor had I known clocks in and around Donnegal Square were set at impressively inconsistent times. I *did* know I had to wake up my children on Father's Day morning to get us to Paddy's cab in time to drive up the coast to Giant's Causeway. A sensible person might have invested a few bucks in a cheap watch along with the hefty Euros and pounds sterling I'd already devoted to airport coffee and Cadbury milk chocolate. (Note to self: caffeine does *not* enhance my traveling persona.) I did not do that.

Instead, as I packed frantically, hours after Suzannah's graduation, I'd stuffed a small battery-operated bedside alarm clock into my pocket. I hadn't bothered to try to reset it when we arrived in Europe: it seemed easier to just add five hours once we arrived in Ireland.

Oh, and I was traveling internationally with my husband's ashes in a sealed rectangular black box in my backpack.

~~~~~

Father's Day morning arrived. I left the hotel where the children slept, in search of breakfast to fuel them for the day's trip. We were only a block from Belfast's political epicenter, toward which my backpack and I headed. The alarm clock was stuffed into my raincoat pocket so I could be sure to be back at the hotel in time to wake everyone up and get us downstairs to meet Paddy. Rain fell. The streets were empty and storefronts were shuttered. Not a single eatery, nor any of the abundant bars, seemed inclined to consider entertaining guests before 1:00 that afternoon. This was understandable when I considered the merriment and colored lights which had spilled into our room's windows until well into the morning's wee hours.

Finally I spotted a McDonald's close to an empty main intersection, while making a note to myself to ask Noah if he could say 'Donnegal McDonald's' three times, fast.) Before crossing, in keeping with my already obsessive need to take photographs when my husband couldn't, I pulled my wee blue point-and-shoot camera from my pocket and photographed some letter 'S' shapes on a corner building sporting rectangular windows with bright red sills, then took a shot of the domed exterior of the most beautiful--but unfortunately closed--grocery stores I'd ever seen.

And then I took just one last picture. Of a brick.

The design caught my eye as rain streamed down. Mythical beasts clutched a garland of roses and laurel, its leaves arrayed like griffons' lolling tongues. They met in a conjoined clawed foot adjacent to a modern-looking tented triangle.

Then, to gauge whether there was still enough time to dash across the street for food and drinks, I reached into my thin jacket's pocket. It sagged with the weight of the camera I'd deposited there, clattering against an impressive assortment of random Scottish and Irish change. I pulled out the alarm clock to check the time and promptly dropped it on the brick sidewalk. Its front disconnected. The batteries popped out. I picked it up and tried to jam it back together.

In retrospect, I can see that frantically adjusting a small electronic device might have looked a bit suspicious to those monitoring the immediate surroundings of an imminent gathering of global political leaders.

By the time I looked up, realizing I needed to speed back to the hotel, a cheerfully checkered marigold and black armored vehicle had pulled up between me and the crosswalk, straddling the sidewalk. An initial group of three heavily armed men rounded its driver's side. Two more quickly reached me in the space between their boxy vehicle and the building with that photogenic brick. It wasn't just Glocks and batons; they had automatic weapons with the length and heft of a well-fed German Shepard at the top of her training class. The gentlemen had bulletproof vests and were swathed in body armor. And an impressive array of ammo clips, in case the five principal weapons at hand weren't up to the job.

With professional curiosity as to whom they were after, I glanced back over both my drenched shoulders. The street was still empty.

Oh. They seemed to want to talk to *me.*

I was wearing a brilliant blue cotton dress, coral poppies embroidered at its inset waist, under a moss green Irish knit sweater and the droopy and ineffective rain jacket. This topped off the sartorial splendor of lime green socks and bright purple sneakers with magenta laces, both diverted from my daughters' donation piles. Because all my hair fasteners had disappeared somewhere in Edinburgh, I'd braided my hair and secured it with a safety pin and some peach silk thread I'd found attached to my dress's lining. I was about where anyone would picture that ensemble on a spectrum between an inpatient in a locked ward and high-tech global security threat.

"Miss, you were just taking a picture of the bank."

Not computing. Did I take a picture of a bank? And had my *Fodors Guide to Northern Ireland* neglected to mention that was verboten?

"Oh, you mean the building with the red windows and the letter 'S's? I was just taking a picture of that because half my family's names begin with the letter 'S,' a little more if you count Scooter.... " I'd wracked my brain to come up with a suspicious activity I might have engaged in. Babbling ensued.

"No, the picture you just took. May we see your camera?"

"Sure, I'm sorry."

"Are you here for the Summit, Miss?" A second man chimed in. Charming accents, both, but I know when something's heading into good cop, bad cop territory. I also was growing concerned about returning to the hotel in time. I realized I'd failed to leave a note about what to do and whom to call if mom's involved in an international incident. *Dammit.*

"I, uh, no.... I didn't even realize it was going on here until.... "

"Are you on holiday?" It was the first guy, who appeared to be in charge.

"Well, not exactly. I mean, I'm here with my children.... "

The first guy was trying to review my photos, so--probably unwisely, and again not something I'd recommend upon reflection--I reached right over one of those massive firearms to show him how to press the little button. Fortuitously, Suzannah had taught me the photo-reviewing skill a couple of days earlier.

"These are the pictures... and, here... oh, the *brick*? I'm not supposed to take pictures of the brick?"

"That's the bank." A loaded pause from Guy Number One. "It's *unusual* for a person to be taking a picture of the bank." The stress was on the 'unusual,' and the voice on the stern side. I thought he might be warming up for the bad cop part. I didn't let on than I'd been involved in more than my share of interrogations; it seemed such a comment could be misconstrued.

"It's just that my mother's an artist and she likes Medieval motifs and I thought I'd take a picture of the brick for her. Do you want me to erase it?"

He'd completed his review of my camera's largely out-of-focus and distinctly apolitical contents.

"Oh, no, no." Guy Number One had already wound down from any trace of the bad cop façade. The look on his face was similar to the one I got from a cop who'd pulled me over when I was nine months' pregnant and had only just pulled out of a parking lot. He'd mistaken my car for one he'd been pursuing, and ended up sheepishly asking me if I'd like his badge number.

The men looked at each other.

"Do you have some ID please?" Very politely.

Fortuitously, I had the passports on me this time. I fumbled with the stack and produced mine to the head guy, subtly placing it atop my flag-bedecked home ID, the better to convey my devotion to institutional authority.

"Where are you staying?"

I gestured down the block, where the hotel's sign was visible in neon scarlet. They looked at each other in a knowing way.

"How are you getting around? Have you a car?"

"Oh, no." I looked down at my now squishy-from-rain repurposed bright purple sneakers. "Mostly we're walking, and we're supposed to be taking a cab up the coast this morning--actually in just a few minutes."

Number One frowned slightly and Number Two gave it the old college try: "So you're not here for the Summit and you're not on holiday? Why are you here?" He paused, taking in my dubious attire with a light frown. "It's not business, is it?"

By this time, I was becoming a bit frantic about missing the coastal trip--and what my kids were going to think if they woke up and eventually discovered that not only had I not only hadn't found food, but was being held somewhere.

"Oh, no. Dude," I managed to sputter (without actually saying the "dude" part out loud). I lifted my gold chain out of my saturated jacket (probably yet another ill-advised quick movement) and held up Jim's wedding band. "No, it's not that, I mean, it's not really a vacation. It's just we wanted to be here on Father's Day because we wanted to bring some of my husband's ashes up the coast." I realized I was tearing up, but Belfast weather provides perfect cover. "And I was trying to find them something to eat, and I couldn't find anything...."

I pictured my children's faces and wondered how they might go about finding a lawyer in Belfast. Guys Three-through-Five had slunk to the armored truck's rear, leaving Number One with my passport as he turned to speak into a radio. Poor Number Two remained stuck with me.

"It's just we have to be careful, with the Summit and all," Number One said as he beat his hasty retreat.

"Oh, I understand. I've worked with law enforcement back home," I added hopefully.

Number Two shifted uncomfortably. I could see Number One, who'd turned his back to me, and was calling in to whomever was manning the cameras that hadspotted my hapless morning activities. He appeared to be shaking with laughter.

"Um," I ventured. "Please, would it be okay if I just ran into the McDonald's, because I've got to get the kids up. There's a taxi coming for us in ten... well, probably five or six minutes."

Number One, my passport still in his hand, turned back toward me, flattened his face, and pointed across the square. "See there," he said, "That little store, through that door, it's open and you can go in there and get some drinks and something to eat."

"You mean it's okay for me to leave?"

"Oh, that's fine." He waited a beat.

"And you do have my passport." I acknowledged sheepishly.

"I *do* have your passport. I'll just be a minute."

I dashed across the street diagonally, in my best Boston jaywalk, as if evading a snipers' training session but minus the swearing and sustained horn blasts. I blitzed through the tiny store I'd missed. The clerk had just rung up my items when Number One came in, filling the door frame in his beweaponed glory.

"Here you go, Stephanie." He cheerfully called out my name and stepped in to hand me my passport. "Have a pleasant day. Looks like the weather's clearing."

The clerk looked at me.

I sprinted back to the hotel room and the kids were none the wiser. They didn't raise an eyebrow when I scrawled a couple of numbers for them to call just in case there were to be some sort of incident during the remainder of our travels.

~~~~~

I remembered the time, years earlier, when Jim happened to arrive home from work just as I--for completely innocuous work-related reasons--was situating myself in the back seat of a police car as an officer I worked with was going around to its driver's seat. Without missing a beat, Jim parked, got out of his pickup truck, glanced at me in the secured passenger seat, and nodded to the officer, saying, "It's about time."

He continued across the porch and into our yellow house as our children, all outside playing a game on a picnic table near the bird-feeders, laughed.
~~~~~

I could picture Jim watching over this scene, chuckling as I tried to explain myself and my odd architectural interests and misbegotten electronic devices to international security forces. He knew that I, and our children, would need some levity that day, as we said another kind of goodbye. Laughter into tears, and back around again.

*It's not that I'm laughing **at** you, Steph; it's just so damn entertaining to watch you sometimes.*

~~~~~

We left Belfast and started up the coast of County Antrim. Through a steady cycling of sun and increasingly light rain, we saw emerald fields dotted with supremely relaxed cows and clusters of sheep bedecked with neon streaks of pink and Kelly green. We stepped lively across the Carrick-a-Rede rope bridge. Later we careened down a steep, narrow road with multiple hairpin turns, to take a peek at the world's smallest public church, painted bright blue. *That* was a heart-stopping ride.

We stood in awe before a road lined with silver oak trees, their branches reaching across to and clutching one another in a vista out of *Pan's Labyrinth*. And at midday, as rain began to spatter again in weary tears on basalt columns, we gingerly stepped down to the sea and let go of a handful of ashes.

~~~~~

Paddy had told us some of the lore behind the Causeway's columns' formation. Some, Noah pointed out, were pentagonal, not hexagonal. He explained why certain shapes would be inherently more stable. But I also enjoyed the mythology of Finn Mc-Cool, a giant said to have had second thoughts about his face-off with the Scottish giants he was to have met across a bridge of columns spanning the sea to the Island of Staffa.

One enormous set of pillars there is conjoined with a cliff. Others jut out in gradations to the green sea, like stepping stones. We stood on the shoulders of these giants, at first spreading out to scout the Causeway's wonders. I followed heart-shaped puddles to the water's edge, where I stood behind my sons and Suzannah stood above me next to copper-tinted columns as rain began to fall more quickly. Sam and Noah had crept down to the basalt steps where heaven met the sea. My hands were shaking too much to open the box that contained the ashes, so my son did it for me, gingerly lifting the inner box from which I removed a bag and untwisted its gold tie. I shook out some ashes, which burst into a billowing cloud as soon as they touched the water. Just as quickly, they disappeared. Opaque white-gray instantly was replaced by the surrounding emerald water. My sons sat thoughtfully as I retreated to where my daughter stood just above us.

A gentleman approached me from the opposite side of a wide expanse and gestured toward my daughter, asking, "Is she alright?"

It was raining steadily by then, and I nodded as I steered her toward her brothers. My voice broke when I told the man, as if he could have known what I meant, "She's okay. It's just that we miss her dad."

He nodded at me as if he did understand, and repeated in German to a woman whose hand he took, "They miss her father."

~~~~~

You would have loved this place.

It was strangely difficult to leave. I began to worry: would we be able to remember and revisit this exact spot? I climbed higher and looked down to where my sons stood near the sea's edge. From my higher vantage point, I realized we'd always be able to find it, and was certain Jim approved of our choice. At the spot where ashes had turned to water, one large, rounded rock was positioned
~~~~~

just behind another of the same color and texture and size. The two perfectly complementary rocks, shaped like immense inverted teardrops, locked their points where they'd settled into a shallow cove. Looking down from above, they were conjoined in a left-tilting, immovable heart that marks this spot, just as surely as the Causeway's interlocking pillars have and will endure, together and inseparable.

32

The Long Way Home

It was the wee morning hours of the dog days of August and I was thirteen hours into a ten-hour return trip.

Each leg alone had been twice as far as I'd ever driven by myself before. In that sense--and clearly that sense alone--I was already besting myself.

Alone in the baby blue mom van, I'd pulled off a looping highway exit into an abandoned industrial park somewhere in Connecticut. The few nearby light poles were shrouded in sickly-yellow wisps of ashen clouds.

I was lost, but somehow knew not irretrievably, either because or in spite of a quirky and never-updated GPS device Jim had given me years earlier. He knew I could always use assistance in orienting myself. Splurging on a new phone would be a few more years away. I was due at work south of Boston in a matter of hours, but first I had to find my way back home--to the highway, to the Mass Pike, and back to New Hampshire for the first of the days when I'd be a parent without a child at home.

Just my beagles and me.

One leap at a time.

277

~~~~~

We'd left home fewer than 48 hours ago. My daughter and I had loaded up the van before she showered her beloved beagles with last kisses, reluctantly let go, and then we were off.

She rode shotgun and provided the musical score, long sun-gilded curls fanning out through her open window. We made a seamless drive across Massachusetts and upstate New York, skirting the top of New Jersey and meandering along the length of Pennsylvania until we could have walked into Ohio. I was moving my baby girl into her freshman year dorm.

I didn't want to let go of her any more than she'd wanted to let go of Rufus and Brady and Scooter.

I realized I was no longer afraid of highway driving. Or of getting lost.

Buffeted by those years without her dad, somehow I was still standing, although I felt like a relic by the time she'd packed up her own talismans to carry away with her. She'd grown a bit since she followed her father around the garden as he taught her about plants and how to care for them and minister to the bugs and inch-worms she found there. Her now darker red-gold hair fell across a white top above a swirling skirt. The shoes were less practical than the wee sneakers she used to secure with a *scritch* of Velcro over patterned socks on her way out the door to absorb all her dad showed her might need her care and attention in the world. But she was the same bright, fearless force.

~~~~~

Before moving into dormitories for the first time, many universities had begun supplying copies of a single book to all incoming freshmen, who would unite to discuss it after arriving on campus. Noah had been sent Cormac McCarthy's novel, *The Road*, which featured a surviving father and son navigating a desolate post-apocalyptic world together. Before Suzannah opened the package she'd been sent, my fingers traced the distinctive outline of the compact hardcover inside: *The Last Lecture.*

Was she ready to read this? I asked myself. This was followed by a quick figurative head slap: is she ready to *read* this? She'd already lived it.

~~~~~

And there was my no longer little girl, hauling the bins of belongings her dad would have helped carry and packing them into the mom van instead of the black truck, and a ten-hour drive her dad would probably have clocked in under that even while finding places to dawdle with her, taking pictures and exploring along the way. I undoubtedly would have stayed home and tended to whatever needed my attention there. I would have kissed them both goodbye and gone upstairs into her room, which would still have been in the yellow house.

I would have missed moments I wouldn't have known had gone missing.

I wouldn't have heard my daughter excitedly telling me about upcoming concerts and new artists and music. I would not have seen landscapes pieced from sheer planes of jeweled color, with subtle dark undertones, like a Hopper painting. Or rows of wind turbines lined up along a green field's edge against the backdrop of Pennsylvania's blue mountains. I wouldn't even have imagined my little girl calmly taking over the wheel when she sensed I needed a break. Her father wouldn't have needed one, but would have yielded the wheel to her for practice. I wouldn't have known there's a place called 'Pleasant Gap,' or considered what unpleasantness might surround it. I wouldn't have refueled at 'The Promised Land,' which introduced me to the apparently anxiously awaited arrival in that land of live bait vending machines. But I think it is safe to
~~~~~

say both her father and I would have remarked on a sign announcing that a place called 'One Mile' was a mile away.

~~~~~

As older siblings had begun working on degrees in different states and on another continent, it often had felt like the two of us against the world. Teenagers are capable of displaying a bit of attitude, as are grieving adults. But as much as she age-appropriately tested me, my daughter made so many things easier for me. She understood when I needed to sell the only home she'd ever known. She pitched in and went to work painting and assembling furniture in the new one. She even learned to cook (which makes one of us). She helped me when I barely functioned. When I was sick and exhausted; when I needed to be picked up after falling and cracking bones; and when I said the wrong thing and knew her father would have waited for the right words. She comforted me when I stared at funereal dark brown paint that had reasserted itself through a third coat of primer on my new bedroom's walls, the inexplicable final straw that left me in such inexplicable wordless despair that she at first thought I'd grievously injured myself again.

We'd felt the sting of each other's frustrations and displaced anger at the universe. I'll always regret our children have had to deal with my pain as well as theirs. I hold against myself times when she must have felt as powerless to know what to do for me as I was to help her and her siblings. But she has her father's compassion and forthrightness, and has brought so much into our lives-- including the rescue beagles he loved and endless music.

When she was eight, she stood alone on a stage at The Player's Ring and sang *On My Own*, filling the room, sealing the space off from the world around it even though the windows were open to Prescott Park's summer crowds. A little girl in a fluttering deep
~~~~~

purple floral dress, with a voice of transcendent beauty. Afterwards, our friend John came over to her and told her he'd watched her father while she was singing, and no one could have looked prouder. "I know," he told her, "because that's the way I feel when my daughter sings."

~~~~~

Pittsburgh's yellow bridge is a strangely lovely sight. Sunny steel and graceful beauty, not unlike the sixteen-year-old managing the music from my passenger seat.

Early the next morning, we wound around the city in my clunky van until we found her apartment-style dormitory. A temporary parking sign in front was helpfully bedecked with cherry red balloons.

I'd slowed with each trip with her up and down four flights of stairs, not because I'd tired from the weight of what I carried but because I had a sense of the weight I'd feel as soon as I'd left her there.

Finally we stood out front, the van's blinkers on as she gently shooed me away. "I'll be fine."

I looked up at her.

"You'll be fine, too, mom. I love you. 'Bye."

~~~~~

I was still well within city limits when I took my first wrong turn and began needlessly adding to my travel time. For the next many hours I relied on inadequate directions and maddeningly changing radio reception. By the time I pulled over, completely lost, in an abandoned industrial park in Connecticut more than twelve hours later, I'd long given up scanning for stations within range and was weary even of my *Mumford & Sons* CDs.

That was when I began rifling around in the chaotic mess that had long taken over my door's capacious side pocket, though I don't know what I could have hoped to find there.

That was when, in the lot's little, wavering and buzzing overhead light, I caught a glint of gold deep among the pocket's ancient receipts, vintage paperwork, and expired Barnes & Noble coupons.

It was a CD, labeled in Sharpie in my husband's unmistakable hand: *John Hiatt.*

My husband had burned me a CD.

The thing is, I'd never remembered putting it there or ever having seen it before, and was certain I'd never listened to it.

~~~~~

I sat, holding the disc in my still wedding-banded left hand. Its pristine orange-gold was as smooth as the glossy surface of Jim's pond after a sub-zero night had vanquished a strong winter day's sun.

I turned the key in the ignition. I needed to find my way back to the highway, but also sensed I'd reached the point--though quite possibly not until that very moment--when I was meant to listen to what was on it. I took in a fathoms-deep breath and popped in the CD as I began my solo trip home.

~~~~~

Jim had made me a soundtrack of the grief he'd known was coming for me... like a burning spear in one song. Three of the songs he'd chosen for me had titles I'd used for posts I'd written on a blog I didn't create until more than a year after he died.

When I reached home, for the very first time, it would be "just my dogs and me," the subject of another song. I listened to the collection while circling back to a house that would be emptied of children for the first time since I became a parent. The songs captured me as the person he knew better than anyone, and somehow also the person I'd precariously evolved to be during years already without him. He managed to make me laugh aloud, alone at the wheel. There I was in one song, surprising my always calm husband by laughing after I'd slept off some out-sized grudge. In another, *Cherry Red*, my grammatical fanaticism tackled misplaced modifiers.

The last song, as I finally neared home, was *Circle Back*. It has the most upbeat tempo and magnetic beat I can imagine anchoring a song about loss--and involves the highly specific kind of loss experienced by a parent dropping off a child-no-more at school. I was living those lyrics as I drove, with just one small variation: I didn't have to labor at all to see my child's long-ago face as I "drove her off to college," or as I drove back to newly empty space.

~~~~~

Jim knew me better than anyone else ever could or will. He introduced me to most of the music I love.

He knew that when he was gone, gone away, my blue-silver mom van would continue to be a mess for as long as I held onto it and used it to haul our growing children from place to place.

He knew our youngest would graduate from high school and go off to college somewhere, and that I'd be taking over all the driving and helping to move in and settle our children as they left home.

He knew I would continue to get lost, in my head and in unlikely and foreboding places in the grace of day and the dead of night.

He knew I'd habitually arm myself with inadequate directions and an insufficient supply of music.

He could not have known I wouldn't unearth the CD until I was ready to listen to it.

He couldn't have known it would take years of being on my own before I happened upon a glint of gold and sliver of writing
~~~~~

on a return trip from dropping off our youngest child when she enrolled at a university much farther away than I'd ever driven on my own before.

He couldn't have known I'd get just far enough off course, and at that moment would fish around in the paper maelstrom within my reach, when there was just enough flickering yellow light over-head to make the CD call to me.

But somehow, he knew.

Part III: Spirits Divine

Darwin Finch

Photograph by James Glennon

33

Improbable Morning

In addition to the two requests he'd made in the ambulance on our way home, I'd promised my husband three things: I wouldn't keep a loaded shotgun on hand, even if I stayed in New Hampshire; I would try to take care of myself, at least through routine medical maintenance; and I would get outside, preferably with whatever child or combination of them was with me at the time. He offered no guidance on how far any of us should go, and surely knew my first steps would be tentative.

I thought at first that he'd wanted me only to keep moving, to breathe fresh air, and perhaps encounter other people and their magnificent dogs. To have adventures at any scale once he wasn't there to coax me outside settled places and routines. I may have taken his wishes for me too literally.

I think he wanted me to discern, as our children grew and finished school and began moving away, that just as they would never be so far that love didn't transcend distance; he understood that for me the yellow house would contain unbearable memories of his dying and that he'd occupy and could be found in every other place in this world. He wanted me to *want* to venture where he'd never walked with me, to places my formerly fearful self would have balked at exploring even hand-in-hand with him. From our children's commencements to Varanasi's ghats, I could make my way for both of us.

I may occasionally have outmaneuvered myself. It's not as if he didn't see that coming, too. Perhaps that's why he included a medical proviso. But the worst things that happened were not, after all, so terrible. A smattering of broken bones. Hours lost with Rufus in dark woods a few miles from another new home. Altitude sickness in the High Atlas Mountains. Obliviously wandering off an Icelandic path and receiving from my daughter a sharp alert that I was treading upon an active volcano from which sulfuric steam visibly gushed. A run-in with an unhinged Swede in apparent nicotine withdrawal on a return flight from Marrakesh. A confounding 2:00 a.m. escort from a plane during a layover in China, to be sternly questioned in a language I do not speak by seven people in gold-edged green uniforms who then abruptly and uproariously began laughing and remanded me to my sons' custody. The lengthier interrogation (fortuitously in a language I spoke) in Belfast. A bout of hemorrhagic fever from a mosquito bite in Delhi ("Don't worry, mom," my daughter told me, "A first Dengue infection is rarely fatal").

How lucky I've been.

I found the healing power of being still and of taking breaths to counts of three through five. I took steps, then traveled miles which became nearly as boundless as Jim's and stretched twice as far as even his adventurous spirit had taken him while earthbound. I went into the world far beyond my assorted doors and back again to stillness. And I found grace itself in thin spaces. In a riot of overgrown weeds in Dublin, a pair of pigeons atop Jaisalmer's Golden

Temple, and a cat who sat with me for hours before sunrise on a mountain of Sahara sand.

I found serenity when I looked up from careful sandal steps while rounding corners in the world's oldest continuously inhabited city. I saw more and less formal offerings to the Gods present in countless lives. Grace presented itself in people I've met and friends I've found--including some I'd lost for a while due to inattention and not design. We rejoined each other's lives in the aching aftermath of different losses, when nothing but genuine connection matters.

I found the gold that stayed and continued emerging when I could settle my bruised heart long enough to see what insistently remained despite the depth of the darkness. I wouldn't have occupied any of these places, physically or otherwise, without my husband's last and continuing gift to me, which is what he took away.

~~~~~

Although our yellow house had been at a small town's center, it lacked a neighborhood--the true community space and connection we'd last and best felt in Dorchester. For the first time in my adult life, I met people who met only me, not the me who was half of a living couple. If they were to know of Jim's life, it would have to be through me.

When I shifted the place I called home by only five miles, as the crow flies, my window on the world vastly changed. I wasn't the only one. Except for their plaintive reaction when I unfurled the great scarred carpet in its new room, Rufus and Brady seemed less mournfully fixated on what they, too, had to leave behind. Each walk now was a chance to meet new, more citified dogs and their humans; to sniff out infinite (and sometimes perilous) discarded flotsam; and to explore a promising new world upwind.
~~~~~

I began to see things differently, too. Not just predawn hours by the water, but the macro within the micro, which had long called to Jim. Going through his carefully catalogued photographic oeuvre, I noticed he had a frequent pattern. He first zoomed out on a landscape, took a single shot, then gradually zoomed in on elements I might not have been able to identify but for the locating shot.

I also found myself surrounded by naturally occurring works of art to which some source of light always guided me. I might not have noticed them had I not studied how and why my husband situated himself outdoors. I'd been unaware of the extent to which I'd grown to be a denizen of artificial light, often missing the effects of true light on what many people routinely overlook. I watched an enterprising bird weaving a silver lining into its nest by re-purposing a discarded strand of tinsel. Another strode forward, its beak overflowing with yellow-green buds to decorate its home. As the season sprang ahead, sunlight transfigured blue-black feathers to iridescent shades of purple and teal. Each flower, bud, and leaf was a masterwork, brilliantly back-lit in morning light as if glowing from within. Water drops became seed pearls on velvet petals. Puddled rainwater on patched black tar turned my street itself into a modern abstract canvas.

Mornings became electric.

I'd never before sought out or savored the technicolor explosions which would wash over the space between two New England states before dawn, but I'd also never before occupied quite so much sustained sleepless darkness waiting for morning. The displays didn't change so much as the beholder did.

~~~~~
~~~~~

Every morning continued to seem at least mildly improbable after night's tangled time. I awaken, and therefore am still here, even though the man I dreamed of isn't.

Perhaps I simply resigned myself to reaching nightfall once I'd made it through part of another calendar day. I realized only after I'd left the yellow house that all I would have needed to do was leave a window shade up, and I could have looked east through our bedroom window to see sunrise. I wouldn't even have had to brace for the cold of bare feet on a pine floor in winter, or cast off the quilts I'd sewn for the maple bed that became so vast when it became mine and not ours. But even in the yellow house, had I not gone outside and crept to some shore, I would have missed seeing the horizon and the twinned reflections which can only be seen there.

~~~~~

Only after seeing sunrise became much more of a production--often requiring layers of winter clothing, chipping off windshield ice to drive to the waterfront, or being speed-walked by beagles while navigating in the dark along paths of colonial bricks pitched like choppy seas--did I hardly ever miss the sight. Now I know the rhythms of storms and skies, and that the most vivid and colorful light often reveals itself far before dawn, and even longer after sundown. I became a pre-dawn devotee, dedicated above all to no longer missing what I'd missed for so long. Especially the misnomer of a sleeper sunrise: light and color so ephemeral that it's impossible to see its full glory if I'm not already there in pre-dawn blackness and facing the right way.

I'm convinced that predictive weather data can't capture these moments. They are more magical than that. I learned only by being alone on the shore, again and again and again, how a band of brilliant color will sometimes break through a bank of blue-black at
~~~~~

the horizon, then evaporate so quickly that the sleep-saturated will never even imagine it.

It is there for the restless wanderers, not the content who are satiated by restorative sleep.

~~~~~

It took me years of going outside, feeling the air and testing the ground, to learn I can't rely on my initial impression of what awaits me on a given day. I have to look longer, and in each direction.

I've since looked from vantage points I occupy only because I've unwillingly been hurled into this new life, both cleaved from and conjoined with my far more adventuresome missing half. I've watched night arrive and give way from mountaintops on three continents and atop camels in two deserts. From glaciers and waterfalls and volcanoes and the Continental Divide; from the Ganges at dawn; and while standing among Essaouira's shrieking gulls as night fell. I've dallied in a midnight-black span between Kentucky and Indiana until the sky blazed into purple and bright blue with tufts of platinum; crept onto water-slicked limestone cliffs in Pemaquid Point as they turned from gray to tiger-lily orange; and watched iridescent anti-crepuscular rays break through dawn over Delhi.

~~~~~

I began by surveying the skies near home, learning to see light that makes me feel both more at home in this world and more connected to my husband beyond it. But I've also become more reliant on senses other than sight. A student of the quasi-historical blind muezzin in *The History of the Siege of Lisbon* who could not see color, but by climbing a minaret above Lisbon could feel it in "the vibrations of the dawning light." Now I can feel, better than I can see, a harbinger on the horizon. A sliver of bright silver to the northeast, a shimmering fissure in a dense cloud bank. A thin gray-lavender parenthesis on my periphery, signaling that within an hour or so the sky will fill with neon colors--sometimes only for a minute or two--before rain begins in earnest and reduces the heavens to murky slate. I quicken my pace as water comes into view, daring to imagine some distant cosmic source of light and color is waiting for me.

Or perhaps I don't really see anything at all, and these sights are merely figments of hope.

Hope that when the sun rises, it will be miraculous, even if it doesn't stay for as long as I would have wished. That when what is in sight is too painful, something far away continues to balance me, holding me within the pull of what is not quite gravity. Faith that while I'm out there chasing light on a frigid shore, in the visible company of only a gold-eyed owl or the occasional coyote, I'm not alone. I'm still here listening to the dark I've befriended. Still here to see whatever light might break through. Still here to make my way through the night that turns to day and into darkness and light again, with or without me.

34

When September Ends

At street level: a pair of sturdy men's shoes. Thick socks over stocky ankles. Billowing orange tulle, cinched at the waist with a pink satin ribbon and fanned out into a makeshift tutu atop khaki shorts. Autumn-hued fairy wings swirled with gold glitter. Even if aerodynamically sound, they would have been hard-pressed to levitate the police officer to whose reflective neon orange vest they were affixed. He had at least a day's beard growth, wore a pink chrysanthemum-bedecked straw hat, and held a large wand instead of a baton.

Everything sparkled.

Fairy children darted among bright flowerbeds where sunlight transformed lingering dewdrops into tiny strings of lights and made velvet petals glisten with iridescent colors, as if dipped in liquid crystal. A foot-high church awaited acorn guests in their Sunday best. Tree stump homes were adorned with seashells and acorns, dusted with silver spiderweb awnings beaded with thistles.

A monarch butterfly--so rare that year that it was the first I'd seen--brushed my shoulder. It tilted its head toward a scarlet zinnia to which it veered off to pose for me.

How about this?

It flipped itself over and threw its head back, theatrically positioning its wings and waiting for me to zoom in.

And this?

It hopped to a leaf and waved at me, upside-down, so I could capture its stained-glass wings against a backdrop of lush fall grass.

None of this was a dream. I'd needed only to wander a few blocks downtown to a waterfront communal space in my new hometown to find art that crossed over into magic.

~~~~~

I'd once been at a meeting where a doctor explained that elderly people's delirium tends to worsen at night, as a patient loses the bearings and rhythms of a waking routine. Touchpoints evaporate. Perhaps it's also a function of solitude itself, or even just the perception of being alone and apart from those one loves. The psychic toll of mutual missing, even among those still here, can be immense.

When eventually my house began to empty, at least for the academic year, it was quiet but for the howling (which almost always came from the beagles). If I spoke, no human heard me. Our dogs didn't react if I paced and practiced arguments, complete with responses to imaginary judges' interruptions and opposing counsels' phantom protestations.

But if I wept, Scooter, who'd known me only as bereaved, was unlikely to rouse, while Rufus and Brady would pad over to me. Brady would carefully situate himself so as best to warm my feet. I took this as his supreme love language. But I wasn't certain even Rufus understood everything I told him.

After I'd befriended night as best I could; by day I realized I had choices. I could hole up alone or go outside. In my pocket of the world, it made me wistful to see whole families, including parents
~~~~~

with their sprites and fairies and the occasional behavioral grem-
lin. But our family had that once, and for many years. We had our
Sundays in Prescott Park and elsewhere together. Not everyone is
as lucky.

~~~~~

Wandering, unlike exile, implies the availability of a return
trip to whatever one thinks of and longs for as home. In *The Elephant's Journey*, Jose Saramago offered up a uniquely Portuguese
variant on the concept of nostalgia: *saudade*, in which its yearning
aspect is leavened with a whisper of hope that what has been lost
will indeed return someday. I thought surely German would have
an apt word to add to the mix. Perhaps it does, in *sehnsucht*, which
seems to replace *saudade's* dollop of hope with an anvil of existen-
tial recognition that our wanderers will not return any more than,
eventually, will those who yearn for them. In *Wishful Thinking*,
Frederick Buechner added a variant of such metaphorical transportation: "to summon the dead past back into the living present.
The young widow remembers her husband, and he is there beside
her."

I wonder if nostalgia is another way to remember, consciously
intermingling the dead past and the living present, and yearning
for something one knows will never be recoverable.

~~~~~

One need not have a specific faith tradition to consider the effects of indefinite exile upon both those who wander and those
left behind, or to appreciate the way a wish to be welcomed home
is interwoven with nostalgia and death itself. Etymologically, the
word 'nostalgia' entwines memory with pain and a yearning to return home. Its comparatively modern Latin origin pairs the Greek
nostos (return home) with *algos* (pain), although 'home' need not be
defined literally. It can refer to a place or person or past phase of

life. Thomas Wolfe's title, *You Can't Go Home Again,* seems to point to the paradox of what is truly home, because his novel recognizes that everyone ultimately does return there and, in death, everywhere. Death is not what's lost, but all that is gained by coming home. His protagonist explains that to die is in part "to lose the earth you know for greater knowing; [and] to lose the life you have, for greater life," in a place "more kind than home, more large than earth,"

What would we do if we had a chance to come back home, just for a day? I think I know what Jim would choose.

Thornton Wilder's *Our Town* is set in the same New England town where Jim handed off his truck's keys to me after our glorious last day of music and fellowship and laughter at a table that now has two empty chairs--his and our friend Elizabeth's. Mother Gibbs exhorts young mother Emily's ghost not to come home to replay a happy day. She reminds Emily that she won't know what lies ahead of her as she relives her chosen day, and tells her to "choose an unimportant day. Choose the least important day in your life. It will be important enough."

~~~~~

I began to learn that signs from above need not bring me to my knees. The luminous departed might tap on a shoulder, or tickle a heel as turtles splash into seawater. Or send someone on a walk past a six-foot sprite wearing sparkly wings while directing traffic. The messages and messengers our five senses percieve--a rustling doe, a radio song, a curated John Hiatt songlist--tapered off, in increments, in something of a mirror image of the way my husband had taken gradual steps to prepare me for what he knew was ahead in each important ordinary day without him.

This is what I do outside every fall.

My files are set up like this.
~~~~~

You should take my keys.
You'll get through this.

~~~~~

It was not quick. I didn't regularly feel peace for years--not until after I'd moved more than once, and not before my daughter coaxed me out into the much wider world. The path to peace began with consolidation: I began to be able to see the past, and even a glimmer of a future, along with whatever present my husband and I shared.

Instead of Sixth Sense-style visitations, I reached an understanding closer to light itself than a vision. An accommodation among what was, what might have been, and where I stand on any ordinary day. Jim's become more like Rainer Maria Rilke's departed "quiet conjurer," mixing his "bright traces into every seen thing."

~~~~~

Over time, this grief seems to cycle, from the externally visible to the internal and back around again. I could point someone to a moth still aloft after being shorn of nearly an entire wing. To sunlight breaking through stained glass windows on perfectly synchronous Hymn notes. But I can only superficially describe the tangle of memories that carries me away at any given time. I've fiercely resisted widening the space between me and my husband. But, just as he tried to ease us into lives which would go on, I began to think he planned to retreat in precisely this way, and only when he hoped I'd be ready.

At first, my heart tricked my senses into the mind's equivalent of muscle memory. I suspect my beagles-of-very-little-brain (and considerable heart) did the same. For a long time, Rufus and Brady seemed to alert, just as I did, to their hero's expected return from work. But eventually they began to adapt. They'd press their noses to the window at nightfall instead of wildly wagging and waiting to greet him at the door. Or perhaps it was only conditioned disappointment that made their hope stop springing.

Until we moved from the yellow house, I'd swear I still heard his truck on the dirt driveway. I found myself holding my breath, waiting for him to switch off the headlights I knew would never again illuminate the old brick-floored barn as he waited for a song's final notes. I knew I didn't really hear the *thunks* as he dropped his sturdy leather shoes onto the old floorboards, hosts to persistently buoyant rusty antique nails on which his workday socks snagged. But even after moving, I'd hear distant echoes of sounds uniquely his, like the light rattle of ice against glass as he swirled his right pinkie finger clockwise to more uniformly chill his drinks. His presence with me in places he never occupied is always gentle, lighter even than birds perching on thin wires.

~~~~~

Once I'd moved the first time, I was freed of the rawest imprinted memories the yellow house's dining room refused to let go. I was able better to see my husband as a carefree wanderer, exploring glorious places on his own, and sometimes with me and us. The hints were always there. His sturdy, animated ghost, whose left hand bears the the gold wedding band hanging on a chain around my neck, no longer was at my right everywhere I went. Seated next to me on our wedding anniversaries. Settled into the passenger seat while I tearfully drove to work and returned from dropping our children off in distant places. When one of our sons graduated from college, I saw my husband kneeling beside me, his camera positioned to capture the image of our son's face as it would have been had his father been there in the traditional way: more joyful than contemplative, in a robe not pinned with a white remembrance ribbon.
~~~~~

His presence was never less assured and vivid in my dreams. On our first wedding anniversary following my first move, a nightmare inserted itself into memory's dream fog. We were back at the school where we met, between the main library and Chapel during cherry blossom season. Jim was his healthy student self, wearing a brown jacket my waking self hadn't recalled remembering. As I ran to him, he turned away from me, glanced back at me over his left shoulder, and solemnly said goodbye. No explanation. A clean and devastating break. In the dream he was leaving forever at the beginning of our relationship: there would be no marriage, no children, no life together.

I awoke shaken and shaking from the dream devastation. It took time to sort out our beginnings and endings, to filter from my dream its false memory that Jim *chose* to say goodbye. I began to feel that in our world, he'd been trying to say goodbye in a different way--not a breaking off, but a handing off.

You don't need me here with you all the time any more.

He never used the word 'goodbye' when he spoke to me before he died.

There *was* a marriage and a life together, and a family of our own and the world's, and still some measure of life for me.

~~~~~

I'd soon drive the entire circumference of a country he never had a chance to see. Only once during our trip, as I squinted into overwhelming sunshine and crested a steep hill with a view of vast mountains and lenticular cloudscapes, was I overcome with the agony of missing him and of him missing this experience.

"He doesn't want me driving when I'm crying," I told my daughter. Still present tense.

"I don't either," my passenger sensibly said.
~~~~~

"Dad would have loved this trip," I wept after she encouraged me to pull over as soon as it was safe to, just as her father had on a deep winter day in New Hampshire.

"And he'd be glad we're doing this," she rightly assured me.

~~~~~

It will never be all forward progress as I navigate life without the partner who was with me every day of my adult life, until he was not.

I woke up from another dream, repeating one sentence of relief-laden hope, as if about to click the heels of my ruby slippers. In my dream, Jim and I had been packing up our family's things to move back into our yellow house.

It was all a mistake. It was all just a mistake, I heard myself murmuring as I struggled not to wake up and lose him again.

I knew the reality. It was cosmic unfairness, but not a mistake. Another family now lives in the yellow house and might now row in the pond, measure passing hours by the church chimes across the street, light fires in the beehive oven, and open eyes to sun filtered by the lace curtains previous owners left for us and I'd left where they belonged.

~~~~~

A small bridge once made it possible to reach a tiny island just off the Maine coast in Kittery. From my new house I could walk to the New Hampshire side of the span of ocean across from it. Enormous rectangular framing remains underwater, emerging at regular intervals between the shore and the island, but supports nothing. The headless pilings from which the missing wood path has been sheared off still stand upright. The island's lone man-made structure has long been empty, the barren spaces within it expanding over time. Its beams have been weathered down by storms. Foundational stone has spilled back into the sea. Earth has eroded.

You can't get there from here anymore, as Mainers are said to say. Even if you could, there's no longer color or life there, apart from the birds touching down or hovering above it when the wind calms. Yet it is a comforting and enduring presence. When the building's shell is visible only in silhouette, it is indistinguishable from a memory of its former self, when it was whole.

There comes a moment each morning when the rising sun seems to swallow its shell completely, before reappearing in the unforgiving daylight that again lays its emptiness bare. It supplies scale to a rising full moon. By lingering steadfastly in the background, it magnifies and brightens and anchors each sunrise I see as I somehow remain standing, alone on a farther shore.

35

A Late Summer Night's Dream

It took years before I was ready to travel by myself overnight. There was never any question in my mind that my first destination had to include Maine's Bar Harbor.

Apart from my father's sabbatical years, my brothers and I had grown up in Massachusetts. There was the minor curiosity of 'summering' on Long island, but that was restricted to what appeared to be old barracks at a secure nuclear research facility. There, my father had been among what I later gathered was a contingent of physicists from World War II's Allied nations. But despite Maine's proximity to home, we'd never ventured there when I was growing up. We'd only once gone with my father even over the New Hampshire border.

When I was very young, my father would occasionally dispatch me to visit my grandmother in Brooklyn, New York. He'd cap a terrifying, seat belt-bereft dash to Logan Airport by sprinting up escalators to an about-to-close gate and wildly searching for a loading passenger willing temporarily to claim me as a child or grandchild during the flight. This apparently significantly reduced my tickets' costs. For someone who dwelled in the theoretical and everlasting unseen, my father could be quite concretely thrifty.

As our family grew, Jim and I began taking our little ones to Acadia National Park, which we'd first visited during a rare overlapping break. I'd just taken the Bar Exam and was about to begin the job that would turn out to be my life's calling. Our family was just the two of us, and our hearts were certain that one day there would be more.

Jim had driven north in the Olds Delta 88, otherwise known as the Living Room on Wheels. It had a plush red velour interior that prompted far less family-friendly nicknames, and evidently screamed 'short-term renters' when we eventually drove it around while seeking to purchase a first home. A quarter-million miles already were under its fan belt when we liberated it from a Sunapee junkyard in which it faced almost certain compression to a metal cube. Or perhaps two or three. It would prove to be our sturdiest and most dependable vehicle.

~~~~~

Jim always did the highway driving. Always glancing left more than right as he drove. Always keeping the beat of some song in his head.

Highway driving is among the fears I eventually realized I'd jettisoned once I had to take over the wheel for good.

Although that first summer camping trip to Acadia was made with no little beings in our car, that had never dampened my excitement about cloud formations.

"That one looks like a dinosaur--well, maybe more like a triceratops with gazelle horns? Look! An *eclair!* And a banana split, right next to it, by that little pile of cream puffs--Oh! I've got it! it looks like a *croquembouche!*"
~~~~~

"Getting hungry, Steph?" My husband smiled.

~~~~~

The first time we returned to Acadia as parents, our happy, curly-haired one-year-old, wearing red Osh Kosh corduroy and perched in a pack on his father's back, kept turning to face me. It was a rainy early October day. Jim was just ahead of me, taking his assured long strides around the path ringing Jordan Pond.

Sam laughed every time a raindrop tickled his cheek, or a footfall made him bounce and settle back into the green canvas seat of the backpack his father carried him in. I woozily, queasily followed, pregnant with our second child.

We would return there with our sons, and then their sister, and another. Noah would lose his first baby tooth while visiting Acadia. He didn't bat an earnest blue eye at the logistics of navigating the Tooth Fairy's toll-free number to report the need for an extra-jurisdictional collection.

~~~~~

I could still see our young family in every nook of the Park Loop. Our children hand-in-hand with their dad, all in feather-weight summer cotton I'd sewn, traversing wide rocks atop Cadillac Mountain. Skipping pebbles across the water at Sandy Beach, where our Sam and Noah were startled when another mom called out the same names to similarly aged sons. It was a feat not since duplicated in my presence even at sea in Ecuador, where Sam 2.0 disembarked just before Noah 2.0's arrival. I could see in my mind the bright yellow midriff-level flower on the first swimsuit our younger daughter wore in the pond near Bubble Rock where Jim swam with our children and tickled her belly. She'd laughed and laughed, setting off a chain reaction of merriment among her siblings.

~~~~~
~~~~~

It was autumn again. All our children were away, three at school and one doing research across the world. As I began driving north, I realized it was the first overnight trip I'd ever planned by myself. I also realized that, other than hospital stays, I'd never spent a night away from any place we'd called home together in just my own company.

By 3:00 the next morning I'd slipped out of a Bed & Breakfast onto the Park Loop Road to make my way up Cadillac Mountain. There, I turned north by northeast toward the spot where I remembered our young children pointing out land formations and pockets of sea. I was at the highest point of the mountain where the sun makes its earliest appearance on the Eastern seaboard. A thick, bubbling blanket of slate-tinged clouds hovered on the horizon. The spot where the sun would break through was heralded by a thin ribbon of simmering orange sky and a hyphen of brilliant pink light.

~~~~~

By the time most people on the island were beginning to awaken, I was standing on another Eagle Lake's shore, taking pictures of a photogenic bright teal kayak against a backdrop of deeper teal water when the kayak's owner appeared. He took one look at me and, notwithstanding the convenient shadows my Red Sox cap cast over me, said, "You look like you lost your best friend."

The kayak's owner happened to be a retired therapist--evidently a pretty good one--and lived on the Island's other side. Already a practiced seeker of the disappearance of day as well as night, I seized the opportunity to ask where he'd recommend going in search of sunset. Hours later, I followed his careful directions.

At first I missed the sunset spot's well hidden entrance, and continued along the road while fierce wind and rain began sweep-
~~~~~

ing through. Southwest Harbor promptly settled under fog so thick and opaque that I could barely make out a scarlet-beaconed lighthouse only yards away from me. Hoping it would clear, I hiked around the Island and retraced my steps.

Just as the sun began to poke through the woods, I found the trailhead that had been described to me. I began my trek from the main road, which angled into an increasingly claustrophobic path, from asphalt to gravel to dusty earth carpeted with crisped brandy pine needles.

The trail was lined with an increasingly dense collection of trees and overgrown sea grasses, hushing my steps. As bird songs fell away, I saw saltwater-weathered trees. They were deeply bowed, but not broken, and empretzeled over the years into shadowed fairy tale creatures.

Finally, the path veered sharply, an elbow pushing through a regiment of evergreens. I continued past a small orchard of gnarled crab apple trees and black-edged white butterflies whose wings caught the reawakening sun as it dipped. They were surrounded by a cloud of dragonflies' flickering silver-plum flashes.

Almost as suddenly as the path reached another cluster of shadowed deep woods, it emerged at an even narrower razor's edge of space through piled boulders to the rocky shore and a perfect view west to a lingering gold-dusted sunset.

All by myself, but never entirely alone.

This time, I did not cry at every moment. I watched the sun nestle down at the horizon to emerge a half-world away, where my daughter might see it rise. Even the birds were silent as night's royal purple shroud was laid over the sea.

36

Dead Reckoning

Exactly five years after that final March day, I went to the shore before work. This time none of my children was in tow or towing me. By then Jim had not taken thousands of photographs. He'd missed large swaths of our children's lives. The most recent commencement had been especially hard for me, not because it had poured so ferociously, but because it was on the campus where we met, and his absence there seemed so magnified. It had taken me three-and-a-half years to take off my wedding band even occasionally, and two-and-a-half years for me just to manage the transition from the soft, sibilant "passed away" to the occasional abrupt "died."

~~~~~

I'd dined with ghosts before. My friend Tineke remained my standing date for anniversary-dinners-which-should-have-been, but this was an impromptu meeting after my work took me to a State Police lab in her direction. We sat across from each other that night in an otherwise empty Thai restaurant and talked after ordering an unseemly amount of food; she remains dedicated to trying to get me to eat properly.
~~~~~

At one point, she asked me if Jim was at the table, which had an available chair to my right.

I hemmed only for a second and felt myself frown as I slowly shook my head. "Well, he has a lot going on. A lot of places to be."

And I envisioned him in great detail--this time not at my side, but hiking among mountains I'd never actually seen, although they reminded me of Scotland. Assuredly he was somewhere in the great outdoors just then, and not sitting with us in a restaurant in Lawrence.

While it may have been problematic that my mental state was such that I felt I had to apologize to my dinner companion for my late husband's absence from the table, Tineke was unperturbed.

I thought about her question and my answer and realized there had been some shift in the way I looked at empty seats. I hadn't re-flexively saved a seat in the stands for Jim at the most recent commencement. But just a year earlier, at another graduation, I'd felt his presence so keenly that I could precisely describe the space he occupied--five paces to my right, on one knee, balancing his camera on the balcony overlooking the ceremony while waiting for our child's name to be called.

"Is he letting me go?" I asked Tineke, once I realized Jim was neither at the table, nor even in the restaurant.

"What do you think?" She turned the answer into another question, as therapists and lawyers are wont to do. Dinners can take some time.

I think we both knew I really meant, "Am I letting him go?"

On one level I realized it was silly of me to think he had other things to do now--places to explore, and people to greet and watch over, once he did not need to keep an eye on me every second lest I fall to pieces. I no longer wept quite so frequently and unpre-dictably. To some degree I was learning to carry on for both of us.

~~~~~

That was about the time when I realized I needed to move again.

From my bedroom window, the moon was slightly southeast. On clear nights it would hang, bright white, above tall pine trees, balanced like a Christmas star. My next home would be in a larger city and face north by northwest diagonally into sunset. There, I'd have only a three-block walk straight to a harbor sunrise.

Jim's undergraduate thesis research had involved gathering data to discern whether it was magnetite that enables homing pigeons to navigate their way home over great distances and without external cues. I can see him still, as I never actually saw him at the time, wearing a dark blue polo shirt with a white pigeon insignia as he released lavender-tinged gray birds into summer winds far from their Massachusetts home base.

Pigeons remain special to me.

Apparently more recent research had pointed to a way to speed up pigeons' return trips: the "Widowhood Method" places home-bound pigeon spouses in proximity to members of the opposite sex. Pigeons mate for life, and the mere companionship of other pigeons has been suggested to accelerate their mates' already wondrous ability to find their way home.

My husband was always ahead of his time.

~~~~~

I've never been nearly as sure of my coordinates in this world as Jim was. Nor had I felt appreciably less unmoored since the beginning of my years without him.

Kuuk Thaayorre of Pormpuraaw, in Cape York, Australia, greet each other by asking in what direction they are going. Professor Lera Boroditsky noted in an interview that a typical response would approximate "Southsoutheast, in the middle distance."

This ability to locate oneself by cardinal direction requires staying constantly attuned to one's location at a concrete visible scale. With practice, it becomes second nature: Professor Boroditsky found that after spending just a week in Pormpuraaw she could orient herself as Kuuk Thaayorre did, envisioning herself from above as a dot moving on a map.

It is another form of dead reckoning I don't possess. I can't even keep left and right straight.

But I do now have a strangely detailed visual memory of the earth beneath my feet that is preserved in my expanding map of the world, and I now can draw and build on it. If I were to be plunked back into Kyoto, I could retrace our steps and point out the spot by the canal where my children and I saw a mother and four ducklings. I could find my way to the strip of sand near the Irish Sea where a long-haired caramel-and-cream dog the size of an insubstantial sandwich yapped with hilarious ferocity as he stood guard against high winds. I could point to precisely the spot in Dublin where the small seashell filled with Jim's ashes wafted into the water, a spray of them lifted by wind into an arc that glittered in the setting sun against blue on blue so compatible that one would have been hard-pressed to distinguish heaven from earth.

37

Birthdays of the Dead

Before leaving the country for her next adventure, my daughter took me to Iceland, where we found wonders like bubbled lava fields and ashy sulfuric gusts which would burst from a volcano's perimeter, evaporate, and billow again. Like trick candles that can't be blown out. My mind kept revisiting that sight when, not long afterward, it was my husband's birthday again.

We were again approaching winter holidays we'd been celebrating in miniature without him. The mighty mom van had been exchanged for a small car with better gas mileage, fewer seats, and barely enough space for the Charlie Brown Christmas tree Noah brought home from a Yankee Swap at his grandparent's house. Even Scooter remained so tiny that he could nest in a sousaphone's flared bell or be tucked into my jacket for the unparalleled warmth of a heart beating next to mine.

The Lilliputian scale was apt for a surviving spouse of my dimensions. I was dwarfed not only by my husband's towering height but also the bounty and breadth of the family I married into. At every holiday gathering each surface groans (as, hours later, may only slightly regretful overindulgers) with specialties of the assorted houses. Pans of potatoes so dense with cheese that it is a wonder light can escape their bubbling browned surfaces. Platters of spiral-cut honeyed ham. Everything in Glennon households is abundant, unlike us tentative, practical Martins. My parents' teak-shuttered liquor cabinet still housed bottles which had resided there for guests' consumption since my childhood. This would probably be the case even had visitors not noticed that my father, who tended always toward consolidation in his quixotic stand against entropy, would occasionally merge unlike substances--like gin and vodka dregs--within the same wan vessels.

Jim's mark on his family, his work, and the world, is also out-sized.

~~~~~

After we returned home following my cliff mishap in Vik--completely my fault, and my daughter had just again warned me of my footwear's inadequacy--I'd had follow-up x-rays at the hospital where my husband had worked, so the orthopedist could check on the status of my healing bones and I could thereafter make the acquaintance of yet another member of the physical therapy roster.

The hospital receptionist asked me about the daughter who'd accompanied me on my trip. My husband's name came up.

"Oh," she smiled. "I was wondering if you were related to *our* Doctor Glennon."

English does not seem to have a word for a smile accompanied by tears not of the wistful kind. I'm not sure even Old Uzbek does.

~~~~~

Our Doctor Glennon.

He wasn't just ours, and I'm glad for that. He was a loving and loved friend, a brother and son and uncle and nephew and cousin. A physician, a reader, a sharp wit and a gentle prankster. A masterful nature photographer, a musician, a coach and troop leader, and a self-taught astronomer. Years already had passed since his death, and I was glad to be reminded he belongs to others as well, and that they still think about him, too.

~~~~~

Rainer Maria Rilke wrote of attracting the dead by leaving out bread and milk, and of the transformative intersection of the unseen and our visible present: "the magic of earthsmoke and rue." Rilke's native German provides a homophone shared by the words for eyelid (*lidern*) and song (*liedern*). The roses in his self-authored epitaph have folds like closed eyelids, the sleep of death, but they are also luminous and enduring and beautiful, like a song.

Like Rilke's resurrected roses, like the pairing of death's earthsmoke with rue of the healing variety--and perhaps even something like Schrödinger's cat--the dead are at once seemingly opposite things: seeing but unseeing, dark and bright, buried and still and always wandering.

As a transitive verb, 'rue' occupies the same bittersweet space as regret--which, like guilt, seems to lock aspects of grief firmly into place when it's too late to fix what might at least have been eased or better understood. Things not done or said can never be certain to have been understood. Unasked questions cannot be answered. But as a noun, 'rue' is a yellow flower, a medicinal herbal balm. It calls to mind not only Robert Frost's paean to the curative power of a dusting of snow fallen from a hemlock tree, but also the healing power of each leaf, as expressed in Amy Gerstler's poem, *In Perpetual Spring*, which our son Sam read for his father in Phillips Church.

I am not without regret, especially for the places my fears kept me from going with my husband. But I can feel his healing presence wherever I now find myself.
~~~~~

38

Windows on the World

As with many aspects of grace, harmony had a special meaning to Frederick Buechner. He described it in *Wishful Thinking* as the place to which each person is called, where their "deep gladness and the world's deep hunger meet." While hungering for my husband to be here with me, the order changed: my hunger sought out the world's gladness, and I needed to locate it in harmony not only with nature and the beings within my daily orbit, but among strangers and in the much broader world.

Thanks to my peripatetic daughter, I found myself in more than one such harmonious place.

~~~~~

It was only in the high 90s when we traveled from Delhi to Rajasthan on a rickety plane. We sojourned overnight in what appeared to be a bus's overbooked overhead luggage compartment, then boarded a thunderously sashaying seatless train to the desert city of Jaisalmer, composed in layered shades of gold. The 11th Century fort on the hill to our left glowed in powerful sun. Mottled beige and cream cows and goats neither yielded nor looked up as I sat on a motor scooter and placed my arms around a
~~~~~

textile merchant's waist before we careened away and across town. As I glanced back, I saw Emma standing in the store's door-less doorway, stacks of mirrored jewel-colored cotton and waffled silk behind her. Intricate overlays of carved ochre stone framed the windowless overlooks above her.

My mission: to extract negotiable currency from my bank account, the corpus of which lay half-a-world away. I simply could not have left this place without buying some of that fabric for my fiber artist mother. I was wearing my daughter's tea-and-thyme airy cotton kurta, a little worse for wear given our overnight accommodations. It would endure yet more during our trip's next leg, overnight by camel toward the Pakistani border.

I was not wearing a helmet.

My reticent mother would have been appalled by just about every facet of this adventure, with the possible exception of the red embroidered fabric I would bring home to her. My daughter seemed pleasantly surprised. I'm confident her father would have been delighted to behold this scene in a place and space I never would have occupied had he not bequeathed to me some of his spirit of adventure, and had my daughter not shown me there was nothing to fear in exercising it.

Her father would have signed on for the full-week camel safari, not just two days, and tied on a scarf and peered ahead into blinding sun with eyes that had, until the end, given him a better than 20/20 view of the world.

He would have looked back at our brilliant, adventuresome, citizen-of-the-world daughter and turned his head forward again before she noticed, so as not to unnerve her by beaming too brightly at the adult she'd become. If he'd survived me, he would have been there with her and I'd have been at home in New England, still afraid to venture on a single form of transportation among the many which ultimately had deposited us outside the Golden Fort.

Had he been there, our daughter would have been spared monitoring her parent for signs of dehydration, plying me with water, alerting me when I was not permitted to take pictures and what I was not permitted to photograph, and coaxing me to expand my culinary choices.

But there I was. And because I was there, and because our daughter suggested we explore the walled Fort, we'd almost completed our lap around it when she saw a narrow stone stairway to an open air enclosure where we could get hot chai and rest, I found myself sharing a thin space with her.

I sat next to her and looked up from the rich tea and small metal cup that radiated its heat. Just beyond her shoulder, two silver-blue pigeons landed on a spouted spot high on the temple directly across from us.

I'll never be able to explain how, and am unconcerned with why, but I knew from looking at those pigeons that her father was there with us. He didn't say anything this time; he didn't need to.

~~~~~

Emma might have been in Ghana, or possibly Australia, when I next found myself atop a camel; she'd become easy to lose track of. This time I was in Morocco, lured out of my comfort zone by my friend Robin, who we'd met in Ecuador and had fallen into our lives as an enduring friend. This time, a limitless tapestry of rich sand was dappled by hoof prints roughly the size and shape of plump swaddled newborns. With each tread, a spray of pure gold would rise, hover in sunlight, and enfold itself back into the dunes. It wasn't nearly as hot as Jaisalmer, and infinitely drier.

My elaborately wound scarf had not come undone, and neither had I. I'd held steady where some others had lurched, given the
~~~~~

abrupt toe-to-heel reclining process camels seem to favor. I carefully downed 18 ml of filtered water every six minutes, having learned my lesson while hiking in the High Atlas Mountains. I was following rehydration instructions furnished by my new astrophysics student friend from Adelaide, one half of one of the couples who made up our group and have remained my friends. My camera hadn't yet fallen into the towering dune from which its shutter would emerge unforgivingly at sundown, as crystalline sheaths of stars began communing. A grain of sand embedded in its lens filter would appear like a hurtling meteor in the upper right corner of every shot I later took.

Meanwhile, I hewed to the guide's newly coined 'Stephanie rule,' which required I maintain both hands securely atop Geronimo's Berber rug saddle--even when he paused photogenically and cast his magnificent shadow across the dunes.

I was starting to get this camel safari thing *down*.

It's among phrases Jim couldn't remotely have thought I'd be likely to think or speak during the days, years, and likely decades when he could no longer be at my side.

~~~~~

Night in the desert was far from silent. Nomadic, highly allergenic cats mewed before curling up to nap upon campers' chilly feet. Our astrophysicist narrated the heavens for us. Bare feet thudded on rugs dotted with sand lagoons.

Even at a distance, I discerned that Geronimo, splayed with somewhat less grace than his regal sphinx-like brethren, had borborygmi.

It could have been my recent bout of altitude sickness; as unaccustomed as I am to hallucinogens, I suppose it also could have had something to do with the sprig of *Artemisia absinthium* that had adorned our cups of mint tea. But whatever its organic source, for
~~~~~

the first time in my life I had waking hallucinations while sleepless in the Sahara.

I saw filigreed ochre arches morphing into imaginary birds and horned magical creatures and back again, a Möbius of ancient design melting into myth. I'm glad for my memories of the long-disappeared artistry, which far outweigh the temporary malaise. I somehow acutely experienced every sense of each moment as the vast past's residuum danced before my eyes.

~~~~~

As I watched the sun slowly set before being swept away on a lavender-orange wing of clouds, I felt kinship with a Kiran Desai character in *The Inheritance of Loss*, who "seemed not to have traveled forward in time but far back," and "in attendance upon infinity," like "a creature of the Galápagos staring over the ocean." Once again I found myself in an ancient landscape that I surely wouldn't have occupied had I not found myself wandering in a world I no longer feared. I understood that beautiful and terrible things will continue to unfold, with or without me, and no matter where I am and have been and may be.

And I no longer asked Jim one of two questions that most tormented me: *Where are you now?*

I had my answer. He's everywhere we are and everywhere I'll ever be for both of us, including ancient forts with partnered pigeons and the narrow beach by the Irish Sea where red-gold sand dunes are bracketed by watercolor skies.
~~~~~

39

Widow's Walks and Rambles

"Wish you were here..."

It was a header on an email my husband sent me while he and our daughters were off on planes big and small after fortifying themselves with shots against mosquito-borne illnesses. Their adventure had neatly combined my fears of needles, deadly infectious diseases, and aircraft. Jim was deliriously happy to have had a chance to take a trip with them, and I was equally as glad to volunteer to stay home with Brady, who'd been anxious and destructive during his first weeks with us. Being *Beagle Quarterly* cover-boy handsome only got him so much mileage in those days.

Jim rarely went away on his own, and when he did it tended to be for an annual three-day medical conference. Such an absence was more than enough for things to fall apart at home. I'd become embroiled in a project and forget to turn off the stove until I smelled something burning or heard an emptied kettle clattering. Although this was expressly the reason he'd given me an eardrum-piercing high-frequency shrieking tea kettle, it only had so far a range, and sometimes I think deeply.

Invariably at least one of us would get very sick as soon as there was no doctor in the house. Jim's clothing would turn shades of pink, including a particularly hideous muddy hue if it had started out gray or khaki. I favor bright red and have never been discriminating while tossing in loads of laundry. He would occasionally look at his formerly white socks curiously, but he was a practical man and did not tend to discard things for mere aesthetic failings.

He and our son Noah once returned from a weekend of sub-zero camping in the White Mountains and located me at my desk in our shared office space. High winds and dense snow *whooshed* in through a broken windowpane to my right as I occupied myself at the computer next to it. I wore two puffy winter coats, one of them Jim's.

I saw the question forming and explained I'd swatted at a fly on the window. With a stapler. He nodded thoughtfully, in that way of his.

I see.

A car battery would die because I'd left an interior light on after searching for misplaced keys. An essential and shockingly expensive vehicle part would hurl itself onto the highway. The latter happened at least twice, and the former with some frequency. More than once, I managed to lock myself out of the house, in slippers and alone with the beagles in an ice storm. Food would burn and spoil. Pots would be encrusted with black starch, requiring the strength of a solidly muscled human to scour them. I would leave the clattering mountain to soak in the sink until Jim returned. The printer would jam or run out of ink when I was working under an urgent and immovable filing deadline. Electricity would short out somewhere crucially important to the household's functioning.

Brady or Rufus would somehow escape, and I'd search the woods for hours, pitifully calling out *"treeeeaaaaat"* (always, but always, in a downpour). Something or someone inside--usually the newest canine addition to the family--would overflow in epic fashion.

Two or three days without him had been nearly impossible. And when he left with our daughters for that trip, they'd be gone for ten days.

Ten whole days.

When I moved the second time, it had been more than two thousand days since he'd come home.

~~~~~

The day after Mother's Day, a few days before driving to Pennsylvania for another graduation, I moved again. My new surroundings were by no means out of my comfort zone. I chose another New England seaport town brimming with clapboard and brick homes from the 1600s through 1800s. Most recently I'd maintained an 1860s home base for my children, and at least one of them had always lived there with me. But, like grief and Tralfamadorian time, historical relocation is not always linear.

~~~~~

This time I headed back to 1802, a few years before the yellow house had been built. I also went south, circling back and closer to the place I still also thought of as home: where I was born and grew up, worked, and began my life with Jim.

I packed up everything, including what seemed like cubic tons of Emma's books. She was on another continent and had needed to be able to travel as lightly as her father had when he'd carried a hammock and backpack into woods. For the second time, I found myself at the crest of a hill, atop a sturdy granite foundation. This time, the house was sided with bricks. Two centuries of fierce regional storms had neither felled it, nor even made it list. Narrow roads radiated from the waterfront and ascended to my new home like a folding fan's monture.

It seems impossible to resist peeking through the street-facing windows of such houses when walking dogs at night. Simulated candles hold blandly steady, never flickering in wind, as Colonial candles must have when wind swept in through seams and horse-hair plaster. I correctly suspected adorable local mice might continue to find their way inside through fieldstone foundations.

Closer to the water, according to my beagles' eyes and noses, much larger and more floridly scented creatures roamed. On the busy main road where magnificent colonial houses soldier on, many of the oldest and grandest are topped with a widow's walk. Were they at ground level, where neighbors wander to shops and farmer's markets, they'd resemble ordinary porches. Aloft, they're both majestic and eerie. Some have ornate carved balustrades painted ghostly white. Elevated above the old Captains' houses, the small enclosures occupy their own solitary plane, like the crow's nest outlook on an old sailing ship's mast. I imagine lachrymose long-departed wives standing and casting thousand-yard stares down toward the port to which their spouses never returned. They would have floated above their neighbors, having ascended those extra steps closer to heaven. Outside any fray and steeped in solitude.

I studied these houses every day on my own earthbound path, always chosen by a certain beagle who still hilariously fancied himself an alpha dog.

"But why does he always look so sad?" I remembered asking Jim.

"Because he's a beagle?"

When he'd walked them, Rufus and Brady used to run ahead of my husband, until one or the other realized he was too exhausted to proceed. They'd never merely walked with him; nor did they pull him. They did both with me. When I moved this time, Brady hadn't visibly aged, but Rufus's muzzle had whitened enough that other dog people--and my new hometown proved to be the Best Dog Town anywhere--instantly recognized him as a vintage model. Although he rarely would run anymore, Rufus would pull me at a steady, quick clip downhill to the waterfront park, nose burrowed in particles of the past until we reached it. There, he'd round the same old granite post, thicker than two tombstones, then proceed to the low boardwalk railing, where he'd raise his deep brown eyes to scan the sea and sky.

By October the harbor would be empty of all but the most stalwart working vessels. Summer pleasure craft would be hoisted on hanging belts and lifted from frigid water. I'd look up where the space between the waterfront and the old white church spires on the hill above it was filled with masts and rigging, a graveyard of ships out of water shrouded in heavy white plastic that reflected harsh sunlight and glowed in moonlight.

~~~~~

Meanwhile, my daughter continued to send me an occasional snapshot of the world far, far outside my changing windows' frames. She'd seen white nights in Russia, a bright green flash at the horizon's vanishing point, and a rare Queen of the Night cactus whose buds flower only for moments in the middle of a single midsummer night. In one photograph she was at the bottom of the sea, a neon-striped blue and yellow fish obscuring her. She photographed golden temples in Myanmar and tagged giant fruit bats in Africa and Australia and East Asia. She described the briefly detained bats as "giant sky puppies" whom the research team named after viruses, as she had with smiling Ruby (short for Rubella), whom she fed drops of fruit juice before returning her and her companion to their high havens.
~~~~~

"Mom," she'd asked while planning one summer's research, "How would you feel about my catching plague rats in Madagascar?"

Her father's daughter, allowing me to marvel at some of what she'd discovered.

~~~~~

Much closer to each home, alone, I continued to witness countless feats both of light and decay. I've stumbled across a tiny strip of beach when the cloud cover was, just for seconds, so perfectly apportioned that it encased the rising sun with a diaphanous curtain that then pulled back from both sides. *Ta da!*

The more I pushed myself to get outside, the more I felt that it is not just that Jim wanted us to linger before such panoramas, but also to take in whatever we see along the way--including the wreckage. Each season's flotsam contained infinite one-of-a-kind creations collapsed into each other. So much lost and so much left behind to reconstitute itself. Everywhere I've gone--even when a step in any direction would plunge a bare ankle into a garbage-filled, fetid hole--I've been surrounded by naturally occurring wonders.

Station Eleven, a novel of a post-pandemic world, described a version of this paradox and of the "beauty in the decrepitude" of "[t]his dazzling world."

Still spinning.
~~~~~

40

God's Golden Eyes

Our lives catch on assorted nails. (In my husband's voice, I hear, *"You say that like it's a bad thing."*)

Zooming in on a memento, or the pixels or paint strokes or other renderings of a work of art--like one of my husband's photos--I see the stunning color, the patterns, the movement, and the life that existed as of one moment in time on both sides of the lens.

Jim took a picture of a Galápagos dove during his last December. In flesh, feather, and delicate bone, this beautiful bird must long ago have soared from this mortal coil. But there he is, still with us through my husband's eyes. A blur from purposeful forward movement on black-tipped coral feet; a dab of yellow and a streak of vivid magenta above earth-toned wings, as if he'd brushed against a freshly painted canvas. Animated bright eyes. Pulling back, he is part of the landscape and the contained world where our family took its last trip together. Part of an enduring species found only in such warmth and isolation. A majestic messenger among the legions of creatures whose sounds I listen for every day.

Accumulating birthdays of the dead are among these sometimes rusty nails. I still write to Jim, especially on his birthdays.

Just after midnight, when the calendar calls up that day, and whether it's tepid or frozen rain taps like weakened woodpeckers against black windows, I speak aloud to the magical intersection between past and present.

It's your birthday, I always begin....

~~~~~

Dear Jim,

I was awake long before you would have hoped for me. This morning, I was in one of my favorite places, just beyond the dunes only a few miles from here. Somehow, we never stopped there, even when we went across the bridge from Salisbury that day we went for breakfast when Suzannah was a baby, then brought the kids to the boardwalks at the Wildlife Refuge for the first time. It was so cold, but you were glad to have the whole island shore to ourselves and point out the heartier winter birds.

Today the sun broke through the clouds on my way back from the marsh and made a spotlight on a gold-eyed snowy owl who turned and looked straight at me before he closed his eyes again.

As you know, subtlety isn't my strong suit. A few years ago, I picked up a novel because of it's title--The Inheritance of Loss--and discovered Kiran Desai, an author I wish I'd found in time to introduce her to you. She described a mother whose son had left her, not forever, but only for another continent. She "was weeping because she had not estimated the imbalance between the finality of good-bye and the briefness of the last moment" with him.

I don't need to tell you why those words will stay with me.

Of course, I still have the soundtrack you left me for what comes after a final goodbye, and I've seen you quite a bit since then. I saw you at graduation and at Jazzy's wedding in Wiscasset, and with my father at Mount Auburn. I see you wherever I go to take pictures, especially in winter. The quiet helps me focus on what only you and I can see. I listen to
~~~~~

*the music you left for me and the music that somehow keeps being writ-
ten.*

*I've taken your place as best as I can for everything you would have
spared me. I've learned to do some of the less backbreaking chores you did.
Finances still give me agita, but I muddle through. I held it together to
have the conversations you would have had with my father, and then my
mother, so I could take charge the way you would have when the time
came.*

*Although I imagine you're still watching over us carefully, on the off
chance you haven't noticed the new return address, after I finally moved
back here your sister Catherine told me you told her you knew I'd need
to--obviously way before I knew. You were right.*

*This morning Rufus, who I think misses you the way I do, looked so
sad after I cleaned up a mess he'd made. I recognize that's a fine line away
from his "Are you sure you haven't forgotten my mom-is-going-to-work
treat?" face, and I told him what you would have: "You're still a good boy.
Just be the best beagle you can. It will always be good enough."*

*I'm sorry I didn't work harder on being the person I should have been
when you were here. I'm sorry I was such a blubbering mess from the moment you were diagnosed. I'm sorry I didn't find your black-and-white
photos for you when you had time, even though never enough time, to
work with film again and play your guitar and do anything you wanted
to do. I'm sorry for everything I didn't adequately treasure when I could
have. But of course, you didn't think there was anything to forgive, because that's the stuff you're made of.*

*That day you came home from the hospital, I told you I'd miss you
every second of every day. I caught the very quick wince. I think I understand now. It's not that you thought I was exaggerating. It's that you
knew I wasn't. You didn't want the rest of my life to be defined by the
missing. The dark negative space always pulling me in. You hoped I'd*

find a way to understand you'd still be with me, keeping me imperfectly afloat.

I'm doing my best.

Love always and always,
S.

41

Riding with Royalty

When we began acquiring canine family members, we negotiated how related duties would be carried out. Jim understood my line in the sand: if there ever came a time when one of our dogs was so ill as to need dispositive veterinary intervention, Jim would be the one to hold him and see him through. Even felony prosecutors are only so tough. And no matter what defense counsel may say about me, even off the record, I'm not in fact entirely heartless.

But that would fall on me, too--the first time, just six weeks after I'd moved back to Massachusetts and into a home I chose in large part because it had a fenced garden where the beagles would be safe. And I knew Brady would love to smell the flowers, especially the pink roses.

~~~~~

Tom Brady, Male tri-color
Age: 1 - 1 1/2
Why here? Stray, found in Nottingham
Responds to Name: Yes
House trained: semi
~~~~~

The Stratham SPCA card's penultimate question's answer was a bit of puffery and its last would prove inaccurate. And he was a *beauty*: heavy on the caramel, tinged with russet-gold. Stunning cinnamon eyes. When he curled up to sleep *just so*, dappled black swirls on the purest white created an M. C. Escher image of intertwined platypuses. He was snipped before we were permitted to bring him home to us and to Rufus, who we'd adopted a year-and-a-half earlier ("from a K-I-L-L shelter in Indiana," we always whispered if asked, spelling out the offending word even if the beagles weren't listening). After his operation, with its impingement upon his capacity to, well, tomcat around, we decided to cast off the 'Tom' as well. He became Brady.

Brady of Nottingham, a gentle prince among beagles.

Brady's needs were relatively simple, but his phobias were entrenched. He'd been on his own in the woods, perhaps a hunter's puppy who'd run away or been discarded: anyone could see he was incapable of harming a fellow creature. He was highly motivated by food, or any substance bearing the most tangential resemblance to it. His IQ, which our children carefully measured, was sub-optimal. Nonetheless, he was at least an accessory to, and quite possibly a principal in, the Great Sausage Calzone Disappearance of 2015. His emotional intelligence was off the charts. He howled with heartbreak when Jim's soul slipped from our home, then came to me and quietly nuzzled me as I sat, stunned and broken, on the kitchen floor. I would swear there were tears in his eyes as he bowed his cloud-soft head into my lap.

He was a lover, not a fighter. Suzannah said she'd never name a favorite among her beloved beagles, but Brady "was by far the sweetest, never started fights, never deliberately disobeyed or tried to get away with thing (*Ahem*, Scooter). He was always the pushover of the group, always giving up his beds and treats if one of the others wanted them. He may not have had the best listening or learning skills or bladder control but he still always tried his best."

During his years with us, his fear of men in SUVs abated. He remained pathologically afraid of thunder and fireworks. We'd have to bundle him in blankets and hold him as he shook, his white-tipped tail locked between his legs.

He loved to lick the floor, an odd habit that dovetailed nicely with my disinterest in cleaning.

He developed a curious tendency to show up at one's feet and park himself quietly there for as long as the feet were willing to stay in place. He was a most excellent foot warmer.

And in the last six weeks of his life, Brady seemed the most content he'd ever been. He adored basking in his new garden, smelling each late spring and early summer bud. He let the bright pink bleeding hearts tickle his glorious ears, and wandered among successive blooms: magenta peonies, four shades of roses, plate-sized orange tiger lilies. The blush pink roses were his favorites. He spent hours stopping to smell the roses.

Until that Sunday on the July 4th weekend, he loved to ride in cars, blissfully sniffing the great outdoors, his ears flapping in the wind. Even when we were on our way to the vet. He'd enjoyed a normal breakfast and walk. While I tended to some work, one of my sons noticed he seemed to be having difficulty breathing. The vet's office would be closed until after the holiday, so I called the veterinary hospital that had performed emergency surgery on puppy Scooter several months earlier, after he swallowed a foreign object and very much regretted his choice. They said to bring Brady in to be checked. With the luxury of being alone with me, he was perky enough to pull me for a very short walk before getting into the car. Then, instead of jumping on the seat to poke out his nose and take in the scents, he settled silently into a space on the floor, a darkened cave among bankers' boxes of transcripts.

It was a blur once we reached the hospital. Oxygen. "Has he had heart trouble?"

IV fluids. "We may be able to bring down some of the edema."

X-rays. "Could we get a room?" the veterinarian asked as she nodded meaningfully to the receptionist when she came out to talk to me.

"He's not responding as well as we had hoped."

Images. More waiting, now on high alert. "Congestive heart failure."

His heart was too big.

It pressed up into his trachea, making it nearly impossible for him to breathe. I looked at his abdominal x-ray through the lens of scarred experience: "His lungs shouldn't look like that," I said. "And are those white shadows something else?"

And, finally, after a suggestion of overnight hospitalization to see if he might improve, and learning he would not, "Can you make him not suffer?"

The doctor assured me he wouldn't, and asked me if I wanted to be with him.

"Of course. Can I go in and see him now?"

She warned me he was agitated and said he they'd bring him to me as soon as possible. She said all the moms she'd ever asked that question wanted to be there.

A woman in puppy-print scrubs carried Brady into a colorfully painted "Comfort Room." He looked sluggish, but instantly alerted to me and settled into my lap. He relaxed as I hugged him and stroked my velvet boy's head and told him how much we love him, how lucky we were to have had him come home with us, and how sorry I was for when I hadn't been patient enough. That he's the best of beagles, he's going to see his human dad again, and now at last he can safely run off leash.

When I told her we had to let Brady go, one of my heartbroken children, 3,000 miles away, said it wouldn't have been right to have him continue to suffer, and that from heaven at least he wouldn't have to be afraid of the July 4th fireworks that night.

~~~~~

For weeks Rufus keened for Brady. He'd go to the door to our backyard garden, stand at the sill, and howl a sustained note I'd never heard from him before, not even when Jim died. Within a few days he gave up trying to track Brady in the garden, where he'd wander in elaborate circles, his nose buried where his brother's had been before. He must have understood by then that Brady was not there to be found.

He stood on the open door's sill and howled into the sky.

When we walked around town, he'd pull me down every path and street which might have carried some hint of Brady's presence. Once those routes had been exhausted several times over, he pulled me farther and farther away, to sniff out whether Brady had gone somewhere without him, and where he might still be able to find him. One day, he pulled me into an unfamiliar forest trail. We didn't find our way out until almost seven hours later, when in the dark we finally made our way home from two towns away. I held Rufus tightly when he saw that Brady hadn't also found his way back home.

~~~~~

Clarabelle, a stunning blonde, had regally roamed a large SPCA enclosure. An Australian Shepard, she may have been in search of subjects to herd. To Clarabelle's right, a wildly yippy Jack Russell terrier had been barely contained within his own barred space on a corner crate's second tier. His unending barks sprayed evidence of his discontent. He was not a satisfied prisoner of circumstance.

Needs attention, does not get along with other animals or young children, the terrier's card unsurprisingly read.

Between the impressive arc of spittle punctuating Jack's non-stop yaps and the lure of the puppy window diagonally across the hall from him, it would not have been hard for visitors to miss the no-longer-quite-a-puppy beagle who soundlessly pressed himself against the back wall. His name was Rufus.

1 1/2 - 2 yrs, trained, responds to his name.

Suzannah and her father spearheaded the ensuing negotiations and visits during a campaign to get all family members on board with our first adoption. Every time Rufus haltingly padded out to meet one of us, he did the same thing: he waited for us to slowly approach, then promptly rolled over on his back to await a belly rub that dissolved his anxiety. He would close his eyes and point his quivering nose to the heavens with a smile of pure contentment, transformed from a beleaguered rescue trucked all the way from Indiana into Snoopy dancing in a field of pure green.

Rufus. King of Belly Rubs.

~~~~~

Rufus's upcoming birthday, or its approximation given his not entirely clear provenance, would fall in late August. All three colors had faded to cream with just a dollop of coffee. Although he was completely deaf, I constantly talked to him. He had so many listening skills beyond those dependent on sound.

Even as he began to give signals that something more than sheer antiquity was amiss, he never missed a walk. During a July heat wave he still tugged with improbable force per vintage pound, and increasingly insisted on walking more than halfway as far as he could manage. I had to twice cradle and carry him home. During
~~~~~

those weeks I found myself talking to him even more than I usually did, about his human dad and Brady, whose bright traces he never stopped searching for.

~~~~~

Scooter had moved across the country with his true human mom as soon as she could keep him with her at school, so it tended to be just Rufus and me, daily greeting his many friends in town. I talked to him at some length every time we walked together. He remained a terrific listener.

When July arrived, and with it an anniversary of Brady's loss--which also happened to be the date when Jim and I first saw the Master of the Universe Boston surgeon--I talked to Rufus about Brady. I remembered how often Brady had run away when we first got him, and how craftily he had done so notwithstanding his lack of guile.

"Remember when *you* used to run away, too, when we first got you?"

Rufus would pause our walk and glance up at me. *Of course, I remember, mom.*

He'd adored riding in Jim's first, rusty white pickup truck. Window down, nose to the open air, ears aflutter. In his youth he'd been such an escape artist that he more than once managed to extricate himself through a sliver of the truck's window space. He'd once jumped onto a nearby haystack, making a break for the hills after Jim had parked to buy garden supplies.

"Remember the time you ran away and I panicked and yelled for you to come back and you kept running and I was sure we'd never see you again--and then your dad put his hand on my shoulder and dropped down to one knee and just calmly called your name? And then you stopped running and looked back over your
~~~~~

shoulder and you saw him holding his arms out? And you turned around and started running back to him."

I still see them both, Jim enfolding young Rufus in his arms and holding him against his own still-beating heart. I don't think Rufus ever ran away from Jim again. And when we adopted sweet, fearful Brady, the two best buddies would enter nirvana every time Jim sat down to put on his running shoes. They waited, white-tipped tails wildly swishing on the slate floor, until he grabbed their branched leash. Off they ran, up the hills.

When Noah's Boy Scout troop learned of Jim's diagnosis, they organized a gathering and presented him with a hand-decorated flag of very special design: *You can do this,* it urged, underneath a drawing of him and the beagle boys running up the hill by our home.

"Someday," I told Rufus, looking away so he wouldn't see me cry, "You're going to see Brady again, and you're going to be able to run with him anywhere you want. And you'll see your dad, too. He's missed you as much as you miss him."

~~~~~

On what I didn't know would be our second-to-last walk, Rufus took me only to the midpoint of a short jaunt. He initiated a meet-and-greet with a weeks'-old foster puppy named Delta in a snazzy orange harness. She eagerly nuzzled him with her bright mahogany head, which bobbed atop a pure white body that seemed to vibrate with the joy of being outside and finding a new friend. After that, Delta bounced happily along and Rufus stepped into the shade of a plant that had bloomed overnight. Its bright magenta and violet buds arced rakishly over one lush ear, like a fascinator at a royal wedding.
~~~~~

He paused and looked up at me and waited expectantly. He knew I'd want to take some pictures of him. He was very patient that way.

Then he inexplicably looked up and away, directly into the sun, and stretched, with the opposite trajectory of a downward dog pose. It was as if he were being gently lifted by his front paws.

And he smiled. I swear he smiled.

I looked in the direction where his deep brown eyes seemed to have been directed, but it was far too bright, and hurt my eyes. Then Rufus lowered his front paws, nuzzled me just under my knee, and canted his head back toward home. He ordinarily resisted turning around so quickly.

It's okay, mom. I'm good now. I'll be okay.

We returned home, through the door where, suddenly and only recently, Rufus had stopped baying for Brady. He lay down on the cool white marble of the kitchen fireplace's floor. He'd eventually worn out Brady's smaller sleeping mat, which he'd crammed himself into beginning on the first night Brady didn't come back home.

~~~~~

When Rufus looked for all this world as if he were just sleeping, I kissed him goodbye and whispered in his ear, because I knew he could hear perfectly again. I told him Brady must be so happy to see him and that I knew they'd want to run and run together, but that every now and then he should look back over his shoulder, because his dad would be waiting for him, too, and might not be able to keep up with those strong young pain-free legs as Rufus zoomed away in the hills with his little brother.
~~~~~

42

Our Fathers

On the first Father's Day without their father here, our children and I had hiked on gentle paths not far from home and raised our water bottles atop a mountain we'd all climbed together many times. As Father's Days began to accrue, whichever of us could be together always found our way outside. On one of those days, my sons were hiking with me in mid-Maine when I received a call that would change our direction.

One-thirty-one: my father's mathematically lyrical birth date. A few days earlier, my subconscious had hovered over the date of six-one-six-one-six as I waited to pick up my brother at Logan Airport. Shortly before that, my father, who'd recently become immobilized by Parkinson's Disease, had haltingly spoken the same five words my husband had not long before he lost consciousness. Although there hadn't been any overt sign my father's death was imminent, intuition spoke.

"It's just my gut, and my gut's been wrong, but I think you should fly out this week." I told my older brother.

And so my brothers and I found ourselves laughing, giving each other a hard time, and telling stories and finishing each other's sentences as we surrounded my father's bed during his last days. He smiled, too.

~~~~~

My grandmother Helen, one of ten siblings, had eventually landed in New York City, where she met her husband Harry, a young Austrian immigrant who then enlisted in the Army and served in a World War. Family legend has it than when my grandmother held her first-born son, she announced--against all objective probabilities--that he would be going to Harvard. Not only did he enroll there on a full ($300) scholarship at sixteen, but he had his Doctorate in Physics and was an Assistant Professor by the time he was twenty-three. He remained at Harvard for more than a half-century and was its first Dean of Applied Sciences. My father's enduring friend and colleague Irwin introduced him to an artist, musician, and graduate student named Ann, who would become his wife. They married in Copenhagen. Or at least, they assumed they were married. My father reportedly had a fever so high as to have triggered hallucinations; both parties were surprised to find themselves at a ceremony conducted by three somber men in black robes; and neither was sufficiently fluent in Danish to translate the document they were handed and thereafter insisted had recorded their marriage (notwithstanding my cross-examination skills) but has not shown itself since.

Over the years, other interesting items have gone missing from my parents' home--including a work of art my mother and Jackson Pollack jointly painted upon a *Sunday New York Times* magazine. My favorite picture of my parents, among the few I ever saw, is of my mother wearing a mod polka-dot dress and art deco hat and tickling my father with a feather at a party at Irwin's apartment. Their friend (and future Noble laureate) Roy is next
~~~~~

to them, dressed up like Inspector Clouseau. Who would have thought physicists could be so wild?

I am the only daughter of a father who had no sisters, and a mother who had no brothers; neither had experience being around young children. My grasp of the hard sciences has yet to emerge, but when I was a toddler I excelled at pushing my father's buttons. He could not carry a note, let alone a tune, but enjoyed warbling the description he thought suited me best: *There was a little girl, who had a little curl right in the middle of her forehead/ And when she was good, she was very, very good, and when she was bad she was horrid.*

Well, maybe he did get me.

We did not once attend a father-daughter dance, or know of their existence, but he took me to some pretty fancy meetings of the Academy of Arts and Sciences. We 'summered' at what I now know was a secure nuclear research laboratory. But best of all were the Physics Department picnics in rural western Massachusetts, where the physicists would gather inside a barn while their little ones ran around outside, performing dangerous stunts and otherwise engaging in applied physics for toddlers. Nearby roads would be marked with handmade signs with arrows, reading *Theoretical Picnic this way*.

Think about it.

My father had one of the world's most beautiful minds and was one of the Commonwealth's most terrifying drivers, which is saying something. He could solve any complex problem but was baffled by teenagers and flummoxed by those not guided by accurate objective data. He could envision aspects of time and space and matter--condensed and otherwise--that no human could see, but had difficulty locating matching socks. He loved his work and family and friends the best he knew how, which is all any of us can do.

~~~~~
~~~~~

That Father's Day began, as it had for some time, with a search for the right place to honor my children's father. We'd previously been close to home and very far away, and had settled on a trip to botanical gardens encircled by mountain paths cushioned year-round by fallen pine needles. The sunny great outdoors suddenly shifted to my father's bedroom, windows shut and shuttered, when I received a call from my little brother as I hiked with my sons. A visiting nurse told me of my father's coughing spell and assured me his temperature was normal and his vital signs were good. No need to rush back, I was told. I'd become his medical proxy years earlier, as I soon would for my mother.

That evening, my father seemed contentedly to fall asleep.

Arguably better than anyone else, physicists understand their place in the universe; the human body's nature as a temporary repository of energy; and that a last breath here is only the first breath of the everywhere out there.

~~~~~

My father-in-law, the youngest of five sons, married the Lady in the Red Dress. He's said to have attended a dance when he was a student at Boston College Law School, and there glimpsed a beautiful brunette in a red dress as she swirled behind a wide column. When a nursing student who spoke in a long-voweled French-Canadian cadence emerged on the other side, he asked her to dance. Only then did he realize it was a different young lady.

They went on to marry and have five children of their own, in roughly Irish twin increments. I'm told my husband displayed only the lightest dusting of disappointment by the time his fourth younger sister arrived and no brother was to be found. But he was by temperament well-suited to be the one retreating to a quiet room of his own amid the mysteries of so many sisters. Somehow my father-in-law--one of five brothers--was in complete equipoise
~~~~~

within this very full household of little girls, so foreign in many ways to his own boyhood just outside Boston. He was both stoic and expressive, practical and extravagant. Contained and available, bound to his faith and understanding of those who did not practice it. Hardworking and relaxed. Financially canny and prone to wild splurges--always for the benefit of others, whether family or strangers.

Barely out of my teenage years, I married into this second family. In many ways I grew up with them more than I had in my parents' household. When my husband told his father of his diagnosis, my undoubtedly devastated father-in-law arrived at our shell-shocked home to brave the morning traffic and drive us to certain surgical confirmation of what we faced. He read my soul and said six words.

"You'll always be my daughter, too."

~~~~~

Two years after losing his son, my father-in-law suffered a catastrophic stroke. My compassionate husband was no longer there to navigate his father's care and soothe his and the rest of our hearts, as he also would have done for my father. It has not infrequently astonished me that my father-in-law was able to endure the hardships of his recovery. I've grown to wonder whether he held on through those years with us in order not to subject us all to another profound loss so soon.

I cannot imagine he sang to his children when they were young, but when his first granddaughter was on his knee, he sang to her his customized jig (*"Little Emma, one shoe on and one shoe off...."*). With *gusto*, as she stared at him intently with bottomless brown eyes. Only the first five grandchildren then graced his world, and he looked up at his son and beamed, perfectly content. He said, "I'd just like to live long enough to see how it all turns out."
~~~~~

He meant that he would like to see the next generation begin to grow into their independent selves, and he did that. None of us contemplated his outliving one of his children. And then he was there for our children when their father couldn't be, for milestones when they would feel that aching absence. He made sure to celebrate with them as they chose and graduated from schools, entered important relationships, and began to find their way as young adults.

I realized only in speaking to my children after he had passed away that, like his son, my father-in-law taught me many things I couldn't fully understand until looking back at the shape of his long life. Among them, he taught me the breadth and meaning of a calling. It was so easy to see a calling in a career path like my father's. He was born to be a theoretical physicist. There was simply nothing else he could have been: he was called to a life of the mind that was profoundly internal, making practical things like remembering meals and rearing small children--particularly yours truly-- far more mysterious. My father dwelled where his attention was, provisionally in his office at school or at home. Slightly more traditional family life transpired at least a floor away, physically, yet seemed to me far more puzzling to him than the unseen universe. In truth, he was rarely fully present in the visible world. He occupied the limitless cosmos, even as his physical world shrank to a single bed in an overly shaded room as his disease attacked his body and only just had begun to tinker with parts of his amazing mind. Since their early childhoods I've seen the seeds of my sons' and daughters' devotion to assorted STEM fields. I've never viewed my own work as only a job. My father-in-law ensured every one of his children received the support and the education they needed to do whatever work spoke to them; a lion's share has dedicated their professional lives to teaching. They all are parents, and have enduring marriages conducted by a rotation of their priest uncles.

Papa Dick supported his family by enduring a daily commute on the Southeast Expressway for decades, working with great accomplishment and contentment in an accounting firm, and eventually moving to Washington, D.C. for six years before retiring back to New England when our second son was born. He always quietly served his church and those in need. He and Grandma Jackie had downsized when their own nest emptied; they up-sized when they moved back to New England. With more than a baker's dozen of their grandchildren yet to arrive, they found a home that somehow would have space for all of them. Three daughters and brothers-in-law also settled within easy driving distance and began raising their families.

We would go to Papa Dick's house every Sunday for family dinners after all the cousins had exhausted themselves playing games on the lawn, eventually settling in groups all over the house. Some, thumbs locked in cupid mouths between fire engine-red cheeks, napped in cribs under Grandma Jackie's quilts. Toddlers cradled newborns on the big yellow couch as parents hovered within lurching distance. Children clustered around early-generation computers in Papa Dick's office, its walls papered with family photos and children's artwork. Above them was always the hand-hammered silver letter "G" his own little boy had forged for him in elementary school. It still hung on the wall of his room when he peacefully passed away to rejoin his son. Once we parents were dramatically outnumbered, there were occasional incidents--like the enduring mystery of the pencil-stabbing of Papa Dick's well-worn leather footstool. (There was a lead suspect, but the statute of limitations has long run.) He would put on a stern show, but I think even the toddlers could sense the laughter underneath. Nothing in life delighted him like these grandchildren, and there was no greater gift he could have given them than the loving bonds of friendship they forged on those Sundays.

It is not, I realized, that his work was or was not what he would have thought of as a calling. And perhaps a calling is not what we do so much as who we are. His calling was his family. Though my father-in-law lived a generation longer than his son, they shared the completeness that comes with the absence of regret. No different calling, and no different life, would have suited either them or my father. Long-lived and not, their lives are causes for continuing celebration. Neither grandfather would have done anything differently while making any choice that mattered--including attending a mysterious ceremony in Copenhagen, and extending an invitation to dance to the Lady in the Red Dress.

43

To the Lighthouses

To the extent obsession is problematic, I've developed a bit of a lighthouse issue. A fluency in Fresnel lenses, colored and clear, glittering with rounded rainbows where the sun skirts their layered crystal rings. An appreciation of the unique counted measure of each lighthouse's cycling strobe, a perpetual beat no less melodic than a heart's.

The eponymous, inanimate lead character of Virginia Woolf's *To the Lighthouse* emitted a steady beacon, notable perhaps above all for its assurance of coming around again. Its core is the light; the surrounding darkness carries no negative freight. A lighthouse delivers a slice of light that is the visible counterpoint to Woolf's lightly sleeping heroine's understanding of the whole of hidden darkness that makes up any human's reductive essence.

~~~~~

I'm a fan of clouded, stormy skies, and not nearly as interested in blinding lemon sun that in daylight nullifies these sentries' steady swoops of teal and white and red. I like to get to my lighthouses well before sunrise, and watch the darkness recede as light reappears in increments so reliable that their past and future paths
~~~~~

coalesce. Their insistently cycling memory creates a *trompe l'oeil* of soft daylight long before the sun appears.

With these quiet guardians, there's nothing to fear in the not-quite-night of solitude. When standing near them, in inky black and the deepest blue, it's as if I can see the whole of the earth and sea bathed in moon-gold. Jagged limestone cliffs, working harbors, ports where pleasure craft are moored while people dream in distant places. The light is alive but noiseless, and even at their fiercest measure, the waves wash in without capacity to startle us. If we look out to sea, we're able to see them coming.

Alfred Lord Tennyson understood darkness and light, and there's some evidence he understood the sleeplessness of the bereaved. In *Dark House* he wrote of "A hand that can be clasp'd no more—/ Behold me, for I cannot sleep,/ And like a guilty thing I creep/ At earliest morning to the door." I've never been afraid rising from non-sleep and going out the door, even in the supreme fresh desolation of heading out unaccompanied by beagles. Whenever possible, I first make my way to the world's nearest empty edges. Such vast spaces were once the stuff of my worst childhood fears, as may be true for many of us smallish humans. Now I'm compulsively drawn to landscapes without end, where gold-plum cloudscapes overcome any divide between heaven and where we stand. Where the moon still ceaselessly cycles, and the sun dependably arrives on its own time.

A beautiful, and no longer a fearful thing.

~~~~~

I dejectedly told a friend and colleague how sad I was to have missed sunrise before work that morning. How extraordinary the color had been, bright sunflower waves seeping into hot pink and neon orange. It was, I told her, similarly as saturated as the Valentine's Day sunset I'd once chased into her west-facing office
~~~~~

(from my windowless one), taking the liberty of sliding her vertical blinds aside and pointing to the enormous bruised purple heart cloud floating on a sea of yellow-peach crepuscular rays.

"Mmmhmmmh." She nodded politely.

Quite rationally, she wondered how I could so vividly describe a sunrise I'd missed. It took me more than a few beats to realize I hadn't missed it. I'd seen it at its glorious peak as I exited the highway just as the sun was about to emerge on the horizon. What I had missed was the chance to take a picture, to commemorate a part of it and be able to share it with someone who had indeed missed out on the sight.

Even when I'm able to collect sunrises, I do so imperfectly, without being able to convey their synesthesia. My photos cannot dance with the indigo diamonds of accelerating cross-wakes as fishing boats chug out to deeper waters. Living things become one-dimensional shadows. A viewer can see only the most recent vogue pose struck by a cormorant atop a mast. Looking at a picture, it's impossible to taste salty air or crunch over underwater barnacles or feel morning light lyrically unfolding. It is also that way with far greater losses. All I can ever capture of my husband and all other missing beings who've become part of me is what I can put into the language of words and other art forms.

~~~~~

Is there a possibility that the wake of deep loss might lead us not back to the capacity to feel joy as we once did, but cause us to retrain ourselves to see joy as ours to experience in *more* places? Can we learn to see it better, to cast off some of what stands between us and joy? It's taken me years to begin to understand the still unsettling possibility that devastation might in some ways allow us to learn to love *better,* or at least to be open to better shar-
~~~~~

ing what we learn through loss. It unsettles me because any such understanding necessarily comes too late to express to the lost.

I thought about the space between the cup of the Psalms which overflows with blessings, and the cup of roiling wrath that provides the context for Matthew 26:42. Does great loss affect only the way we inhabit negative space, or might it help us better inhabit the world, and to experience joy along with love and grace different in kind from what we'd known? Could making friends with the dark, and with our own scars, allow us to augment the light we might still bring to this world?

~~~~~

When we decide not to go out at dawn, we forego not only the chance to see a one-of-a-kind display of light and color, but also deprive ourselves of what we may have found within more somber and muted surroundings.

Acceptance of risk and dark fate has never been my strong suit. When we mortals face each morning, and like Vizzini in *The Princess Bride*, we simply cannot know which cup will be handed to us, or from which cup we safely may sip. We choose to partake--or not--of that night and the day that follows it, but each day hands us what it will. When we reach out to other beings, it can be sublime. It also may prove disappointing or maddening or break our hearts. We may be betrayed or injured in innumerable ways, sometimes so terribly that we're reduced back to zero.

We may maintain ourselves within the reasonably safe and manageable known unknowns, in the land of the closely held amygdala. But the banal pleasant present of (spoiler alert) *The Good Place* has been shorn of its peaks as surely as its dark vales have evened out, and therefore disappeared, and it is no longer a vibrant and interesting place. Or we can take a page from the not-so-
~~~~~

Cowardly Lion as he reclaims courage, or the hero of Edgar Albert Guest's *It Couldn't Be Done*, and try and try again.

Reaching out--and dealing oneself in--can be like a cross between *The Lady or the Tiger?* and Bertie Bott's Every Flavour Beans: will it be the grass flavor or the vomit, cinnamon or cement? Will you be handed the cup that runneth over or the vessel of down-to-the-dregs bitterness?

Some element of choice remains within the micro and macro of each day. I choose to get outside and contemplate the horizon. Even when winter wind turns my hands powder-blue and all the sea and sky I can see is rendered in dusky gray. I never regret going out to greet ordinary skies. I have regretted not taking the detour. And sometimes--say, one in forty mornings and nights--I'll dally at the shore and be there to see it bloom into color almost no one will believe is untouched when I share its image. We don't get to choose the result; we do get to choose where we stand, and sometimes what we put ourselves in a position to see and to risk feeling.

"This mounting wave will roll us shoreward soon," Tennyson wrote. His seafarers yearned for waves to bring them home again; the signs leading them there were likely a matter of dead reckoning. Maybe it is not only the lighthouse-illuminated waves which continuously call me and convince me I can never live far from the sea, but the hope of what they might one day return to us.

44

Enduring Ephemera

I performed a questionable parking maneuver, not the first committed while armed with a camera. From across a field near profusely double-consonanted Pepperrell Cove, my peripheral vision had registered a dazzling sight. A shadowed far corner was alive with twinkling lavender and bluebell fireflies who'd gathered just this once to celebrate bright morning instead of convivial night. As one, they formed a flowing sail heading out to sea in following winds.

I snapped a picture to preserve what I saw, which was never actually there. That morning I'd had an inexplicable impulse to drive in the opposite direction before heading south to work. I happened to have glanced right, toward an open field, instead of left to a dank gas station. So now it's not I alone who can see morning lights sparkling and dancing before turning to steam in late summer's rising sun.

The vision was there for the taking.

~~~~~

It was a trick and treat of the light. Ordinary things rendered extraordinary, whether or not someone had been there to behold
~~~~~

them. Plastic meshing had been draped to protect wire-girded greens from being consumed by wildlife. Overnight rain had doused the layered grids just enough to leave plump water drops on their surfaces as the sun's fiercest light made its way above the tree line. The sun had finally traversed the field and lit up the last lingering pearls as I glanced that way.

What I'd seen was not, after all, a portal to a magical world. It was an unassuming mass-produced piece of webbing that had lost its hold on a thin metal post and collapsed over an unflowering garden of monochromatic green.

The sky had clouded over again by the time I sprang back into my less than artfully discarded car and zipped off to the highway and work. The scene re-assumed its Clark Kent persona. But, for those few seconds, and just as I happened by, a constellation glittered there within my reach.

~~~~~

In *The Idler*, Samuel Johnson wrote, "Our brightest blazes of gladness are commonly kindled by unexpected sparks."

We may be inclined to think of sparks as young love, or signaling transfiguration into something richer. As something we uncertainly await, or that resides in our long-ago pasts. Something either yet to ignite, or once incendiary, and now extinguished after having burned too brightly. An irresistible and uncontrollable force, but not one likely to remain, in the present, visible. An intense relationship that doesn't last. The July 4th fireworks which stayed silent for deaf Rufus and made Brady quiver under a blanket, but neither now hears from heaven.

Sorrow can be suffused with dazzling, fleeting sparks, too.

~~~~~

Driving back from my solo trip to Bar Harbor, I first heard The Weakerthans' *Left and Leaving*, with its bittersweet catalogue of what a lover left behind with a partner-no-longer. Poet Rebecca Lindenberg, who also curated *The Museum of Lost Objects*, listed a lost partner's continuing signals to her in the present tense in her *Catalogue of Ephemera*.

Now I see such signals as gifts, and I see gifts everywhere. And I see the greatest gift is what my husband took away, by relieving me of lifelong fears. He did this not only by living in a way that showed me fear is fruitless--although he also did that--but by showing me fear is powerless in the face of grace, and that love can transcend it and fill whatever space has been given over to it.

Signals from the beloved stay in the present tense at least as long as those attuned to receive them are here. I can see their sparks in our children and in my dreams, and almost everywhere I look or remember.

~~~~~

You give me Giant's Causeway's interlocking pillars, descending and flattening into steps across the sea to Scotland. The stairs of Genovesa, the pure blue of island birds' feet, and the sea lion that slid up behind our daughter and nuzzled the sun-kissed gold curl that dangled behind her ear.

All the colors and their permutations, forest green and emergent orange and fragmentary blue.

You give me peeper frogs chirping and silence and a purple-black mussel shell with a serrated edge, tiny shark's teeth where I rub my thumb, but never deeply enough to bleed.

Cantilevered stones high on a path along southern Maine's rocky shore, on a clear sub-zero December night when you faced the ocean and I faced you and we talked about and named the children and life we hoped to have together--which you gave me, too.
~~~~~

A vegetable garden that wasn't a portal to a magic world of fairies and sprites, but to all we had within and outside the yellow home we shared.

You give me a full heart and a still one and a Mother's Day card you left in your desk along with one for your mother. And pauses to count and catch my breath and excruciating pain and reminders you would prefer I take better care of myself.

You give me sun pillars and lightning. Clouds shaped like mythical beasts and extravagantly patched with rainbow sun dogs. A riot of green leaves laced with dancing raindrops. Flowers and shadows which curve into descending doves and hearts.

You give me the way to the shore and to watch the storms, and paths where I lose myself and eventually find my way back.

You give me ways to see the world with our children and on my own. A handful of white feathers and an entire shorn wing fallen on Vik's black sand, its underside turned up to the sky. High cliffs where Pacific birds nest. A corner rounded in Varanasi as our daughter led me to a shrine where a water buffalo stared at me in air so wet it was more like the ghats' rising waters, which had etched milky-green ghost leaves into a stone wall from which they must just have receded.

You give me the camera in my hand, and the eye to capture sights I've been left to see. The vaulted roof of St. Andrew's Church and the view from the top of Arthur's Seat. A blue heron wading in the river at Droghedah, water turned to fire by the setting sun's reflection in the windows of an ancient stone church.

You give me sleepless nights and serene mornings and strength. You give me memories that make me laugh and make me feel like I'm drowning; sometimes they're one and the same.

You give me beagles with behavioral issues and neuroses and the purest good intentions. Sepia flowers which come back to life.

A pair of pigeons in Jaiselmar, and camels named Geronimo and Doniel.

You give me a solar eclipse through a triangle of green glass in the observatory next door to our son's graduate school apartment, which you never saw.

You give me stories and the words they're made of, about the before and after and the great middle. You trust me to do justice in the telling.

You give me a handmade card with the last picture of us both smiling, and a John Hiatt CD when I need to find it.

You give me yourself, still and forever, and this life with and without you.

You give me the family and friends who loved and love you.

You forgive me everything.

And you take away my fears of all but one thing.

So I can get through this, as you gently remind me many people do.

Acknowledgments

Welcome to the world, James Millstein, who shares his name-sake's birthday. We know you will fill those big shoes, just as you fill your family's hearts.

Thanks to Dr. Nicholas D. Garcia, who encouraged me after reading my very early and raw writing, and the Reverend John Hudson, of Sherborn's Pilgrim Church, who has cheered me on in telling this story. Thanks to the Reverend Robert Thompson, who supported our family and presided over and lent his magnificent voice to the perfect Closing Ceremonies. My heavenly complement includes the Reverend Deborah Duval.

Thanks to the extraordinary Bethany Van Delft, who told me as my heart thundered before taking the Moth Mainstage to just look at her between the bright lights directly in front of me, adjust the mic, and I would be fine. She's shared her beautiful family and golden heart, given me the confidence to share more stories, and gifted me with a magical surprise John Hiatt concert. We'll never forget the music, the kindness, and the soul-deep understanding.

Love to all of our Deering friends for absolutely everything. I marvel at my good fortune in being forever connected with all of you.

A special thanks to Portsmouth Clipper Band leader Eric Gagnon, who always found the time and the music and provided the shoulder when we most needed it.

Immense thanks to the two Jessicas, K. & P., who, respectively, swiftly responded to a first query late on a Saturday night, and gave me the excellent advice to cut at least 30K words. I needed that.

Love to the Lonely Hearts Writers and luminous leader Gae Polisner, who assembled us over great distances and made magic happen, with Chris, Marie, Eli, and Kate (and their four-legged family members, and at least one surprise guest Texas snake). When I first read a section of what I'd written about my husband to them, Eli gave voice to the singular purpose I hadn't yet realized fueled my writing during so many difficult years, telling me that although they'd never had a chance to know Jim, they felt they saw him. No feedback could have meant more to me.

And thank you to my wonderful Writing Battle friends around the world, all brought together by tireless leaders Max and Teona.

Our gratitude goes out to Dr. Mike and Dr. Patty and each compassionate health care professional, along with many kind strangers we'll always remember. We will try our best to pass it on. Finally, please treat yourselves to the poem *Kindness*, by Naomi Shihab Nye (*Words Under the Words: Selected Poems* 1995).

Stephanie Martin Glennon, May 2026

Notes & References

~PART I~

Page 6: William Shakespeare, *Julius Caesar* (Oxford Univ. Press 2001); p. 12: Edward Gorey, *Amphigorey Also* (Congdon & Weed 1983); p. 13: J. Lambrechts, "*The Problem of Groundwater and Wood Piles in Boston, An Unending Need for Vigilant Surveillance*" (Wentworth Inst. Technology, AC 2008-1977); p. 14: *See* William Blake, "Auguries of Innocence," *Poets of the English Language* (Viking Press 1950); pp. 18 & 62: John Irving, *The World According to Garp* (E.P. Dutton, 1978); p. 38: *See* Randy Pausch & Jeffrey Zaslow, *The Last Lecture* (Hyperion 2008); pp. 54 & 175: Oliver Sacks, *The Mind's Eye* (Vintage 2010); pp. 64 & 132: *See* José Saramago, *The Stone Raft,* translated by Giovanni Pontiero (Harcourt Brace 1995); pp. 64 & 68: John Irving, *Last Night in Twisted River* (Bloomsbury Publishing 2009); p. 70: *See* Samuel Taylor Coleridge, "*The Rime of the Ancient Mariner,*" accessed via Ginsberg, Jacob, *LitCharts.* 26 Nov. 2016. Web. 31 July 2022; Page 72: William Shakespeare, *The Winter's Tale* (E. Maynard & Co. 1890); pp. 73 & 122: Kurt Vonnegut, *Galápagos* (Delacorte Press/Seymour Lawrence 1985); pp. 74, 189, 269 & 287: Frederick Buechner, *Wishful Thinking* (Harper One 1993); p. 79: *See* Atul Gawande, "Letting Go," *Annals of Medicine, The New Yorker* (Aug. 2, 2010); p. 80: *See* Stephen Jay Gould, "The Median isn't the Message," *Virtual Mentor.* 2013;15(1):77-81. doi: 10.1001/virtual-mentor.2013.15.1.mnar1-1301; p. 86: *See* R.T. Smith, "Sourwood," *The Atlantic Monthly,* May 1998, Vol. 281, No. 5, p. 76; p. 111: *See* Gérard Miller, "*Rendez-vous chez Lacan,*" produced by Leslie Grunberg and Gérard Miller. 2013; p. 143: *See* Louis Sacher, *Holes* (Farrar, Straus & Giroux 1998); pp. 131-132: Primo Levi, "In the Park," *A Tranquil Star* (W.W. Norton & Co. 2008); p. 137: José Donoso, *The Obscene Bird of Night* (David R. Godine 2003).

~PART II~

Page 154: *See* Pablo Neruda, "If You Forget Me," *Love Poems* (Editorial Losada 1958); translated by Donald D. Walsh (New Directions 2008); p. 154: *See* Nicholas Friedman, "Not the Song, but After," *Poetry Magazine,* issue no. 71499 (Nov. 2012); p. 156 & 157: Andre Dubus, *Dancing After Hours* (Vintage 1997); p. 156: Elif Batuman, *The Possessed* (Farrar, Straus & Giroux 2010); p. 156: Arthur W. Lindsley, "C.S. Lewis on Grief," *Knowing and Doing: Life and Writings of C.S. Lewis* (C.S. Lewis Inst. 2001); p. 160: *The Collected Tales of Nikolai Gogol,* translated by Richard Pever & Larissa Volokhonsky (Pantheon 1998); p. 161: *See* Lawrence Block, *A*

Drop of the Hard Stuff (Mulholland Books 2011); p. 163: *See* Horace, *Ars Poetica*, translation by D. R. Shackleton (Univ. of Cambridge 2001); p. 163: *See* "Burns' Heir," *The Simpsons*, Season 5, ep. 18; p. 169: C.D. Wright, "More Blues and the Abstract Truth," *Steal Away: New and Selected Poems* (Copper Canyon Press 2002); p. 170: *See* Lois Lowry, *The Giver* (Houghton Mifflin 1993); p. 175: *See* Macdonald Critchley, *"Types of Visual Perseveration." Brain*, Vol. 74, Issue 3:267-299 (Sep. 1951); p. 176: Marilynne Robinson, *Home* (Farrar, Straus & Giroux 2008); p. 176: José Saramago, *The Cave*, translation by Margaret Costa (Mariner Books, 2003); p. 186: Greg Brown, "Canned Goods (live)," *One Night Year* (Red House Records 1983); p. 186: Pablo Neruda, "Cierto Cansancio," *Esquire* (March 1974); p. 190: Barbara Kingsolver, *The Poisonwood Bible* (Faber & Faber, 2000); p. 190: *See* José Saramago, *Death with Interruptions* (Mariner Books 2009); p. 190: *See Monty Python's Flying Circus: Complete & Annotated (All the Bits)*(Black Dog & Leventhal Pub., Inc. 2012); p. 192: *See* John Hiatt, "Before I Go," *Crossing Muddy Waters* (Edel 2000); p. 200: Fernando Pessoa, *The Book of Disquiet*, translated by Richard Zenith (Penguin 2003); pp. 201 & 269: José Saramago, *The Elephant's Journey* (Mariner Books 2010); p. 204: Mary Oliver, *Devotions: The Selected Poems of Mary Oliver* (Penguin Press 2019); p. 207: José Saramago, *The Year of the Death of Ricardo Reis* (The Harvill Press 1992); p. 209: Alfred Noyes, "The Highwayman," *Collected Poems of Alfred Noyes*, Vol. 1 (Frederick Stokes 1913); p. 209: *See* Richard Thompson, "1952 Vincent Black Lightning," *Rumor and Sigh* (Sunset Sound, Los Angeles & Konk Studios, London 1991); p. 211: Anne Stevenson, *Poems 1955-2005* (Bloodaxe Books 2005); p. 221: James Joyce, *Dubliners* (Penguin 1993); p. 223: "Sunday Best," *Boardwalk Empire*, Season 7, ep. 5; p. 224: *See* Vijay Seshadri, "Bright Copper Kettles," *Poetry* (Dec. 2010); p. 227: Geoffrey Chaucer, *Canterbury Tales* (Penguin Classics 2005); p. 227: Louis Untermeyer, *Father: An Anthology of Verse* (E.P. Dutton 1931); p. 229: *See* "Philip Glass on Legacy," *Fresh Air*, NPR, April 6, 2015; p. 230: Elie Weisel, *Night* (Hill & Wang 2012); pp. 234 & 236: Kurt Vonnegut, *Slaughterhouse-Five* (Delacorte Press 1969); p. 238: Alejandro Zambra, *Ways of Going Home* (Farrar, Straus & Giroux 2013); p. 239: Carol Ann Duffy, *Collected Poems*, p. 415 (Picador 2019); p. 240: Michael Franti & Spearhead, "I'm Alive (Life Sounds Like)," *All People* (Capitol 2013); p. 240: *See* James Joyce, *Ulysses* (Wordsworth Editions Ltd. 2010).

~PART III~

Page 265: José Saramago, *The History of the Siege of Lisbon* (Harcourt 1997); pp. 269-270: Thomas Wolfe, *You Can't Go Home Again* (Harper & Bros. 1940); p. 270: Thornton Wilder, *Our Town* (Gardners Books 2004); p. 282: *See* "Lost in Translation: The Power of Language to Shape How We View the World," *Hidden Brain*, NPR, January 29, 2018; p. 286: Ranier Maria Rilke, *Sonnets to Orpheus*, translated by Edward Snow (Farrar, Straus & Giroux 2004); p. 286: *See* Amy Gertsler, "In Perpetual Spring," *Bitter Angel* (North Point Press 1990); p. 286: *See* Robert Frost, "Dust of Snow," *Robert Frost Early Poetry Collection: 1913-1924* (public domain); pp. 291 & 299: Kiran Desai, *The Inheritance of Loss* (Atlantic Monthly Press 2005*)*; p. 297: Emily St. John Mandel, *Station Eleven* (Vintage Books 2014); p. 318: *See* Virginia Woolf, *To the Lighthouse* (Harcourt, Brace & Co. 1927); pp. 319 & 322: Alfred Lord Tennyson, "Dark House," *In Memoriam A.H.H.* (1849); p. 319: *See* Tom Pirozzoli, "A Fearful and Beautiful Thing," produced by Willy Porter (2020); p. 324: Samuel Johnson, *The Idler* (London, Universal Chronicle, 1758-60); p. 324: The Weakerthans, "Left and Leaving," *Left and Leaving* (G7 Welcoming Committee 2000); p. 325: Rebecca Lindenberg, "Museum of Lost Objects" & "Catalogue of Ephemera," *Love, an Index* (McSweeney's Publishing 2012).